WYSIWYG GUIDE
What You See Is What You Get

THE WAY WORD FOR THE MACINTOSH® WORKS

WYSIWYG GUIDE
What You See Is What You Get

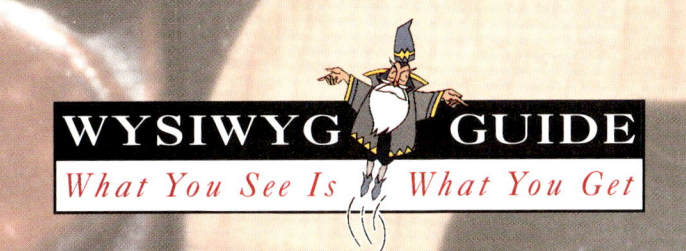

THE WAY
WORD
FOR THE
MACINTOSH®
WORKS

Peter Gloster

Microsoft PRESS

Copyright © 1994 Dorling Kindersley London

Conceived, edited, and designed by DK Direct Limited and Microsoft Press.

Published by Microsoft Press.

All rights reserved. No part of the contents of this book may be reproduced or transmitted in any form or by any means without the written permission of the publisher.

DK DIRECT

Series Editor: Robert Dinwiddie; **Series Art Editor:** Virginia Walter
Project Editors: Kathleen Fahey, Maxine Lewis; **Editor:** Edda Bohnsack
Art Editors: Nigel Coath, Jenny Hobson; **Designers:** Stephen Cummiskey, Jacqueline Greene, Poppy Jenkins
Production Manager: Ian Paton

MICROSOFT PRESS

Acquisitions Director: Dean Holmes; **Acquisitions Editor:** Lucinda Rowley; **Technical Director:** David Rygmyr
Assistant Managing Editor: Nancy Siadek; **Project Editor:** Katherine A. Krause; **Technical Reviewer:** Marc Young

ADDITIONAL CONTRIBUTORS

Illustrators: Anthony Bellue, Nigel Coath, Peter Serjeant, Andrew Green, Janos Marffy, Coral Mula
Airbrushing: Janos Marffy, Roy Flooks; **Model Making:** Sean Edwards; **Photography:** Tony Buckley, Andy Crawford, Mark Hill
Computer Support: Simon Grey, Mark Gugliemetti, Sam Segar; **Typing Assistance:** Margaret Little

Microsoft is a registered trademark of Microsoft Corporation. Apple, the Apple logo, System 7, Macintosh, and Power Macintosh are registered trademarks of Apple Computer, Inc. All other trademarks used in this book are the property of their respective owners.

The persons, organizations, businesses, and products referred to for the purpose of practice examples in this book are fictitious. Any resemblance to real persons, organizations, businesses, and products is unintentional.

Library of Congress Cataloging-in-Publication Data

Gloster, Peter.
    The way Word for the Macintosh works / Peter Gloster.
      p.   cm.
    Includes index.
    ISBN 1-55615-672-3
    1. Microsoft Word. 2. Word processing. I. Title.
Z52.5.M52G57 1994
652.5'536–dc20   94-26959
                                                                                     CIP

Color Reproduction by Mullis Morgan, UK

Printed and Bound in the USA

123456789 QEQE 987654

Flexibook

CONTENTS

INTRODUCTION

6 ABOUT THIS BOOK

CHAPTER ONE

Getting Started

Welcome to Microsoft Word! In this introductory chapter you'll get to know the program and learn how to use it. You'll work with the mouse and learn about the Word application window with its toolbars, menus, dialog boxes, and other features. Then you'll take the plunge and create your first Word document — a simple letter.

10 WELCOME TO WORD FOR THE MACINTOSH

18 YOUR FIRST LETTER

CHAPTER TWO

Up & Running

Master basic word processing techniques: Practice opening and saving documents and entering, editing, and revising text. Also learn how to manage and organize your files efficiently.

26 TEXT ENTRY

30 TEXT SELECTION

32 TEXT REVISION

40 TEXT CHECKING

44 MANIPULATING WINDOWS

48 FILE MANAGEMENT

CHAPTER THREE

Looking Good

Learn how to enhance the look of your documents by applying formatting and adding graphics, tables, and charts.

54 FORMATTING PRINCIPLES

56 FORMATTING A DOCUMENT

66 ADVANCED FORMATTING

72 ADDING A LOGO

78 TABLES AND SORTING

82 CHARTS

86 BE CREATIVE

CHAPTER FOUR

Perfect Printing

Discover different printing techniques and find out how to best use your printing options. Learn how to use Word's Mail Merge feature to print personalized form letters.

90 PRINTING DOCUMENTS AND ENVELOPES

96 MAIL MERGE

100 PRINTING MAILING LABELS

CHAPTER FIVE

Timesavers

Practice using Word's timesaving features, such as templates, styles, and macros, that can help you speed up the tasks you frequently have to perform. Discover also how to optimize your Word tools to suit your personal working style.

104 TEMPLATES AND WIZARDS

108 STYLES

110 AUTOCORRECT AND AUTOTEXT

112 MACROS

REFERENCE

Reference Section

116 TOP TEN SHORTCUTS

117 OUTLINING

118 INSTALLING A PRINTER

119 FONTS

120 CONVERTING FILES

121 MANIPULATING YOUR FILES

122 OBJECT LINKING AND EMBEDDING

124 CUSTOMIZING WORD

126 INDEX

About This Book

Welcome to *The Way Word for the Macintosh Works*, an easy-to-follow guide containing all the basic information you'll need to create a variety of documents using Word — and plenty more too!

This book is designed to make your introduction to Word version 6 as smooth as possible. It shows you how to use the most important features of Word and provides practical advice about many day-to-day word processing tasks. Throughout the book, you'll find step-by-step instructions for all the tasks you are asked to do; and you'll also find shortcuts, examples, and tips to make life even easier.

BUILDING YOUR CONFIDENCE

This book is organized so that you begin with the easiest tasks and move on to more advanced topics later. First you'll learn about the program itself and the elements you can see in the Word application window. Then you'll learn a few basic skills for creating your first Word document — a simple letter. As you move through the book, you'll perform a variety of more complex tasks, like designing images for your documents, performing a mail merge, incorporating charts into documents, and much more.

THE WYSIWYG CONCEPT

By the way, my name's the WYSIWYG wizard, and you'll find me popping up quite often throughout the book, handing out a few tips on getting the most out of Word.

One of the first questions you may be asking is: What does WYSIWYG mean? Well, WYSIWYG stands for "What You See Is What You Get." It was coined some years ago to describe programs with a special feature — namely that *what you see* on the screen is the same as *what you get* when you print it out. In this book we'll be turning the WYSIWYG concept around a little bit. Throughout the book, the practical instructions for learning about Word are accompanied by visual prompts (such as the screen shots and fragments shown on the next page) showing exactly what is happening on your computer screen. In other words, *what you see* on the page is the same as *what you get* on the screen. Step by step, you'll find out how to get the most out of Word.

Creating Pictures
Find out how to create colorful images to enhance the appearance of a document on pages 72 to 77.

Character Shaping
Discover how to use Word's Formatting toolbar to create special typographical effects, such as making a word italic or bold, on pages 56 to 57.

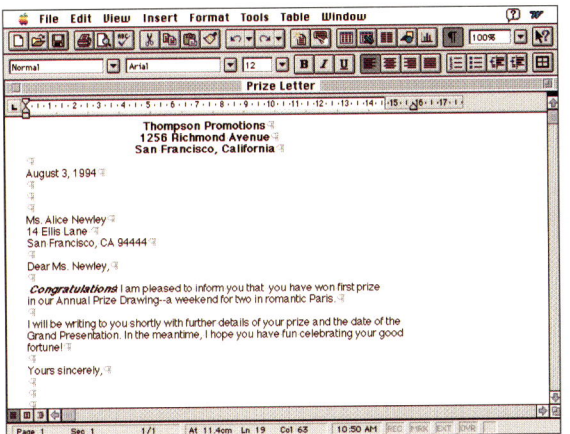

SCREENS AND FRAGMENTS
Sometimes, an instruction will be accompanied by a screen "shot" (like the one at left) showing how your screen will look at a particular stage in an operation. Or you'll see a smaller box within the screen (like the one at right), called a dialog box, that allows you to specify a number of different options for the command you're performing. Alternatively, as you follow a set of step-by-step instructions, you might see an accompanying series of screen "fragments" (like those shown at right); these home in on where the action is taking place.

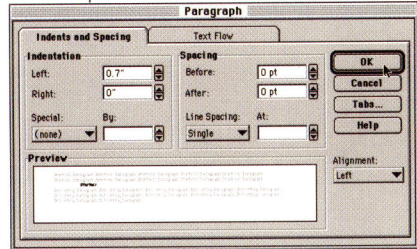

SPECIAL KEYS
On the Macintosh, the modifier keys are the Command key (sometimes called the Apple key), indicated by the and ⌘ symbols on the keyboard; the Option key (sometimes called the Alt key); the Shift key; and the Control key. This book refers to them as the Command, Option, Shift, and Control keys throughout.

TIPS AND SHORTCUTS
You'll see various tips in colored boxes scattered throughout the book. The *pink* boxes contain warnings about some common pitfalls you may run into when using your Macintosh and Word. The *green* boxes offer advice on anything from troubleshooting common problems to useful shortcuts and tips.

REFERENCE SECTION
At the back of the book, there's a useful Reference Section. This includes important information, such as how to install a printer and convert and manipulate files. At the end of the Reference Section, you'll find a comprehensive index to the whole volume.

EASY READING
The only way to become comfortable with any new program is to get hands-on experience. By the end of the book, you'll feel confident using the many features of Word, and you'll be able to create a wide variety of different types of documents — from impressive business reports to bright and colorful party invitations. Read on!

No Spaces!
You can't include any spaces in your bookmark name — only letters, numbers, or the underscore character (_). Choose a name with 1 to 20 characters, beginning with a letter.

Missing Something?
If you can't see the Standard toolbar or the Formatting toolbar, open the *View* menu, and choose *Toolbars*. In the *Toolbars* dialog box, click in the boxes next to *Standard* and *Formatting*. Then click on *OK*. If you can't see the Ruler, choose *Ruler* from the *View* menu.

1

CHAPTER ONE

Getting Started

This chapter introduces you to Word 6 for the Macintosh. In the first section you'll learn how to start up the program and how to use the menus, tools, and other elements that appear on screen. You'll also learn how to obtain on-screen help as you work on your Word documents and how to close a document and quit Word. In the second section, you'll find out how to create, save, and print a simple letter. Here you'll learn the essential steps involved in producing virtually any document using Word.

WELCOME TO WORD FOR THE MACINTOSH

YOUR FIRST LETTER

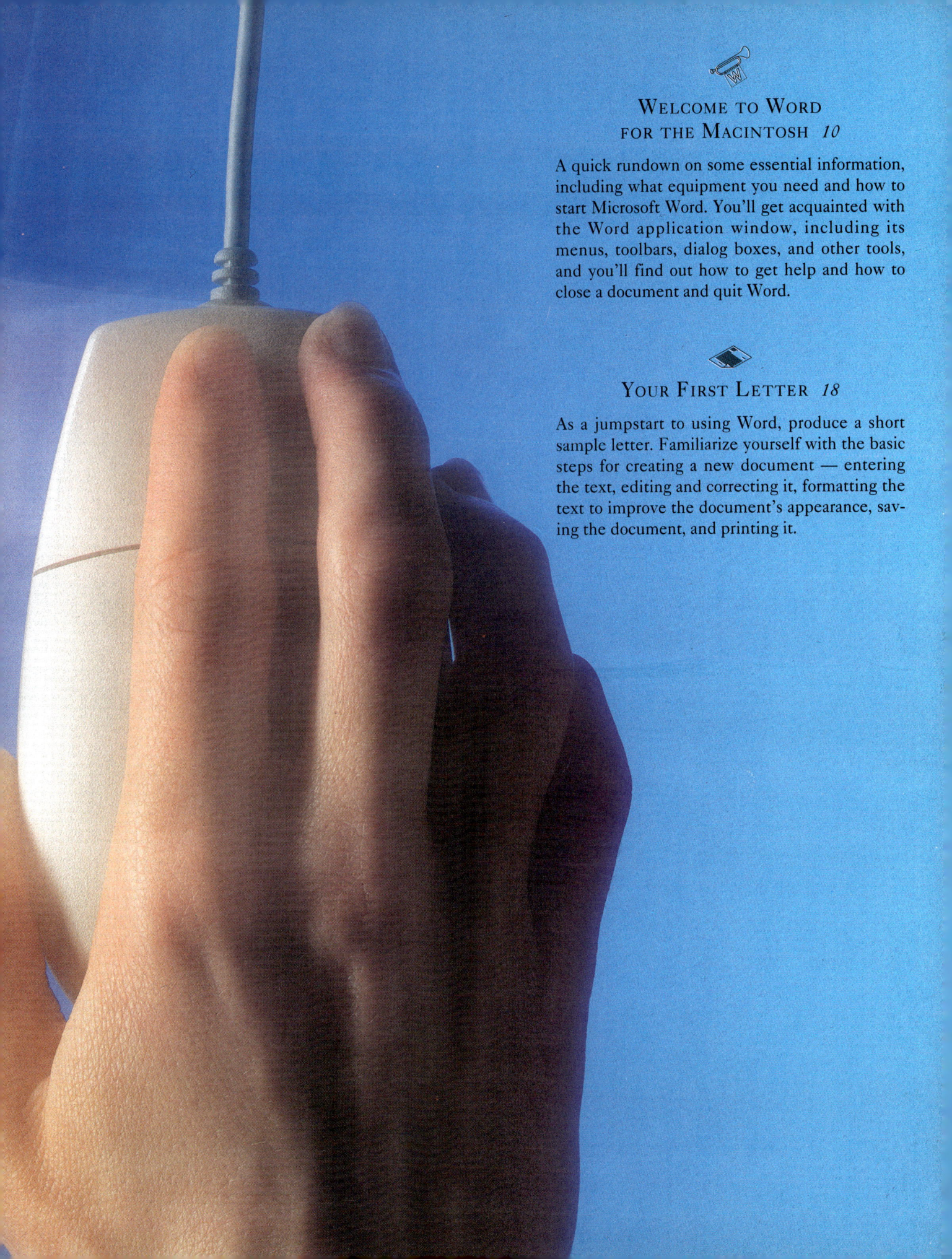

Welcome to Word for the Macintosh 10

A quick rundown on some essential information, including what equipment you need and how to start Microsoft Word. You'll get acquainted with the Word application window, including its menus, toolbars, dialog boxes, and other tools, and you'll find out how to get help and how to close a document and quit Word.

Your First Letter 18

As a jumpstart to using Word, produce a short sample letter. Familiarize yourself with the basic steps for creating a new document — entering the text, editing and correcting it, formatting the text to improve the document's appearance, saving the document, and printing it.

Welcome to Word for the Macintosh

WHEN WORD PROCESSING SOFTWARE was first introduced it was very simple and was used mainly to enter and store text and not much else. But times have changed. Microsoft Word for the Macintosh provides a powerful, modern solution for integrating text and graphics. Unlike earlier word processing software, Word can display your document on screen exactly as it will appear on the printed page — producing the results you want.

Design to Impress

Word provides tools so that, with a little practice, even the most inexperienced user can create all sorts of professional-looking, well-designed documents. You can experiment with a variety of typefaces, sizes, and styles; add pictures, graphs, and charts; and draw rules and borders. You can also make sure your document reads well by using the program's spelling-check, grammar-check, and thesaurus facilities. With Word, you have your very own desktop publishing system that is easy to learn and use.

Window Display
Rather than displaying a blank screen when you start up your program, the Macintosh displays a "desktop" made up of windows and icons, allowing you to point to what you want rather than remember complex keyboard commands.

What Equipment Do I Need?

In order to run Word 6 for the Macintosh you must have the correct hardware and system software. Minimum requirements include:

■ An Apple Macintosh computer with a 68020 microprocessor or higher or a Power Macintosh.

■ At least 4 megabytes of RAM (random access memory).

■ At least 5 megabytes of hard disk space for minimum installation; 18 megabytes for complete installation.

For software, your computer must have System 7 or later installed, along with Word 6 for the Macintosh itself.

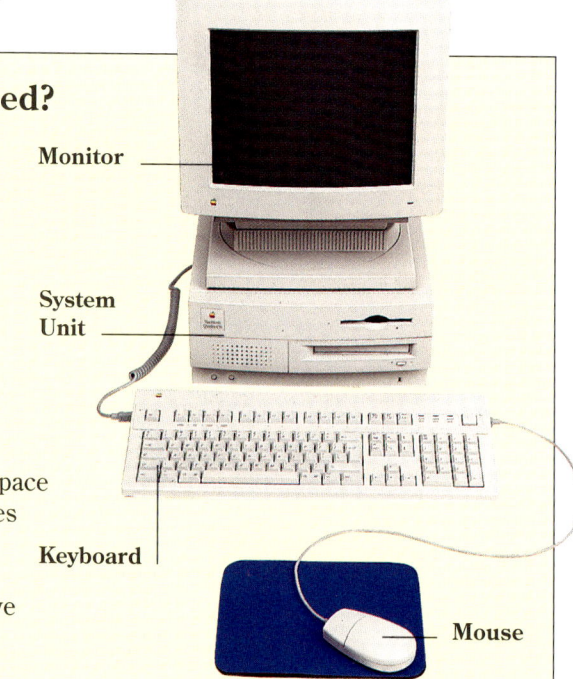

Monitor

System Unit

Keyboard

Mouse

? Do I Need a Special Printer?

The type of printer you choose to print your Word documents depends on the quality of documents you want to produce. If you want to produce crisp, professional-looking documents, you'll probably need a laser printer.

Using Your Mouse

Word for the Macintosh is specifically designed to be used in conjunction with a mouse. This hand-held device, which is connected to your Macintosh's keyboard, controls a pointer on the screen. The Macintosh mouse has a single button. The four main actions you'll perform with your mouse are moving, clicking, double-clicking, and dragging.

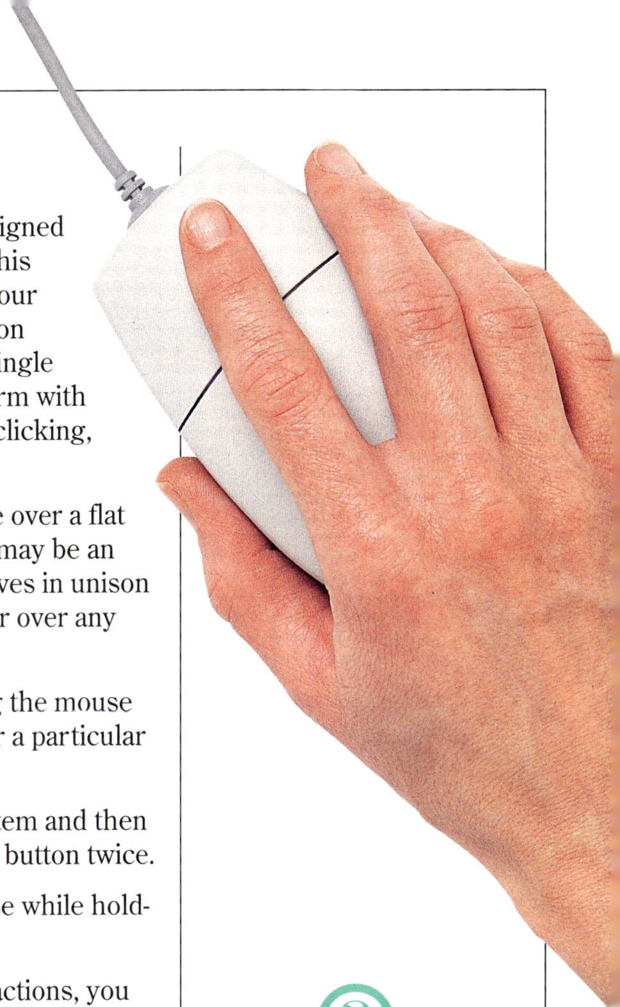

■ *Moving* consists of gliding your mouse over a flat surface. As you do so, a pointer — which may be an arrow, an I-beam, or another shape — moves in unison on the screen. You can position the pointer over any on-screen item.

■ *Clicking* entails pressing and releasing the mouse button when the pointer is positioned over a particular on-screen item.

■ *Double-clicking* entails pointing to an item and then quickly pressing and releasing the mouse button twice.

■ *Dragging* consists of moving the mouse while holding down the mouse button.

Using one or a sequence of these mouse actions, you can open and close files, negotiate your way around your document, move blocks of text, draw objects, and much more — all without having to type in any keyboard commands.

Running Word

Once you have installed Word version 6, you are ready to start the program and begin working on a document. Just follow the steps below:

How to Open Word 6

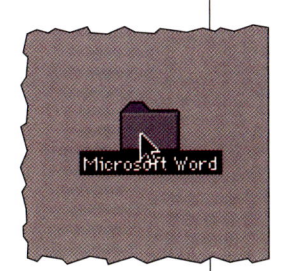

1 Double-click on the *Microsoft Word* folder to open it.

2 Double-click on the *Microsoft Word* icon. The Microsoft Word application window appears on the screen.

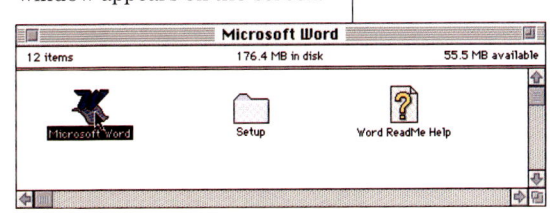

Pointer Problem?
If the pointer does not move on the screen when you move your mouse, check that the cable is plugged correctly into your Macintosh's keyboard. Remember that the mouse must be plugged in before you start your Macintosh.

Hidden Folder?
If you haven't double-clicked on the hard disk icon, you won't be able to see the *Microsoft Word* folder or icon on your desktop. When you double-click on the hard disk icon, the hard disk window opens, displaying a collection of folders and icons including the *Microsoft Word* folder.

WELCOME TO WORD FOR THE MACINTOSH

The Application Window

When you start Word, the program automatically displays a box entitled *Tip of the Day*, which provides you with a tip about how to use Word more efficiently. If you want to see another tip, click on *Next Tip*. If you don't, click on *OK* to close the box. A new, empty document window, which is given the name *Document1*, then opens. Above this name is a collection of menus, buttons, and tools. If you move your mouse pointer up to this area of the application window, the pointer becomes a black arrow. Pointing the arrow at a button or menu name and clicking or pressing on the mouse button chooses that item. These are the features that you will use as you work on your Word documents.

Here we briefly describe the elements you should see on your application window when you start Word. If your screen does not look like the one shown, refer to "Let's Synchronize" at right.

Close Box
Click on the close box to close the document window. Although the window closes, Word is still running.

Selection Bar
On the left-hand side of your screen is an invisible "bar" called the selection bar. You click here when you want to select certain amounts of text (see page 30). You know when you're in the selection bar because the mouse pointer changes to a right-pointing arrow.

Formatting Toolbar
This displays buttons you can use to change the appearance of your text. Using the Formatting toolbar, you can specify different fonts, styles, point sizes, text alignments, and so on.

View Buttons
Clicking on these buttons gives you different views of your document (see page 66). Make sure you are in Normal view by clicking on the far left button.

Status Bar
This displays information about your position in the active document, the current time, and about certain options that have been chosen. The status bar also displays information about selected commands.

Apple Icon
If you point here and press on the mouse button, a drop-down list appears showing standard Apple menu items and any applications that you've chosen to put in the menu.

Standard Toolbar
This contains a collection of buttons that speed up the most frequently used operations in Word.

Menu Bar
This contains eight menu names. If you point at one of these and press the mouse button, a list of commands appears. Choosing a command tells the program to perform a certain action.

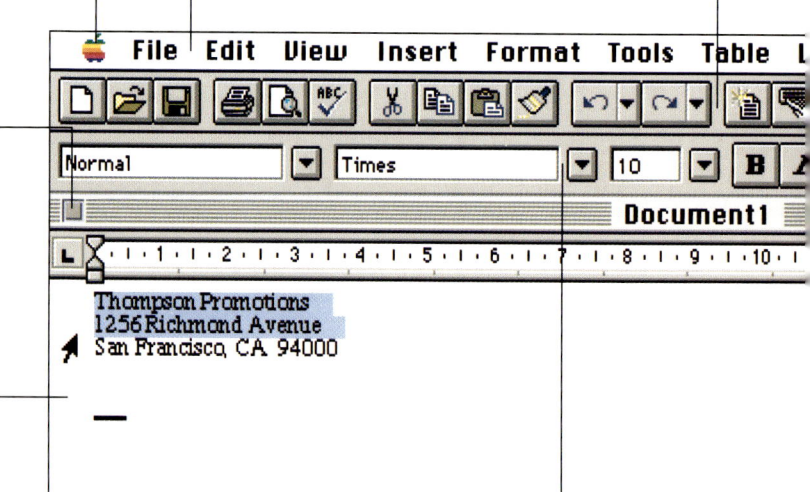

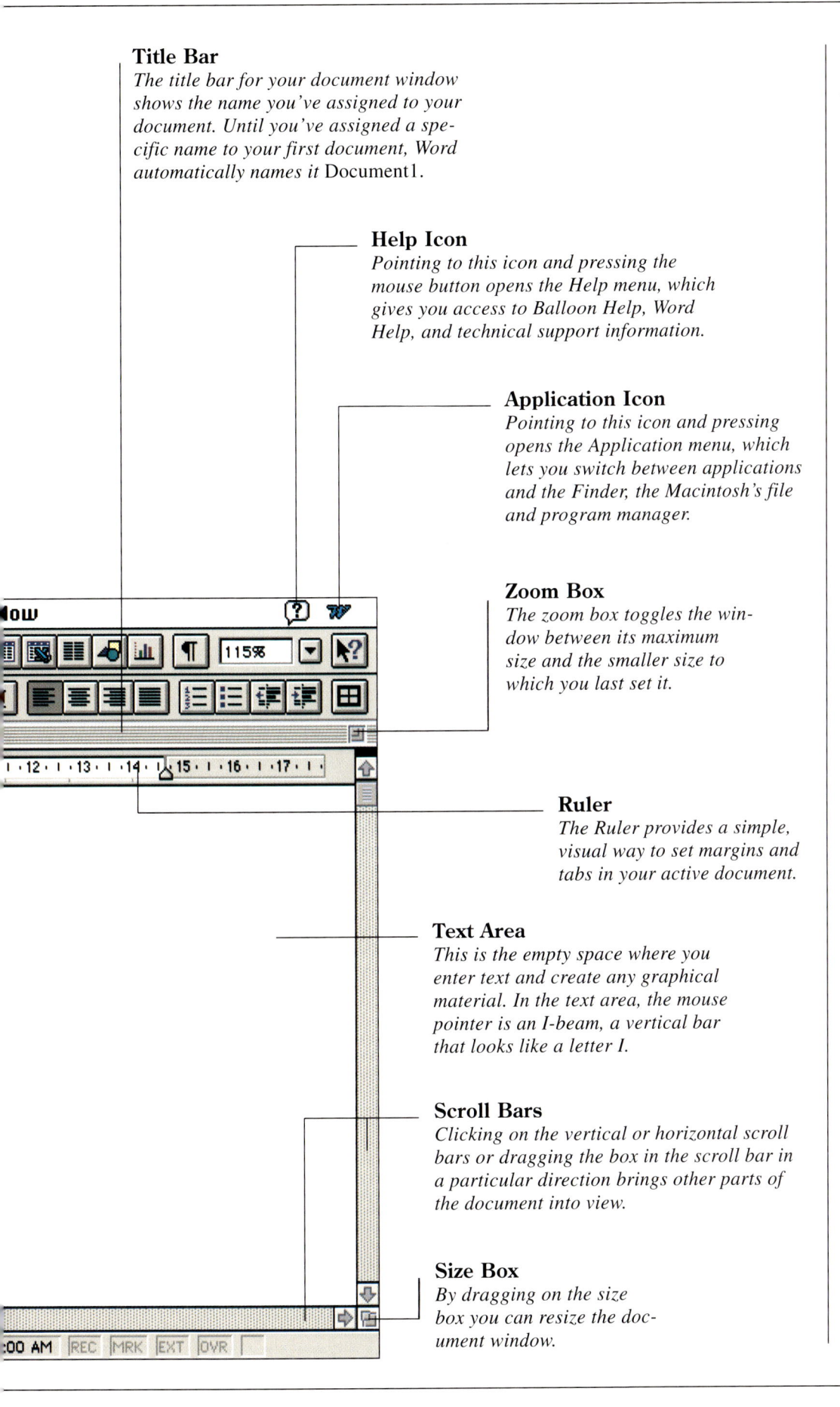

Title Bar
The title bar for your document window shows the name you've assigned to your document. Until you've assigned a specific name to your first document, Word automatically names it Document1.

Help Icon
Pointing to this icon and pressing the mouse button opens the Help menu, which gives you access to Balloon Help, Word Help, and technical support information.

Application Icon
Pointing to this icon and pressing opens the Application menu, which lets you switch between applications and the Finder, the Macintosh's file and program manager.

Zoom Box
The zoom box toggles the window between its maximum size and the smaller size to which you last set it.

Ruler
The Ruler provides a simple, visual way to set margins and tabs in your active document.

Text Area
This is the empty space where you enter text and create any graphical material. In the text area, the mouse pointer is an I-beam, a vertical bar that looks like a letter I.

Scroll Bars
Clicking on the vertical or horizontal scroll bars or dragging the box in the scroll bar in a particular direction brings other parts of the document into view.

Size Box
By dragging on the size box you can resize the document window.

Let's Synchronize

To make your screen look as much as possible like the screens in the book, you should do the following things:

■ When you start Word, make sure that the document window fills the screen. If the document window doesn't fill the screen, you should click on the zoom box to maximize the window.

■ You'll notice that highlighted text appears as black against a blue background throughout the book. This makes it easier to read highlighted text. If you have a color screen you can set your Macintosh to display highlighted text in the same way by choosing *Control Panels* from the Apple menu, double-clicking the *Color* icon, and then changing *Highlight color* to blue.

If your screen still does not look like the one shown at left, you may have a version of Word other than version 6 installed.

Missing Something?
If you can't see the Standard toolbar or the Formatting toolbar, open the *View* menu, and choose *Toolbars*. In the *Toolbars* dialog box, click in the boxes next to *Standard* and *Formatting*. Then click on *OK*. If you can't see the Ruler, choose *Ruler* from the *View* menu.

WELCOME TO WORD FOR THE MACINTOSH

How to Use the Menu Bar

If you point to a name in the menu bar and press the mouse button, a drop-down list appears that displays a selection of commands. To choose a command with the mouse, move the mouse pointer down to highlight the command and then release the mouse button. If you choose a command followed by an ellipsis (...), Word displays a dialog box in which you specify the options you want. Some commands in a menu list are followed by the name of a key or combination of keys. Pressing the specified keys achieves the same result as choosing the command with the mouse. You can close a menu by moving the mouse pointer off the menu and then releasing the mouse button.

Choosing a Command

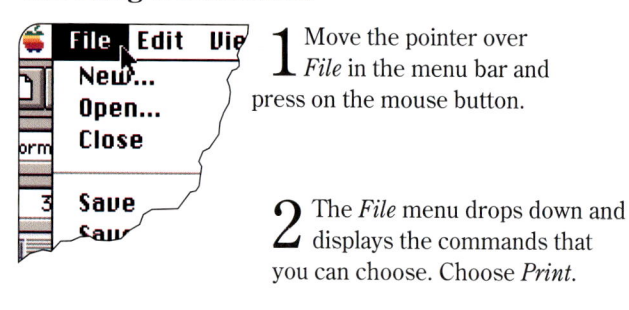

1 Move the pointer over *File* in the menu bar and press on the mouse button.

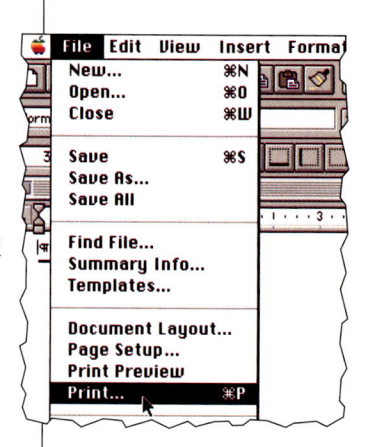

2 The *File* menu drops down and displays the commands that you can choose. Choose *Print*.

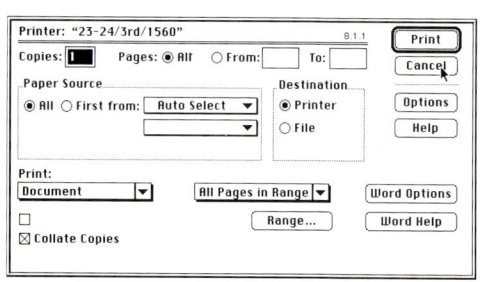

3 For now, click on *Cancel* in the *Print* dialog box to make it disappear.

What Does the Wristwatch Mean?

When you choose certain commands in Word, you'll notice a wristwatch symbol on the screen. This tells you that the program is in the process of performing some action. When the watch disappears, the action has been carried out.

Fingertip Control

You can use the keyboard to choose a menu command. Press the Command key and the Tab key together to activate the menu bar, then press the underlined letter in the menu item you want to select.

You can also use the Right and Left direction keys to select a menu, and the Up and Down direction keys to select items on a menu. Press Return to activate a menu item you've selected.

No Response!

If a menu command is dimmed, you won't be able to select it — Word is telling you that the command is not relevant to your current activity and so is unavailable.

Using a Toolbar

A toolbar is a selection of buttons displayed in a bar. Some buttons provide shortcuts to dialog boxes for commonly used commands. Others are shortcuts around dialog boxes. With a single click on a button you can save a file, print a document, and much more. Clicking on a button may also display a pop-up menu that gives you a list of options.

You can make the Standard toolbar float on the screen by double-clicking anywhere in the toolbar (except on a button). Double-click anywhere in the toolbar again to make the toolbar return to its normal position.

At right we show the buttons on the Standard toolbar. The Formatting toolbar is shown on page 56. To see a button's function, move the pointer over the button — a yellow box with the button's name appears, and an explanation of its action appears on the status bar.

14

DIALOG BOXES

If you choose a menu command that is followed by an ellipsis, a dialog box appears. A dialog box is a special window containing a variety of options that you choose in order to tell Word how to carry out the command. The dialog box displayed when you choose the *Print* command from the *File* menu illustrates some common features of dialog boxes.

Command Buttons
Clicking on a command button performs a particular action. Dimmed command buttons are unavailable. The default command button has a bold border. If you press Return when the dialog box is active, the default command button is activated.

Text Box
A text box lets you type in information. Clicking anywhere inside a text box causes a text insertion point to appear. In the From *and* To *boxes shown here, for example, you can enter the numbers of the page range you want to print.*

Option Buttons
These buttons represent mutually exclusive options, like the buttons on a car radio. If you click on one of the options, the others are automatically switched off.

Check Boxes
Clicking on a check box chooses that particular option, and an X appears in the box. To switch the option off, click on the check box again. Check box options aren't mutually exclusive.

Pop-Up List Box
Clicking on a list box that has a down arrow next to it displays a list of options from which you can choose.

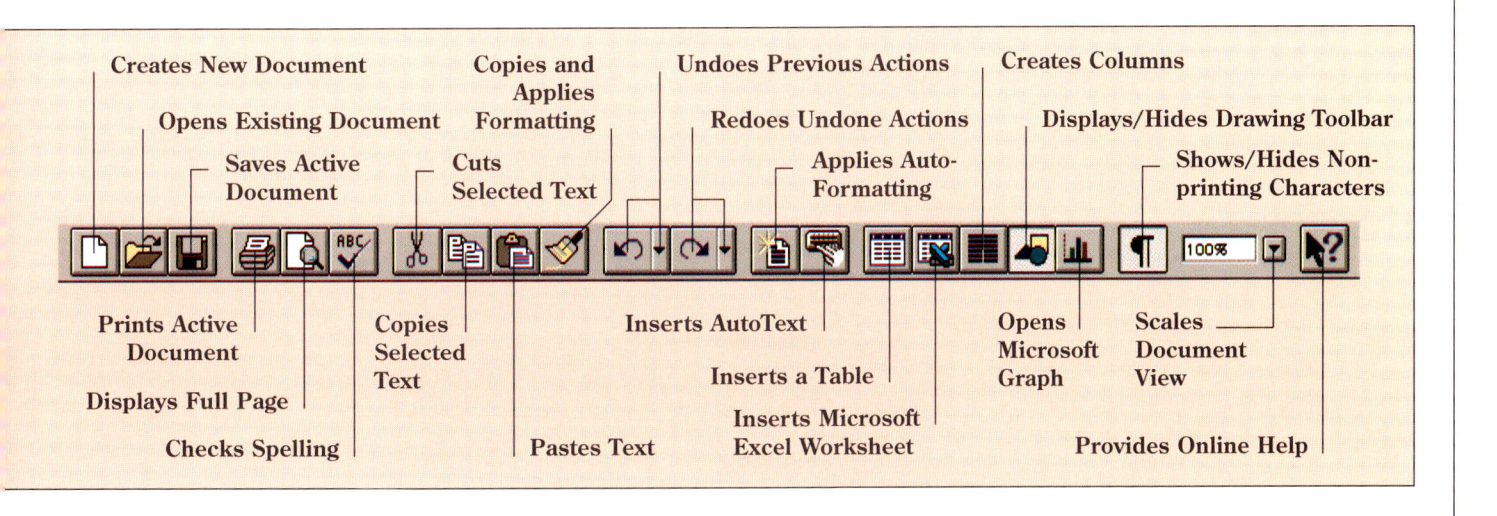

- Creates New Document
- Opens Existing Document
- Saves Active Document
- Prints Active Document
- Displays Full Page
- Checks Spelling
- Copies and Applies Formatting
- Cuts Selected Text
- Copies Selected Text
- Pastes Text
- Undoes Previous Actions
- Redoes Undone Actions
- Applies Auto-Formatting
- Inserts AutoText
- Inserts a Table
- Inserts Microsoft Excel Worksheet
- Creates Columns
- Displays/Hides Drawing Toolbar
- Shows/Hides Non-printing Characters
- Opens Microsoft Graph
- Scales Document View
- Provides Online Help

15

WELCOME TO WORD FOR THE MACINTOSH

How to Obtain Help

If you need help at any time when working on a Word document, you simply have to ask for it! Word can supply instant on-screen help for a variety of tasks. You can ask for step-by-step instructions for performing a particular procedure, get a definition for a word you don't understand, obtain detailed information about a command, and much more.

USING THE HELP POINTER

Clicking on the Help button on the Standard toolbar turns the mouse pointer into the help pointer. You can use this pointer to get an explanation of what menu commands, buttons, or other tools do. Follow these steps to get help on the Save button:

1 Click on the Help button on the Standard toolbar.

2 The mouse pointer changes to the Help pointer. Now click on the Save button on the Standard toolbar.

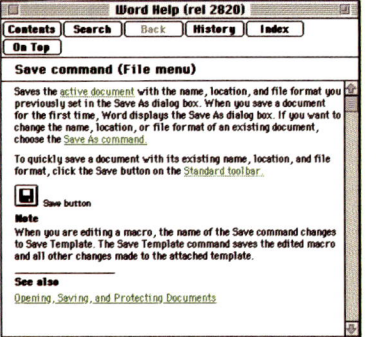

3 A *Word Help* window appears, displaying information about the *Save* command. You can click on any words that appear underlined and green to bring up more information on that topic.

4 When you have finished reading the Help information, click on the close box in the *Word Help* window to return to your Word document.

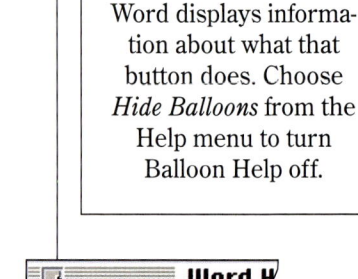

Balloon Help

To get help about interface elements (such as dialog boxes and buttons), choose *Show Balloons* from the Help menu. When you move the mouse pointer over a button, for example, Word displays information about what that button does. Choose *Hide Balloons* from the Help menu to turn Balloon Help off.

Word Help Contents

You can also get help by choosing *Microsoft Word Help* from the Help menu. A *Word Help Contents* screen appears, showing the kinds of information that are available.

■ *Using Word* gives you step-by-step information about specific tasks, such as adding a header to a document or creating a document template.

■ *Examples and Demos* are online tutorial programs that help you learn Word.

■ *Reference Information* gives you general reference help, tips, and answers to common questions.

■ *Programming with Microsoft Word* gives you complete reference information about the WordBasic language.

■ *Technical Support* tells you about the support options that are available to help you make the most of Word.

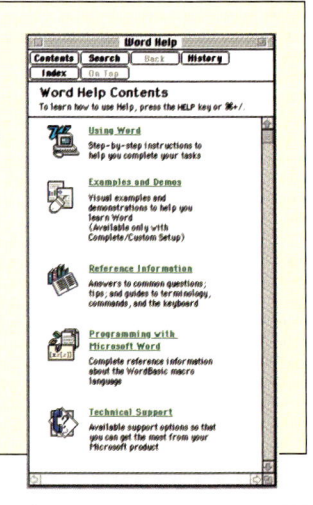

16

How to Close a Document and Quit Word

It is important for you to understand the difference between closing a document, hiding Microsoft Word, and quitting Word.

When you finish working on a document, it's a good idea to close it before opening another one. You can close a document without quitting Word. When you quit Word, you also close all open documents. Whenever you close or quit, you are asked if you want to save any open documents.

How Do I Hide Word?
You can hide the Word application entirely by choosing *Hide Microsoft Word* from the Application menu. Word is still running but is not visible on screen. To display Word again, choose *Microsoft Word* from the Application menu.

Closing a Document

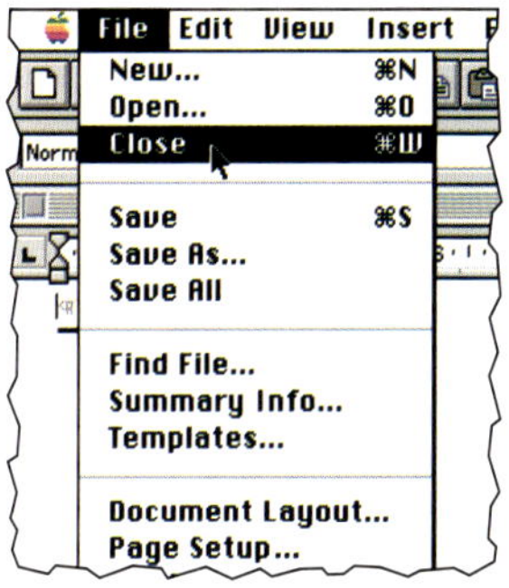

1 From the *File* menu, choose the *Close* command.

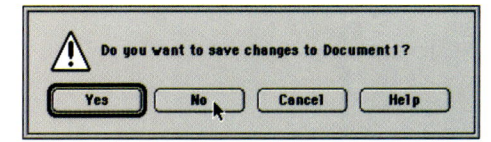

2 If you have entered anything in the document (in this case, *Document1*), a dialog box appears asking if you want to save the changes. In this instance click on *No*. (If you want to save the changes, see "Saving Your Document" on page 21.)

3 The document closes and the document window disappears, but the Word menu and toolbars remain on screen. The menu bar displays only the *File* menu name.

Microsoft Word Application Window

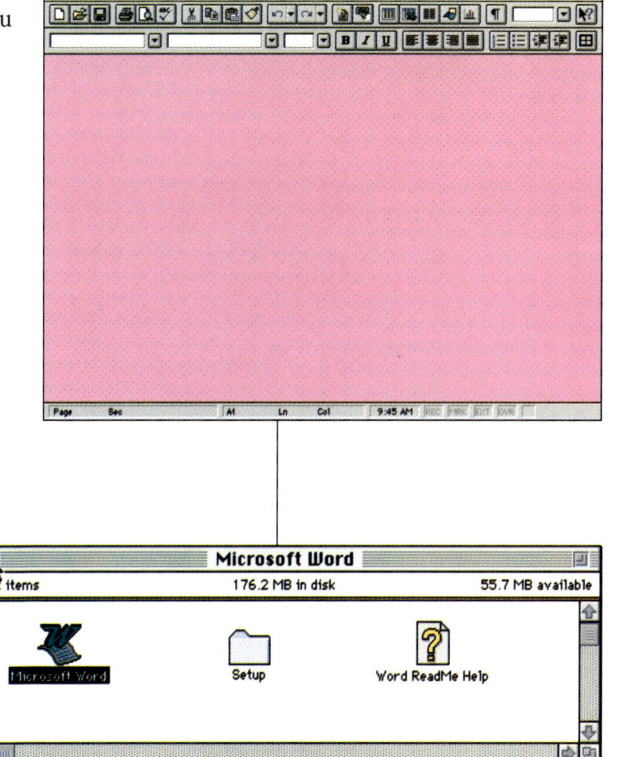

Quitting Word

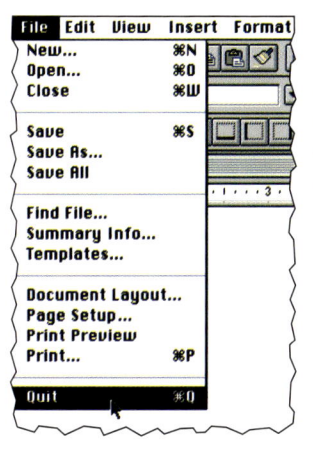

1 To exit Word, choose *Quit* from the *File* menu. Normally, you are asked if you want to save changes to each open document. But in this instance, you have already closed the only document that was open.

2 Word shuts down and the application shrinks back to the *Microsoft Word* program icon. Click on the close box to close the *Microsoft Word* window.

17

YOUR FIRST LETTER

Your First Letter

A GOOD STARTING POINT for learning some basic Word techniques is to create a short sample letter. The steps involved in producing the letter — typing in, editing and correcting, formatting, and printing — are essential steps involved in producing virtually any document using a word processor. Each of these steps is covered in greater detail later in the book, but here we take you briefly through the whole process. By the time you've finished the letter, you'll realize how easy using Word can be.

How to Create the Letter

Open Word (see page 11 if you've forgotten how to do this). An empty window, *Document1*, appears automatically on your screen. Don't worry about naming the document for now — you'll do this later when you save the document. In the *Document1* text area, you will enter the sample letter shown on the opposite page. As you work through your letter, you'll have the opportunity to use several special keys, such as the Tab key and direction keys, that perform specific operations during text entry. Later you'll learn how to format and print your letter.

Text Out of View?

If a document is long, you won't see all of it on the screen. Press the Page Up key to scroll up one screen or the Page Down key to scroll down. Word displays a few of the first or last lines of the previous screen so that you can keep track of where you are.

Steps to Creating a Document

Here are the basic steps you will follow to produce most Word documents.

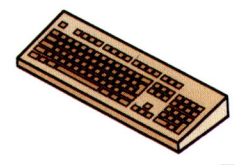

Typing In

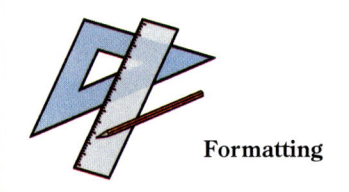

Editing and Correcting

Formatting

Printing

Moving Around Your Document

To move the insertion point (the flashing vertical bar) within a document, you can use the direction keys on your keyboard. If you press the Right or Left direction key, the insertion point moves one character to the right or left; if you press the Up or Down direction key, it moves up or down a line. If you hold down the direction key, the insertion point moves through the document continuously.

If you want to move the insertion point a long distance over an area of text, you'll find it easier to use your mouse. Just move the mouse I-beam pointer to where you want the insertion point to appear and then click the mouse button. You'll find more information on the different ways to negotiate your way around a document in Chapter Two (see "How to Move Around the Text Area" on page 29).

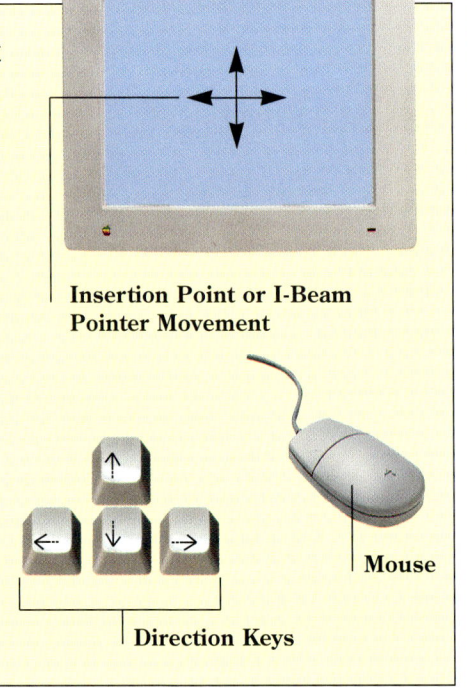

Insertion Point or I-Beam Pointer Movement

Mouse

Direction Keys

Want to Indent?

If you want to indent the first line of a paragraph, you can press the Tab key to move the insertion point a standard measure forward on the line. The standard (default) tab movement is equal to one-half inch. For more information on indentation, see page 61.

18

ENTERING YOUR TEXT

The first step in creating any Word document is to enter the text. In the empty *Document1* window, type the short letter shown below. The text will automatically begin at the insertion point, which you'll see flashing at the top left-hand corner of your screen. Don't worry if the lines in your letter break in different places. Just follow these steps:

Typing In

1 Type the name of the sender, and then press Return to move down to a new line.

2 Type the sender's street address, and then press Return. Type the next line and then press Return twice after the zip code to create a blank line.

3 Type the date, and then press Return four times.

4 Type the addressee's name and press Return. Follow this pattern for the next two lines of the address, pressing Return twice after the zip code to create a blank line.

5 Type **Dear Ms. Newley,** and press Return twice.

6 Press Tab once to indent the first main paragraph of the letter and begin typing. Don't press Return at the end of lines. At the end of this paragraph press Return twice to create a blank line between the paragraphs.

7 Press Tab and type the second paragraph, including the deliberate mistakes in the words **writing** and **celebrating**. Press Return twice.

8 Type **Yours sincerely,** press Return five times, and then type **Simon Swan**. Press Return and then type **Promotions Manager**.

Key Positions
To create the letter shown below, you have to use the Tab key and the Return key. Here is what they look like:

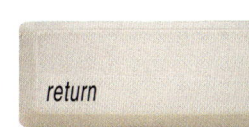

Tab Key **Return Key**

⚠ Point of No Return!
You do not have to press Return to end a line within a paragraph; Word has a word-wrap feature that breaks the line and moves the insertion point to a new line when you reach the right margin.

Thompson Promotions
1256 Richmond Avenue
San Francisco, CA 94000

August 3, 1994

Ms. Alice Newley
14 Ellis Lane
San Francisco, CA 94444

Dear Ms. Newley,

 Congratulations! I am pleased to inform you that you have won first prize in our Annual Prize Drawing -- a weekend for two in romantic Paris.

 I will be wriring to you shortly with further details of your prize and the date of the Grand Presentation. In the meantime, I hope you have fun celegrating your good fortune!

Yours sincerely,

Simon Swan
Promotions Manager

YOUR FIRST LETTER

Correcting Your Mistakes

Don't worry if your typing or spelling is not accurate when you work on your Word documents. It's easy to correct spelling mistakes and typing errors within your document by using the Delete and Del keys on your keyboard. First use your mouse or the direction keys on your keyboard to move the insertion point next to the mistyped character. Pressing the Delete key erases the character to the left of the insertion point, and pressing Del erases the character just after the insertion point. Practice using these keys by correcting the mistakes in the letter you've just created. If you want to delete more than one character at a time, see pages 30 to 33 for instructions on selecting and revising text.

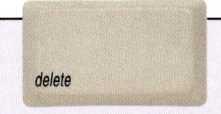

Delete Key

*Click the mouse I-beam pointer to place the insertion point just after the mistyped **r** in the word **wriring**, and then press the Delete key.*

I will be wriring to you ation. In the meantime, I

*The letter **r** disappears, and you can type **t** in its place.*

I will be writing to you ation. In the meantime, I

Del Key

*Now click the mouse pointer to place the insertion point just before the mistyped **g** in **celegrating**, and then press the Del key.*

h further details of your p have fun celegrating your

*The letter **g** disappears and you can type **b** in its place.*

h further details of your p have fun celebrating your

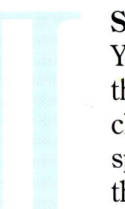

SHOWING NONPRINTING CHARACTERS

Your document includes certain nonprinting characters that do not normally appear on the screen. Nonprinting characters include tabs (→), paragraph marks (¶), and space marks (·). It is useful to see these characters so that you can easily locate them — for example, if you want to delete them or insert text between them.

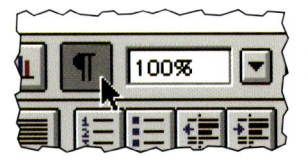

1 Click on the Show/Hide ¶ button on the Standard toolbar to view nonprinting characters.

2 The nonprinting characters now appear on the screen. Move the insertion point just to the left of the word **Congratulations**. Press Delete to delete the tab before the word.

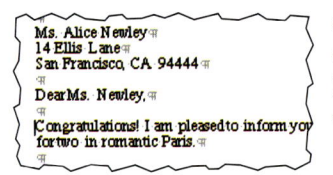

3 The word **Congratulations** moves back to the left margin. Now delete the tab in front of the word **I** in the second paragraph.

4 Click on the Show/Hide ¶ button again to make the nonprinting characters disappear.

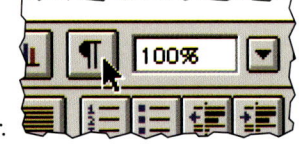

SAVING YOUR DOCUMENT

If you want to return to your document in the future, you need to give it a name and store it on disk. It's best to give it an obvious name that you'll remember easily.

Once you've given it a name, you need to save your document at regular intervals in order to keep any changes you've made. To save your document, you can use the *File* menu to access the *Save* command or you can click on the Save button on the Standard toolbar.

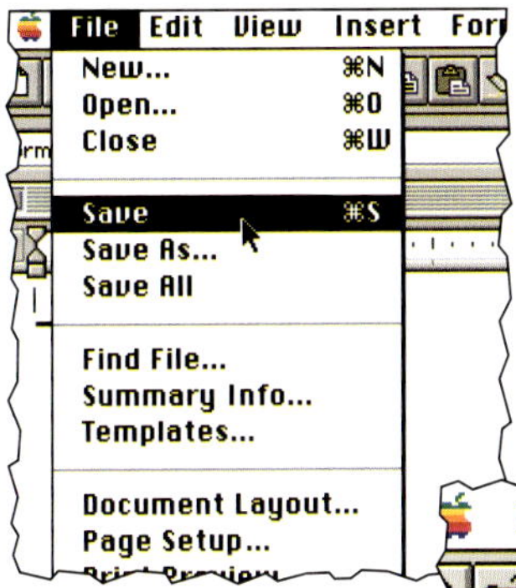

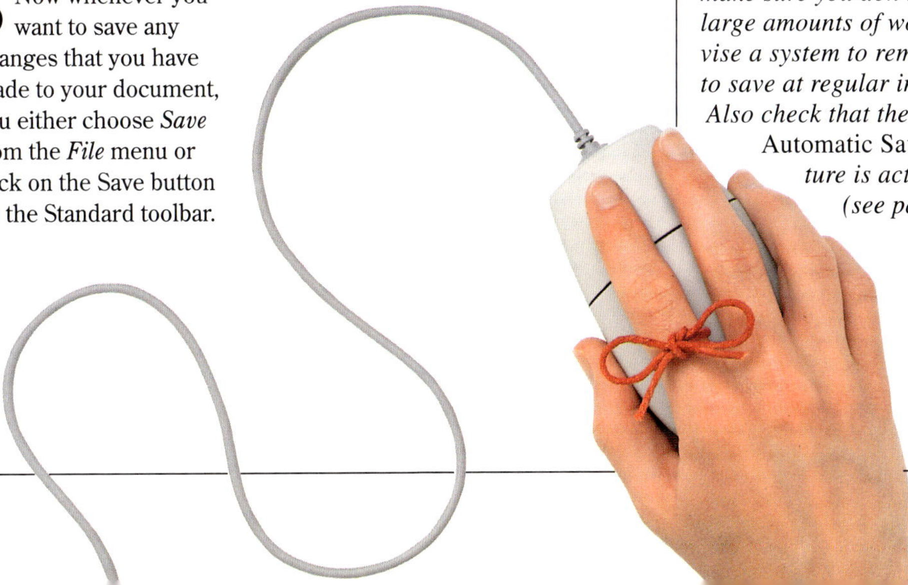

Should I Avoid Certain Characters When Naming Files?
You don't need to avoid any particular characters apart from the colon (:) when you name a Macintosh file. Your file name can be up to 32 characters long and can include spaces.

1 Choose *Save* from the *File* menu or click on the Save button on the Standard toolbar.

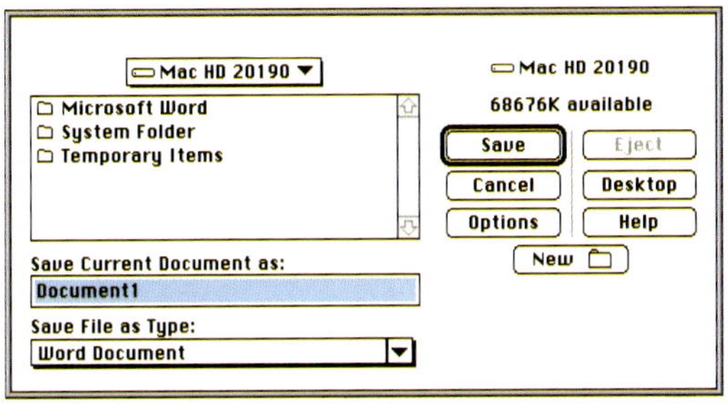

2 When you're saving for the first time, Word displays the dialog box shown at left. Make sure the Macintosh hard disk is displayed in the folders list box at the top. Under *Save Current Document as*, *Document1* is highlighted as a suggestion for a filename.

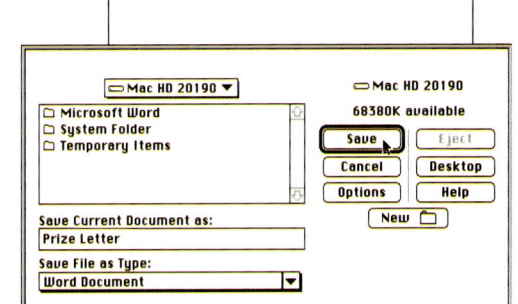

3 *Document1* is too general a name, so type **Prize Letter** in the *Save Current Document as* box and then click on the *Save* button.

4 Your letter is now called **Prize Letter** and the new name appears in the title bar.

5 Now whenever you want to save any changes that you have made to your document, you either choose *Save* from the *File* menu or click on the Save button on the Standard toolbar.

Don't Forget to Save
No computer is completely immune to power failure. If the power fails, you will lose any changes that you have made since you last saved your document. To make sure you don't lose large amounts of work, devise a system to remind you to save at regular intervals. Also check that the Automatic Save feature is activated (see page 27).

21

YOUR FIRST LETTER

How to Format and Print Your Letter

When you have finished typing your letter, you may want to make it more interesting visually. Detailed information on the different ways you can style and format your documents is given in Chapter Three, but here you'll learn how to perform a few simple formatting tasks. When you are happy with the appearance of your document, you are then ready for the final stage of its production — printing.

FORMATTING

Using Word, you can improve the appearance of your letter in several ways. Before you can apply any formatting to an area of text, however, you must select it. You'll find it easier to format your document if the non-printing characters are displayed. First click on the Show/Hide ¶ button, and then follow the steps below:

1 Select the whole letter by holding down the Command key and clicking anywhere to the left of the text in the margin (this area of the screen is called the selection bar). The whole letter is highlighted.

2 Click on the down-arrow button to the right of the Font box on the Formatting toolbar. Use your mouse to scroll up and down the list to see the fonts that are available, and choose *Arial*. Word changes the highlighted text from the default font to the new font.

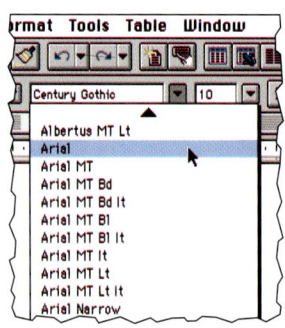

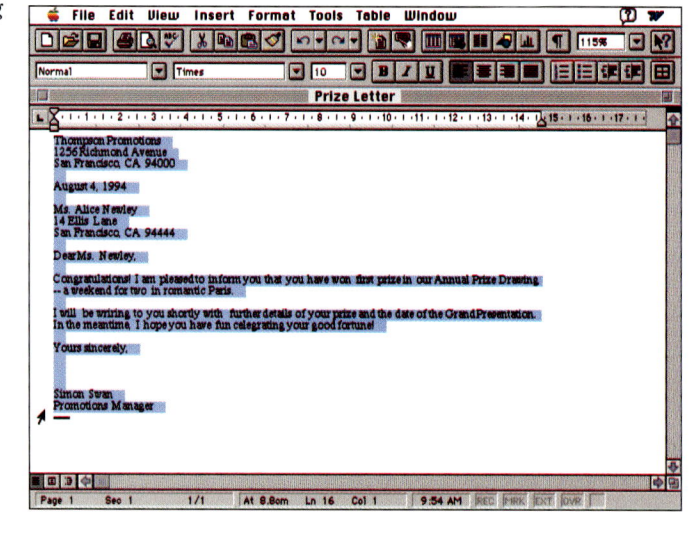

3 Select the return address by positioning the mouse pointer in the selection bar to the left of the word **Thompson**, holding down the mouse button, and dragging the pointer down until the whole address is highlighted. Then release the mouse button.

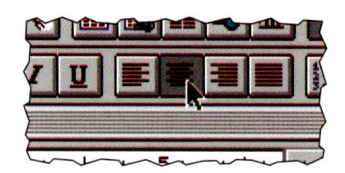

4 Center the selected text on the page by clicking on the Center button on the Formatting toolbar.

22

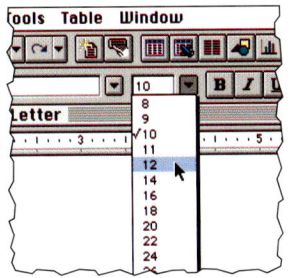

5. While the return address is still selected, click on the down-arrow button to the right of the Font Size box on the Formatting toolbar and choose *12* as the new point size.

6. With the return address still highlighted, click on the Bold button on the Formatting toolbar.

7. Select the word **Congratulations** by double-clicking anywhere within the word. Click on the Bold button and then on the Italic button.

It Works Like Magic
Word can help format professional-looking documents at a touch of a button. Clicking on the AutoFormat button on the Standard toolbar prompts Word to analyze and polish your document for you.

A Stylish Document
You now know how to use some of the tools that help improve the look of a document. The finished letter is shown at right.

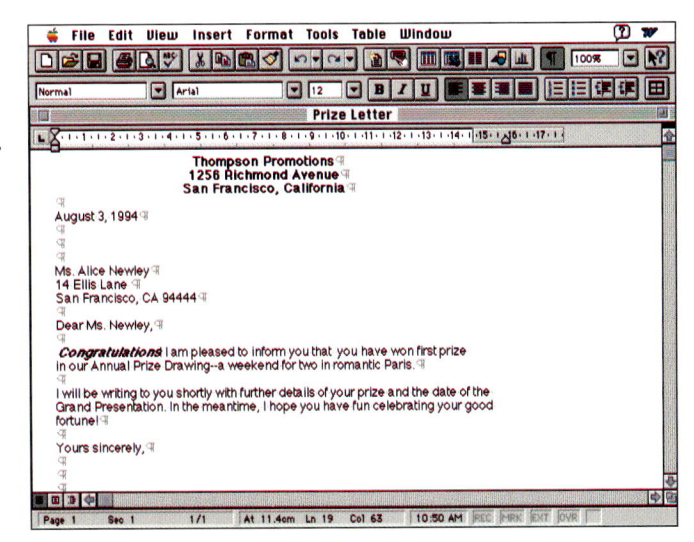

PRINTING
When you are happy with the formatting changes you have made to your letter, you are ready to print and then close the document. Just follow these steps:

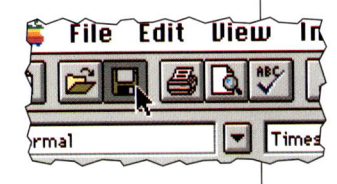

1. Click on the Save button on the Standard toolbar to save the changes you have made.

2. Click on the Print button on the Standard toolbar to print your letter.

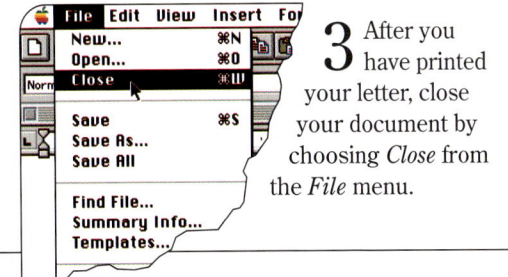

3. After you have printed your letter, close your document by choosing *Close* from the *File* menu.

CHAPTER TWO

Up & Running

In this chapter, you'll be practicing a number of commonly used word-processing techniques by creating and revising an example document — a restaurant menu. You'll learn how to add special characters to your document, move sections of text, find and replace words, check spelling and grammar, and much more. You'll also discover how to use split screens and how to manage your files efficiently.

TEXT ENTRY • TEXT SELECTION
TEXT REVISION • TEXT CHECKING
MANIPULATING WINDOWS
FILE MANAGEMENT

Text Entry *26*

Create a new document — a restaurant menu — and start typing in some text. Learn how to incorporate special items and how to move around your document.

Text Selection *30*

Selecting text is an important step in learning to work in Word. Before you can work with text — moving, formatting, or correcting it — you must learn to select text efficiently.

Text Revision *32*

Learn how to revise text after you've typed it in. You'll see how to insert, delete, move, copy, and paste text; how to search for and replace text; and how to use bookmarks.

Text Checking *40*

Learn about Word's tools to help you perfect your writing — checking spelling, suggesting different words to avoid repetition, and examining grammar.

Manipulating Windows *44*

Explore the possibilities of your Word application window: work in the most convenient way by splitting, resizing, or maximizing your windows; open several documents at the same time; switch between them effortlessly.

File Management *48*

An introduction to the elements of file management. Discover how files are organized into folders on your Macintosh and how to store, find, and delete files.

TEXT ENTRY

Text Entry

TYPING IN TEXT IS PROBABLY the first thing you'll do when creating any new document. In this section, you'll start entering the text of a restaurant menu. Later in the book, you'll format the text and add other items to the menu. When you've finished, it will look like the menu at left. But before you begin, let's learn how to open new documents.

How to Open a New Document

When you first open Word, it displays a new empty document window, *Document1*. If you have a document on your screen (or if you have closed a document but have not quit Word) you can use the *New* command from the *File* menu to open a new document. You should save the document with a name reflecting its content before you enter any text. Doing so will prevent any possible confusion later on.

> **What's a Template?**
> A template is a pattern that helps you create and format a document. Word supplies a variety of templates designed for standard business letters and other documents. You can also create your own templates. See pages 104 to 106 for more information on templates.

Opening a New Document

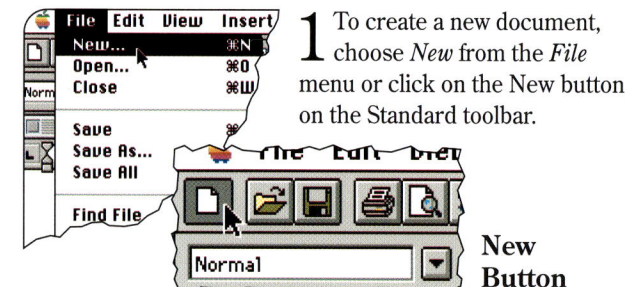

1 To create a new document, choose *New* from the *File* menu or click on the New button on the Standard toolbar.

New Button

2 If you choose the command from the *File* menu, the *New* dialog box appears, asking if you want to use the *Normal* template. Click on *OK*. If you click on the New button on the Standard toolbar, Word uses the *Normal* template automatically.

3 Word creates a new document window, *Document2*, in which you can start typing.

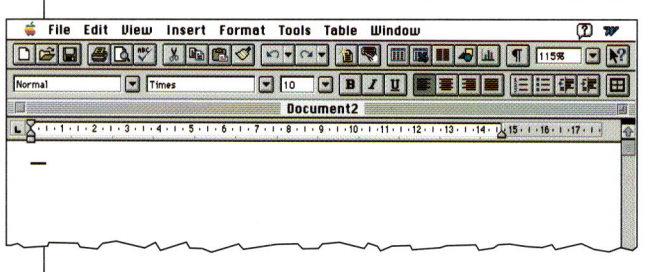

4 Before entering text in a new document, you should save the document. Click on the Save button on the Standard toolbar, name the file **Restaurant Menu** in the dialog box that appears (see page 21), and save it to your hard disk.

26

How to Type in Text

Now start entering some text into the **Restaurant Menu** document file that you've created. Don't worry if your typing or spelling isn't accurate — you can ignore any errors for now because you'll use the spelling checker to help you correct your mistakes later in this chapter.

Word automatically moves the insertion point to a new line when you reach the right margin, so you need to press Return only at the end of a paragraph. Pressing Return more than once adds blank lines between paragraphs. Type the text below, pressing Return only where you see <Return> in the text. If they are not already displayed, click on the Show/Hide ¶ button to display nonprinting characters.

Automatic Save
Word automatically saves a temporary copy of the document you're working on at 10-minute intervals. After a power failure or other problem, Word will display the last-saved copy of that document on the screen. (You'll see *(Recovered)* in the document title.) To change the time interval between saves, choose *Options* from the *Tools* menu. In the *Options* dialog box, click on the *Save* tab. Under *Save Options*, you'll see the checked *Automatic Save Every* box. Change the value in the *Minutes* box to the value you want, and then click on *OK*.

Sunset Bay Grill <Return> <Return>

TRADITIONAL FRESH SEAFOOD (AND PLENTY MORE BESIDES) <Return> <Return>

Like many other restaurants, Sunset Bay Grill boasts a relaxed, anything-goes atmosphere. Open every day from noon to midnight, we will provide the type of service you need, whether you want a quiet meal for two or a fun-filled group night out. For the extra rowdy, we have a large back-room -- soundproofed! Unlike most seafood restaurants, however, Sunset Bay Grill does not dwell on fresh fish and lobster alone. Our forceful (but friendly) chef, Hank, insists that we serve a wide range of interesting and international dishes too! And all at very reasonable prices. We pride ourselves on good value. But be warned: Hank doesn't believe in small portions -- when you come to Sunset Bay Grill, you must come hungry (if you manage three whole courses, we'll be amazed). Long live the Sunshine Coast. Long live Sunset Bay Grill.

OPENING AN EXISTING DOCUMENT

You may need to close your Restaurant Menu document at some point during these exercises. To do so, choose *Close* from the *File* menu and click on *Yes* to save the changes. When you want to open the restaurant menu again, follow these steps:

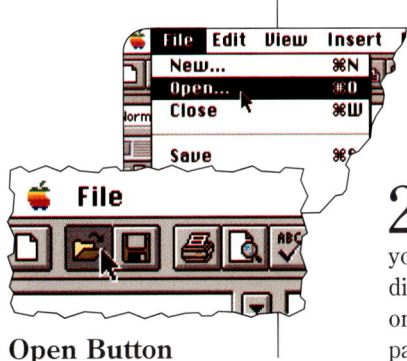

1 Choose *Open* from the *File* menu or click on the Open button on the Standard toolbar.

2 A dialog box appears. From the pop-up list above the scroll box, choose the location of your document (probably your Macintosh hard disk). Then choose **Restaurant Menu** and click on *Open* to open it. (See "File Management" on pages 48 to 51 for more information.)

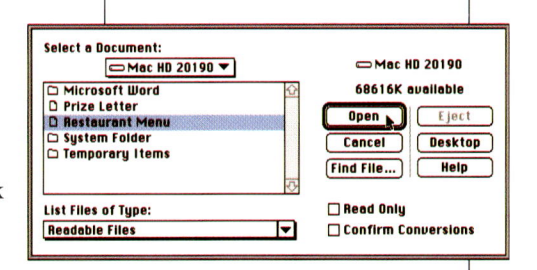

Open Button

TEXT ENTRY

How to Insert Special Items

Some text items, such as accented characters, cannot be typed in using the keyboard. To display and print such special items, you can use the *Symbol* command from the *Insert* menu.

September 15, 1994 <Return>
TODAY'S SPECIAL <Return>
Try our "hungry sailor" menu: <Return> <Return>

Crab soup <Return>
All the fresh pasta you can eat <Return>
Rum and raisin sundae (very large) <Return> <Return>
only $10.95 <Return> <Return> <Return>

Starters <Return> <Return>

French onion soup $2.00 <Return>
Garlic bread $2.00 <Return>
Vegetable soup $2.95 <Return>
Lobster pate with bread $3.50 <Return>
Bay oysters (6) $4.00 <Return>

ADDING ACCENTED CHARACTERS

Before adding any accented characters, let's add some more text to your restaurant menu. Put your insertion point at the end of what you have typed so far, press Return twice, and then type in the text shown at right. After you finish typing, perform the steps below:

1 Click the I-beam pointer just to the left of the **a** in **pate**. Hold down the mouse button, drag the mouse one character to the right, and release the button to highlight just the letter **a**.

2 Choose *Symbol* from the *Insert* menu.

3 The *Symbol* dialog box appears. Make sure the *Font* text box reads *(normal text)*. If it does not, click on the down arrow to the right of the box and select *(normal text)*. Then click on â and click on *Insert*, or simply double-click on â. You'll see the accented character replace **a** in your restaurant menu.

4 The *Symbol* dialog box remains open until you choose *Cancel* or *Close*, so you can scroll to other locations in your document and insert as many symbols as you want. Click in your document and use the same method to insert **é** at the end of **pâté**.

ADDING OTHER SPECIAL CHARACTERS

Your text contains other characters such as double hyphens that you can now modify using the *Symbol* dialog box. To change the double hyphens to em dashes, follow the steps at the top of the next page:

Adding Today's Date
If you want to add the current date to your document, you may find it quickest to use the *Insert* menu. Position the insertion point where you want the date to appear, then choose *Date and Time* from the *Insert* menu. In the *Date and Time* dialog box, choose the date format you want and click on *OK*. To insert the current time, choose one of the time options in the same way.

28

How to Insert Special Characters

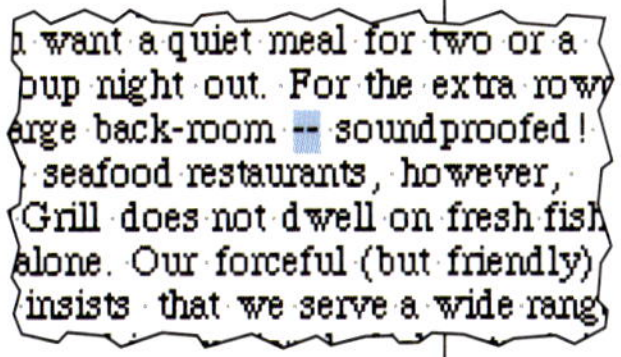

1 Click in your document and move upward in the text using the Up direction key, then select the double hyphen between **back-room** and **soundproofed**. You may need to move the *Symbol* dialog box to do this efficiently. To move the dialog box, point to its title bar, hold down the mouse button, and drag the box to a new position (see "Moving a Window" on page 47).

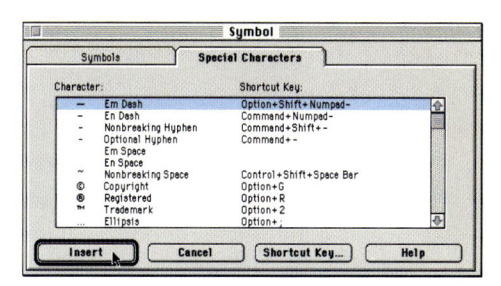

2 In the *Symbol* dialog box, click on the *Special Characters* tab. A list appears showing the special characters you can insert. Select the line representing the em dash (—) and click on *Insert*. Repeat the procedure to insert an em dash between **portions** and **when**. Remember to click in your document before using the Up direction key.

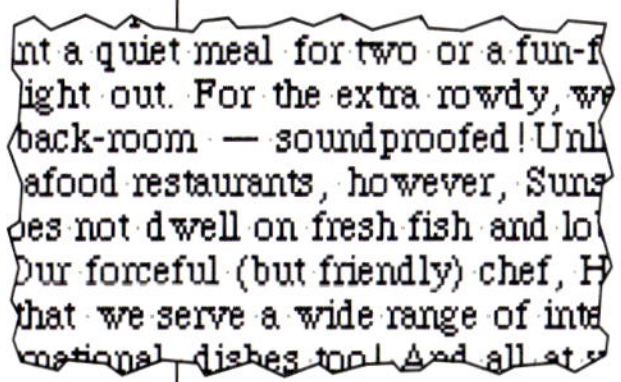

3 The double hyphens are replaced by em dashes. Click on the *Close* button to close the *Symbol* dialog box.

How to Move Around the Text Area

One way to move the insertion point within your document is to move the I-beam pointer to the new position using your mouse and then click on the mouse button (see page 18). But there are a number of other shortcuts to help you navigate around your text:

Moving Left and Right

■ To move to the left or right one character, press the Left or Right direction key on your keyboard. Hold the key down for continuous movement.

■ To move to the left or right one word, hold down the Command key and press the Left or Right direction key.

■ To move to the beginning of the current line, press the Home key. To move to the end of a line, press the End key.

■ To move the entire document horizontally, drag the scroll box in the horizontal scroll bar to the left or right. Alternatively, click on the left or right arrow button at either end of the horizontal scroll bar. Hold down the mouse button with the mouse pointer positioned on one of these arrow buttons for continuous scrolling.

Moving Up and Down

■ To move up or down one line, press the Up or Down direction key. Hold the key down for continuous movement.

■ To move up or down one paragraph, hold down the Command key and press the Up or Down direction key.

■ To scroll the document up or down one screen, press the Page Up or the Page Down keys.

■ To move to the top or bottom of your screen, hold down the Command key and press Page Up or Page Down.

■ To move to the beginning or end of a document, hold down the Command key and press Home or End.

■ To move the entire document vertically, use the vertical scroll box or the up and down scroll arrow buttons.

Smart or Straight?
Word automatically inserts special "smart quotes" (curly quotation marks) when you type quotation marks with the keyboard. If you want to use straight quotes instead, choose *AutoCorrect* from the *Tools* menu. In the *AutoCorrect* dialog box, click on the *Change 'Straight Quotes' to 'Smart Quotes'* box to deselect this option, and then click on *OK*.

29

TEXT SELECTION

Text Selection

BEFORE YOU CAN DO ANYTHING to a section of text — move it, copy it, delete it, or change its format — you must first select it. Learning the most efficient way to select different amounts of text will speed up many of your operations in Word.

How to Select Text

There are a variety of techniques for selecting text; the best method depends on the amount you want to highlight. For example, you might want to select a whole paragraph in order to move it, or you might want to select just one word in order to delete it. In many instances, you'll need to click on an area called the selection bar in the left margin of the screen. Use your restaurant menu to practice the following methods.

Selection Bar

How Do I Deselect?
If you select an area of text and then decide that you don't want it selected, click anywhere outside the selection in the document window to deselect it.

Selecting a Single Word
To select a single word, you double-click on it with the mouse. Place the I-beam pointer in the word **other** in the first sentence of the main paragraph, and double-click on it. The word and any spaces after it become highlighted.

Selecting a Line
To select a line, you click in the selection bar next to the line you want. Select a line in the main paragraph by clicking in the selection bar next to it.

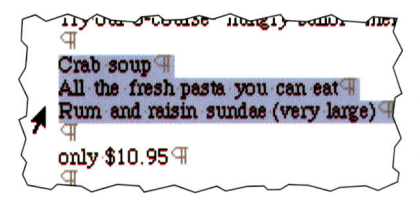

Selecting a Sequence of Lines
To select a sequence of lines, you click in the selection bar next to the first line you want to select and drag the mouse up or down. Hold down the mouse button when the pointer is in the selection bar next to **Crab soup**; drag down to select the next two lines, and then release the mouse button.

Selecting to the End of a Line
To select from the current position of the insertion point to the end of the line, you hold down Shift and press End. Holding down Shift and pressing Home selects from the current position to the beginning of a line. Click the I-beam pointer in front of (**AND PLENTY MORE BESIDES**), hold down Shift and press End.

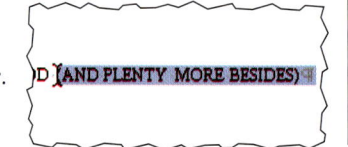

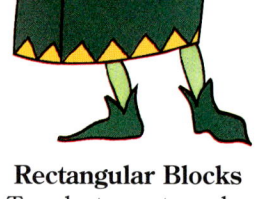

Rectangular Blocks
To select a rectangular block of text of any size within your document, hold down Control and Option, put your I-beam pointer at one corner of the block you want to select, press down on the mouse button, and drag the mouse in a diagonal direction. Release the mouse button when the rectangular area of text you want is selected.

Selecting a Sentence
To select a whole sentence, you hold down the Command key and click anywhere in the sentence. Hold down the Command key and click anywhere in the sentence beginning **But be warned**. Any spaces at the end of the sentence are also selected.

Selecting a Paragraph
To select a paragraph, you double-click anywhere in the selection bar next to the paragraph. Double-click in the selection bar next to the main paragraph that starts **Like many other**.

Selecting the Whole Document
To select the entire document, hold down the Command key and click anywhere in the selection bar.

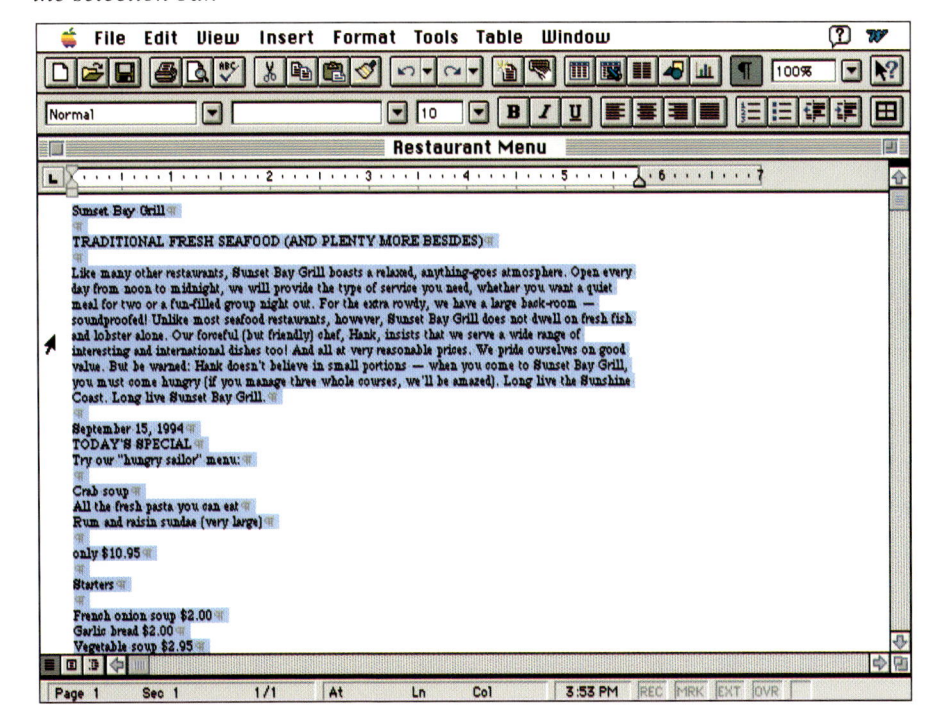

Clear That Box!
If you select by dragging over more than one word, and your selection includes a part or parts of words, Word automatically highlights the whole of each word, as well as any spaces after the words. If you don't want this automatic word selection, choose *Options* from the *Tools* menu, and then click on the *Edit* tab. Under *Editing Options*, clear the *Automatic Word Selection* check box, and then click on *OK*.

Selecting Any Amount of Text
To select just one character or any amount of text, you position the I-beam wherever you want the selection to start, hold down the mouse button, and drag the mouse pointer to the position where you want the selection to end. Then release the mouse button.

31

TEXT REVISION

Text Revision

AFTER YOU HAVE TYPED IN SOME TEXT, you may decide to revise the text in a variety of ways. For example, you may want to insert or delete a sentence, change a word, or move or copy whole paragraphs from one place to another in the document. With Word you can even search for specific text and replace it with new text in one easy step. Let's find out how simple it is to perform these operations by revising some of the text you have entered so far for your restaurant menu.

How to Insert Text

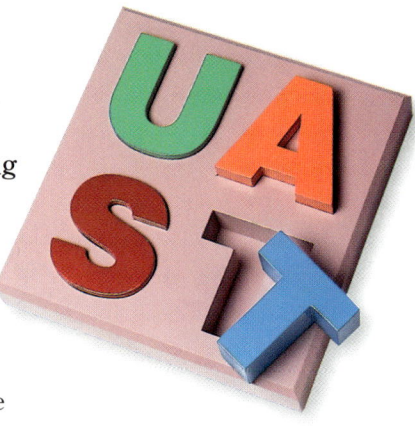

To insert text in your document, all you need to do is position the insertion point at the place you want to insert the text, and then type. As you type, the existing text is pushed along to the right. In your restaurant menu, carry out the following insertion:

Adding Text

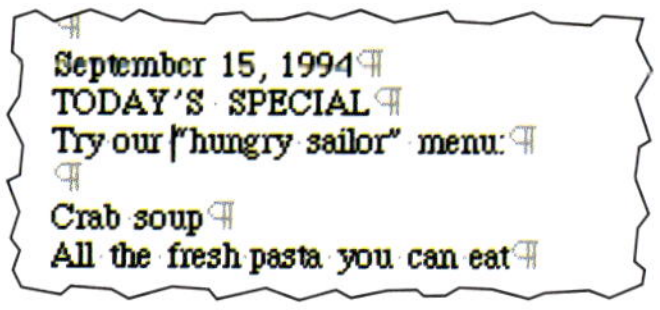

1 Position the insertion point just to the left of the words **"hungry sailor"** under **TODAY'S SPECIAL**.

2 Type **3-course** followed by a space. The text is inserted into your existing text.

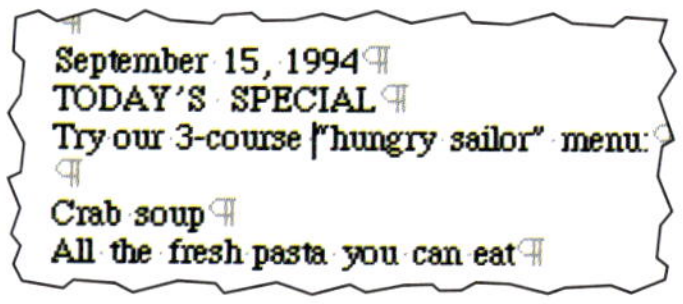

How to Delete Text

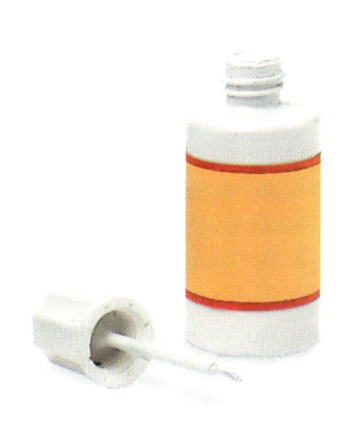

The simplest way to remove small amounts of incorrect text is to position the insertion point next to the text you want to remove and press either the Del key or the Delete key to remove one character at a time (see page 20). If you want to delete more than a few characters, however, Word provides a number of mouse and keyboard shortcuts to make text correction faster and easier.

DELETING ONE WORD AT A TIME
You can quickly remove a single word using the Command key and Del. In your document place the insertion point to the left of the word **fresh** in **All the fresh pasta**, and then press the Command key and Del together.

Lost Your Bearings?
Don't worry if you can't find the place where you were last editing, Word remembers the last three locations where you typed or revised text. Press Shift and F5 until you reach the location you want.

Wrong Word?
If you want to remove a word that you've just typed, press the Command key and Delete together. The insertion point must be positioned at the immediate right of the word.

DELETING SELECTED TEXT

The quickest way to delete whole sections of text, such as sentences and paragraphs, is to select the unwanted text (see pages 30 to 31) and then press the Del or Delete key. Follow these steps to practice this:

1 Select the line **French onion soup $2.00** under **Starters**. Make sure you also select the paragraph mark at the end of the line.

2 Press the Delete key. All the lines below will move up.

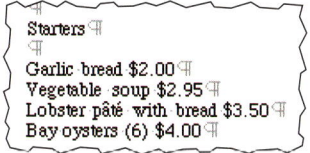

OVERTYPING

You don't have to delete text in order to correct mistakes. Word lets you type over incorrect text with new text. There are two ways of doing this. If you select the incorrect text and then start typing in the replacement text, Word deletes the old text and inserts the new text. Alternatively, if you double-click on OVR on the status bar, Word switches to "Overtype" mode and anything you type will overwrite existing text, character for character. Do the following to practice these two methods in your document:

Typing Over Selected Text

1 Select the word **Vegetable** under **Starters**.

2 Type the word **Crab**. Word deletes the old text as you begin to type in the new text.

Using the Overtype Mode

1 Double-click on OVR on the status bar to switch to Overtype mode. Position the insertion point at the beginning of **bread** in the line **Lobster pâté with bread $3.50**.

2 Type **toast**. Because the new word contains the same number of characters, it overwrites the original word. Double-click on OVR again to turn off Overtype mode.

Unwanted Deletion?

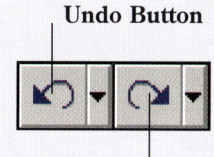

Undo Button

Redo Button

If you make a mistake when you are revising your text, don't panic. Word allows you to undo an action or command. For example, if you accidentally delete a selection of text, you can bring it back again. Simply click on the Undo button on the Standard toolbar; Word will undo the last action it performed. If you then decide to go through with the action after all, you can redo it by clicking on the Redo button.

A Multiple Undo

Multiple Actions
To undo or redo more than one action, first click on the arrow next to the Undo or Redo button. A pop-up list appears, showing the order in which the previous actions were performed. Click or drag to select the actions you want to undo or redo — note that they have to be undone or redone in sequential order.

Check the Status Bar!
Be careful when you are using Overtype mode — if the text you are inserting is not the same length as the text you are replacing, you may type over text you want to keep. You must also remember to turn off Overtype mode when you have replaced the text. If the letters OVR are not dimmed on the status bar, overtype mode is on. Double-click on OVR to turn off Overtype mode.

TEXT REVISION

How to Move Text

Another way you may want to revise your document is to move text from one place to another, perhaps to reorder sentences or paragraphs. Word offers two main methods for moving text. Let's practice these different methods by moving some text around your restaurant menu.

DRAG AND DROP METHOD

If you want to move text over a short distance, the easiest technique is the drag and drop method. You can also use this method to move text or other items from one Word window to another (see "Multiple Windows" on page 46).

What Can I Move?
Text is not the only thing you can move using the drag and drop and cut and paste techniques. You can move any item in your document including graphics, special screen symbols, and items you have inserted from other applications.

Dragging and Dropping

1 Select the line **Crab soup $2.95** in the **Starters** section of your restaurant menu. (Make sure you release the mouse button after selecting text.)

2 Place the mouse pointer over the highlighted text, and then hold down the mouse button. A dotted I-beam pointer and a small box appear along with the pointer.

3 While holding down the mouse button, drag the text to its new position. Position the dotted I-beam pointer at the left margin directly below the line **Bay oysters (6) $4.00**.

4 When you release the mouse button the text drops into its new position.

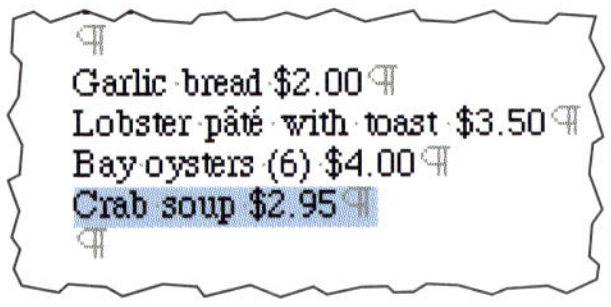

CUT AND PASTE METHOD

This method is better for longer moves over several pages within a document. Cutting erases the selected text and transfers a copy of it to the Clipboard, a temporary storage area. Pasting then copies the Clipboard contents to the new insertion point you choose. Let's practice this method on your restaurant menu.

Cutting and Pasting

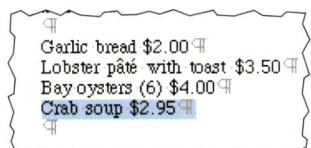

1 Select the line **Crab soup $2.95** again.

2 Choose *Cut* from the *Edit* menu or click on the Cut button on the Standard toolbar. The selected text disappears from your document.

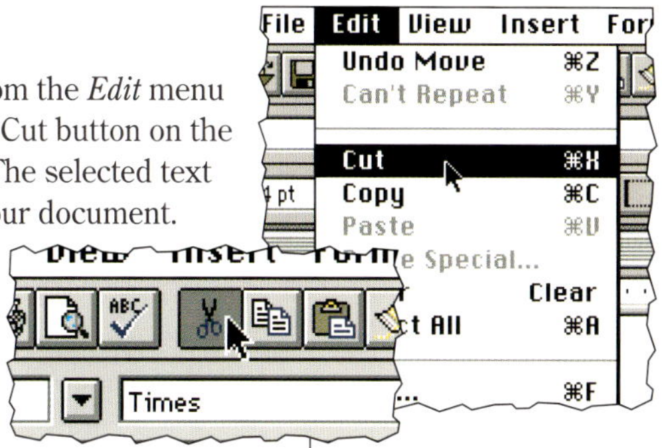

Cut Button

3 Move the insertion point to the beginning of the line **Garlic bread $2.00**, and then choose *Paste* from the *Edit* menu or click on the Paste button on the Standard toolbar.

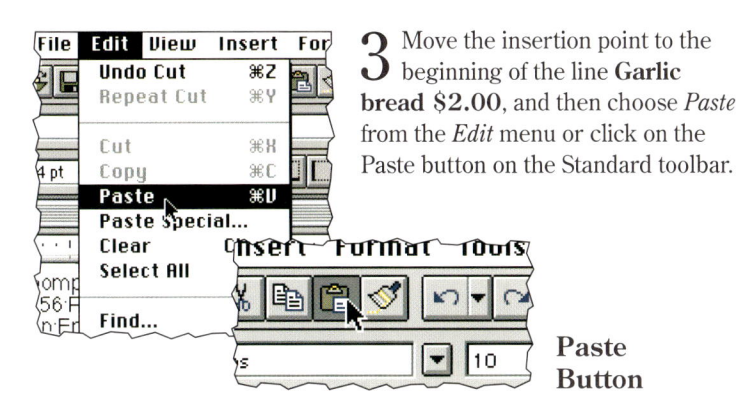

Paste Button

4 The text reappears in its new position.

How to Copy Text

When you are working on a document, you may want to copy sections of text that have to be repeated elsewhere. Copying text is similar to moving text in that you select the text and then use either the drag and drop method or the copy and paste method. Unlike moving text, however, copied text also remains at its original location.

DRAG AND DROP METHOD
To copy text, you use the same drag and drop technique you used for moving text, except you also hold down the Option key.

1 Select the word **Sunset** at the top of your document. Place the mouse pointer over the selected text. Then hold down the Option key and press the mouse button.

2 Drag the dotted I-beam pointer in front of the word **Bay** in **Bay oysters**. Because **Bay** is not visible on the screen, you'll have to scroll while dragging. Drag the pointer to the bottom of the screen; the pointer will stay in place in this position but the screen will move upward to reveal the remaining text.

3 Release the mouse button and the Option key to drop the copy of the text into position.

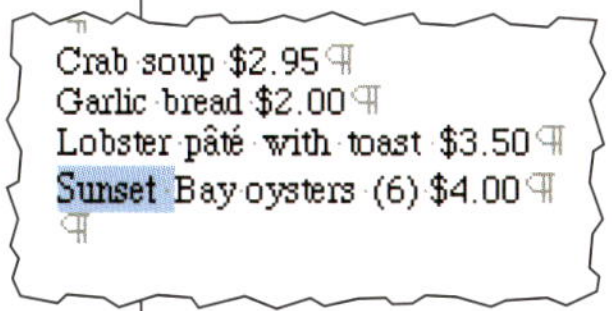

> **?**
> **What's the Clipboard?**
> Every time you cut or copy text, it is copied into the Clipboard, a temporary holding area. The item remains in the Clipboard until you choose *Cut* or *Copy* again, when it is replaced with the new item. You can view the Clipboard's contents by choosing *Show Clipboard* from the *Window* menu.

35

TEXT REVISION

COPY AND PASTE METHOD

As with cutting and pasting, the following method is better if you want to copy text over several pages. For now, let's practice using the technique on your restaurant menu. (Alternatively, you can carry out the *Cut*, *Copy*, and *Paste* commands by using shortcut menus. Select text you want to move, hold down the Control key, and click on the mouse button to open the shortcut menu. Then choose the relevant command.)

1 Select the words **Sunshine Coast** in the last line of the main paragraph.

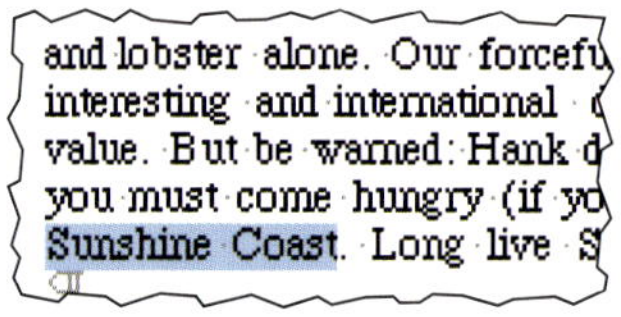

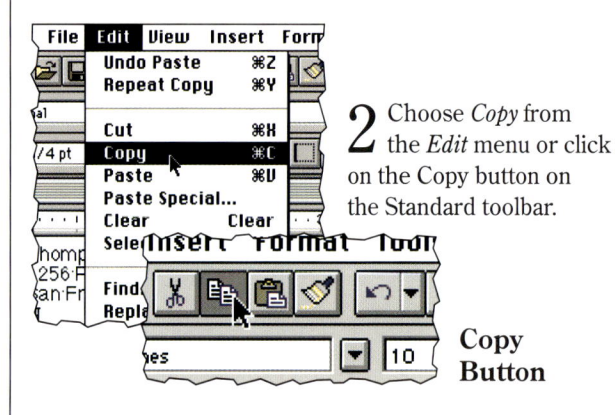

2 Choose *Copy* from the *Edit* menu or click on the Copy button on the Standard toolbar.

Copy Button

3 Place the insertion point at the beginning of the word **restaurants** in the first line of the main paragraph, and then choose *Paste* from the *Edit* menu or click on the Paste button on the Standard toolbar.

Paste Button

4 You'll see the copied text plus a space appear in its new position. Word automatically adds a space to make the text fit its surroundings. (If, for example, you select a word with a space and then paste it to the end of a sentence, Word automatically removes the space in front of the period.)

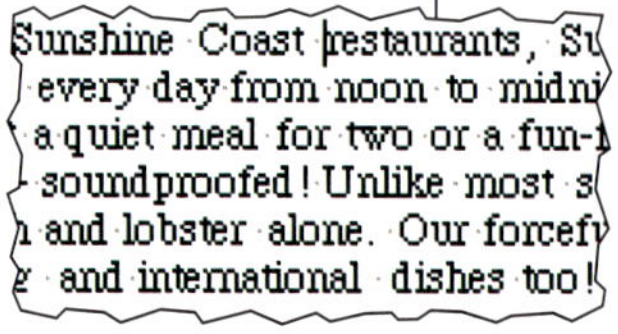

Want to Paste More Than Once?
Once you have copied a selection of text to the Clipboard, you can paste it into your document — or any other documents — as many times as you like. The text remains in the Clipboard until you replace it by copying or cutting a new item.

Spike It!
If you want to move (not copy) many pieces of text to the same place, use the Spike — a feature that is like the Clipboard but holds more than one entry at a time. To move text to the Spike, select the item you want to move and press the Command key and F3 together. You can keep adding to the Spike in the same way. To paste the Spike contents, place the insertion point at the desired place and press the Command key, Shift, and F3 together.

Using Bookmarks

As the name suggests, a bookmark is a "tag" that you can insert into a Word document to find a particular selection of text again. Bookmarks are helpful for navigating around long documents. To insert a bookmark, you have to assign a name to the location you want to tag. Word invisibly marks this location and leads you back to it when you call up its name. Bookmarks don't appear on the screen or when you print the document. You can assign as many as 450 bookmarks to one document.

No Spaces!
You can't include any spaces in your bookmark name — only letters, numbers, or the underscore character (_). Choose a name with 1 to 20 characters, beginning with a letter.

Inserting a Bookmark

1 Position the insertion point where you want to insert the bookmark. In your document, position the insertion point to the left of the word **Starters**.

2 Choose *Bookmark* from the *Edit* menu.

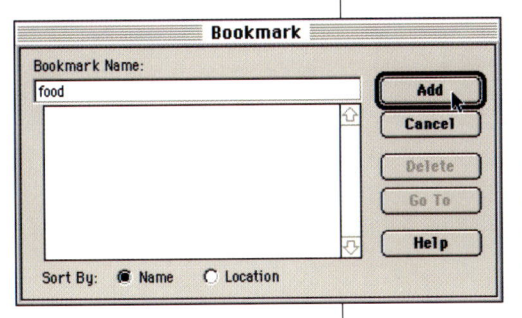

3 The *Bookmark* dialog box appears on the screen. In the *Bookmark Name* text box, type in the name **food** to define your bookmark and then click on *Add*. The location you chose is now named, and the name of your bookmark appears in the *Bookmark Name* list box.

Jumping to a Bookmark

1 Position your insertion point somewhere else in the document, and then choose *Go To* from the *Edit* menu.

2 The *Go To* dialog box appears. Under *Go to What*, choose *Bookmark*. In the *Enter Bookmark Name* box, choose the bookmark you want to go to (in this case, **food**). Click on *Go To*, and then click on *Close*.

3 Word jumps to the point in the text where your specified bookmark appears; in this case, in front of **Starters**.

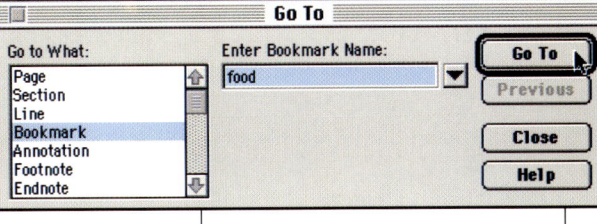

37

TEXT REVISION

How to Find and Replace Text

Word lets you change the text in your document using the *Find* and *Replace* commands on the *Edit* menu. You can use the *Find* command to search a long document for specific words, characters, or other elements, such as graphics. To replace specific items, you can use the *Replace* command. The *Replace* command is most often used for changing text that occurs frequently throughout a document.

FINDING TEXT IN A DOCUMENT
The *Find* command is especially useful if you are looking for a section of text that contains a key word that easily identifies it. Let's use *Find* in your document.

> **Want to Repeat a Search?**
> If you close the *Find* dialog box and then decide to repeat the search you've just completed, you don't have to open the dialog box again. Just press Shift and F4 on your keyboard; Word will repeat the search.

Finding a Word

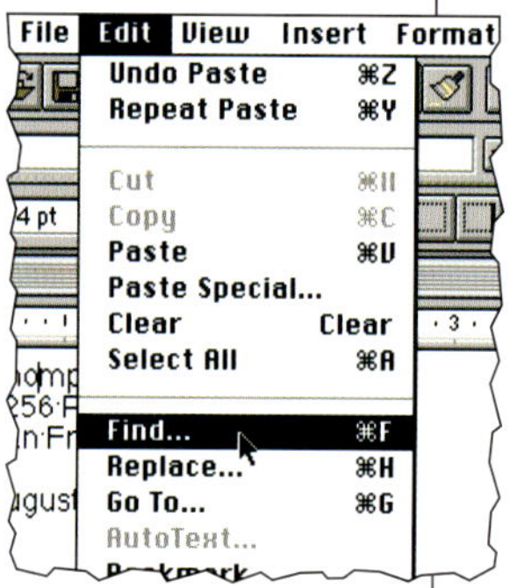

1 Position the insertion point anywhere in your restaurant menu, and then choose *Find* from the *Edit* menu.

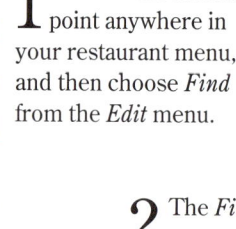

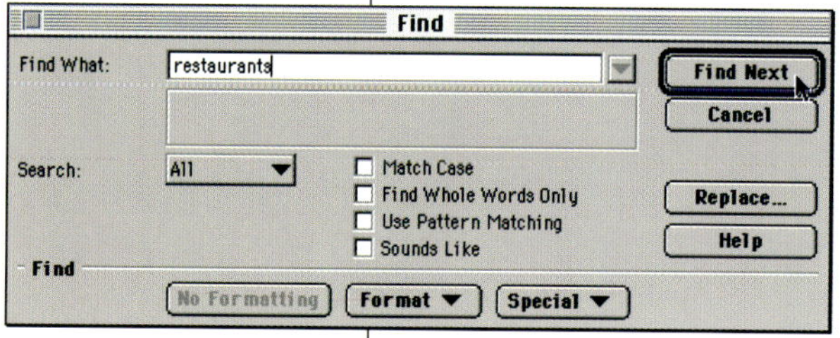

2 The *Find* dialog box appears. In the *Find What* text box, type the word **restaurants**. In the *Search* box, select *All*. Then click on the *Find Next* button to begin the search.

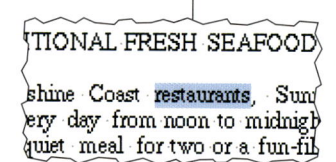

3 Because *All* is displayed in the *Search* box, Word will search the whole document. Word finds the word and highlights it. If you wanted to edit the word in your document without closing the *Find* dialog box, you could do so by clicking in your document and editing.

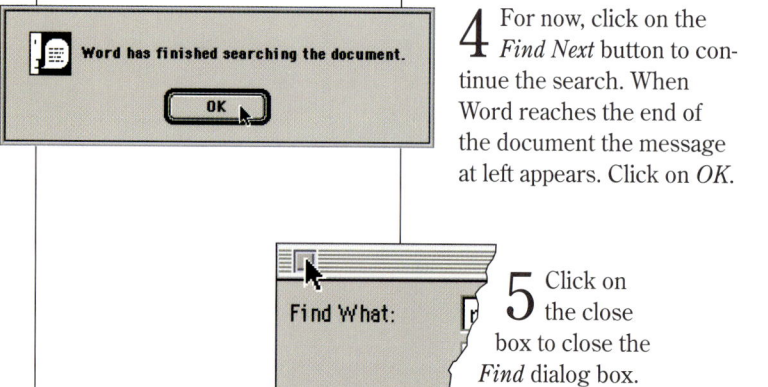

4 For now, click on the *Find Next* button to continue the search. When Word reaches the end of the document the message at left appears. Click on *OK*.

5 Click on the close box to close the *Find* dialog box.

Replaceable
If you want to change your search from finding text to replacing it, you can click on the Replace *button in the* Find *dialog box. The* Find *dialog box disappears and the* Replace *dialog appears in its place.*

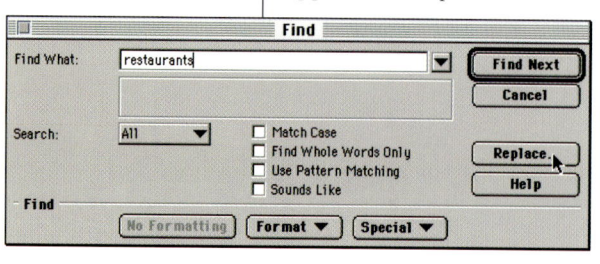

38

REPLACING TEXT IN A DOCUMENT

Word's *Replace* command is a useful timesaver when you want to change an item over and over again in your document. It can search for and replace all occurrences of a specified element in your document in one easy step. Practice using this command to replace a frequently occurring word in your restaurant menu.

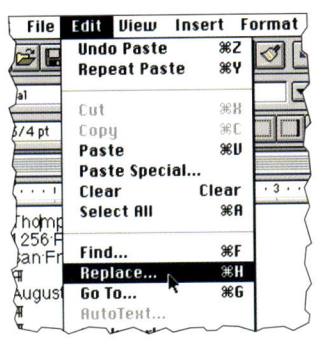

Replacing a Word

1 Place the insertion point at the beginning of your document, and then choose *Replace* from the *Edit* menu.

2 The *Replace* dialog box appears. Type **sunset** in the *Find What* text box and **sunrise** in the *Replace With* text box. Then click on the *Replace All* button to find and replace all occurrences of **Sunset** within your document.

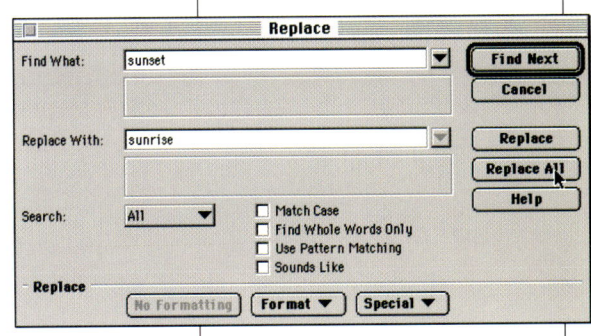

3 The message at right appears, telling you how many replacements were made. Click on *OK*. Then click on *Close* in the *Replace* dialog box.

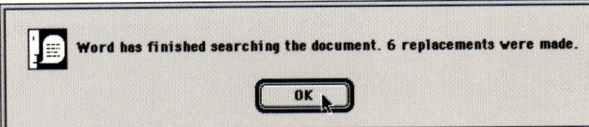

Perfect Matches

In both the *Find* and *Replace* dialog boxes, you'll find several options that make searching for an item more precise. By checking any of these options, you can control the way that Word searches through a document.

■ *Match Case* — If you check this option, Word searches your document and finds only those words with the specified pattern of uppercase and lowercase letters. For example, if you type **Sunrise** in the *Find What* text box, Word finds **Sunrise** but not **sunrise**.

■ *Find Whole Words Only* — This option finds only separate words, not characters embedded in other words. For example, if you tell Word to find the word **sun** without checking this option, it highlights every instance of the word, even if it is contained within another word (**sun**rise, **sun**shine, **sun**dae, and so on).

■ *Use Pattern Matching* — This option, sometimes known as wildcard searching, can be used for special search operations. For example, you can type **r*d** to search for any string of characters that starts with **r** and ends with **d**, or **r??d** to search for any four-letter string of characters that starts with **r** and ends with **d**.

■ *Sounds Like* — This option finds words that sound the same as the text you typed in the *Find What* box but are spelled differently, such as the words **pail** and **pale**.

■ *Search* — By default, the *Search* box is set on *All* and Word searches the whole of your document. You can limit a search by setting *Up* or *Down* in the *Search* box. This prompts Word to search your document from the insertion point to the beginning or end of your document only.

Not Just Words!
You can also use the *Find* and *Replace* commands to find and replace formats, such as bold and italic, and special characters, such as paragraph marks and tab characters. To see the formats and special items you can find or replace, position the pointer over the *Format* or *Special* button and press on the mouse button.

39

Text Checking

WORD provides several tools to help you clean up your text. You can check spelling with the dictionary, look up synonyms with the thesaurus, and even check your writing style and grammar with the grammar checker. Before you use these tools, add some lines to the restaurant menu. First position the insertion point at the end of the current last line of text, press Return twice, and then add the lines shown in the box below. Type the lines exactly as they appear, including misspellings.

Don't Expect Miracles!
The spelling checker cannot identify an incorrectly spelled word that is a word in its own right and spelled correctly, for example, "form" when you wanted "from."

How to Check Spelling

The spelling checker identifies misspelled words by comparing them to a list of words stored in a dictionary file. The spelling checker searches the document and suggests corrections for misspelled words. To synchronize the order of your spelling check with the one shown here, position the insertion point at the beginning of the document and then follow these steps.

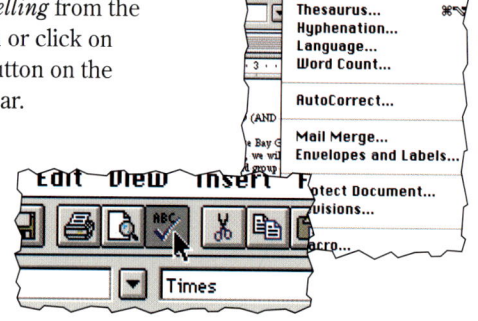

Main courses <Return> <Return>

Swordfish stek $13.95 <Return>
Sunshine Coast lobster $15.95 <Return>
Spaghetti carbonara (pasta with bacon, cream, egg, and parmesan) $7.95 <Return>
Grilled halibut with lime and béarnaise sauce $14.95 <Return> <Return>

All dishes are served with a choice of vegetables of the day or side salad <Return> <Return>

Desserts <Return> <Return>

Rum and raisin sundae $2.95 <Return>
Death by chocolate (a deep layer of chocolate mousse on a sponge base) $3.95 <Return>
Cassata (layers of real Italian ice-fream) $2.95 <Return> <Return> <Return>

why not try a delicious liqueur coffee for only $3.50? <Return>

Running a Spelling Check

1 Choose *Spelling* from the *Tools* menu or click on the Spelling button on the Standard toolbar.

Spelling Button

2 The spelling checker identifies **stek** as a potentially misspelled word and displays the *Spelling* dialog box. The *Not in Dictionary* text box displays the word, and the *Change To* text box offers a likely alternative. The *Suggestions* list box displays a number of other possible spellings.

3 You could click on any word that appears in the *Suggestions* list box to put it into the *Change To* text box. But because **steak** is the word you want, click on *Change* to substitute **steak** for **stek**. The spelling checker will move on to the next misspelling.

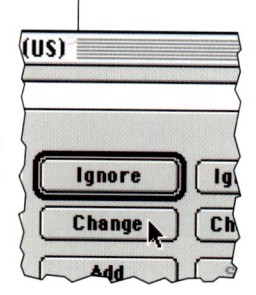

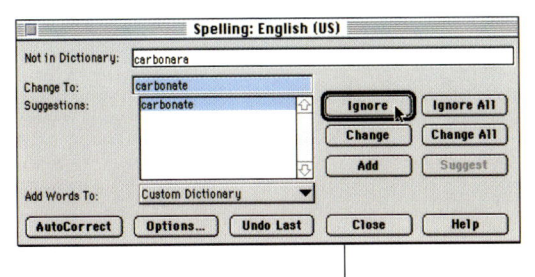

4 The spelling checker queries the foreign words **carbonara** and **Cassata**. Because you don't want to change them, click on *Ignore*. (If you did not insert the accent above the **e** in **béarnaise**, Word will query this word also. Click on *Change* to accept the correct spelling.)

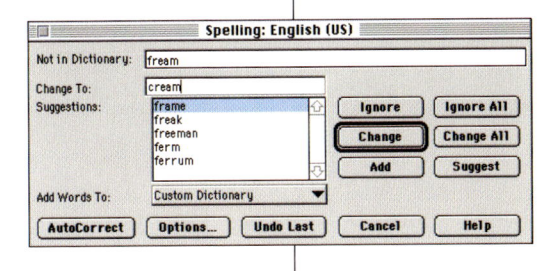

5 Sometimes none of the suggestions are appropriate or no suggestions are made. In such instances, you must type the correct word. The spelling checker doesn't suggest using **cream** for **fream**. Instead it suggests **frame**. Type **cream** in the place of **frame**, and then click on *Change*.

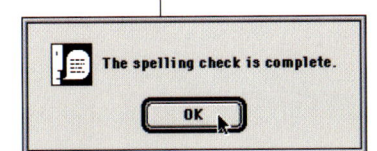

6 The message at left tells you that Word has finished checking your document. Simply click on *OK*.

Common Errors

The AutoCorrect feature (see page 110) can automatically correct spelling errors you habitually make. When an error you frequently make is queried by the spelling checker, click on the *AutoCorrect* button in the *Spelling* dialog box. This will add the error and its correct spelling to the AutoCorrect list, so when you make this error next time it will be automatically corrected as you type.

Custom Dictionaries

In your documents, you might use specialized words, such as foreign words, product names, or acronyms, that are not listed in the ordinary spelling dictionary and are therefore flagged as misspellings. To prevent Word from querying these terms, you can add them to a custom dictionary for Word to consult when running a spelling check. Word provides an empty custom dictionary called Custom Dictionary; you can also create additional custom dictionaries for different categories of specialized words.

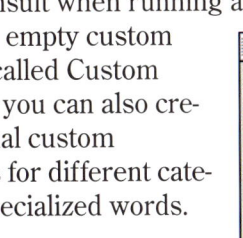

ADDING TO THE CUSTOM DICTIONARY

To add a queried word that appears in the *Not in Dictionary* text box to a custom dictionary, click on the *Add* button. This adds the word to Custom Dictionary, unless you specify a different custom dictionary in the *Add Words To* box.

Want to Check Just One Word?

If you want to verify the spelling of a single word rather than check your whole document, select the word by double-clicking on it, and then press F7.

41

TEXT CHECKING

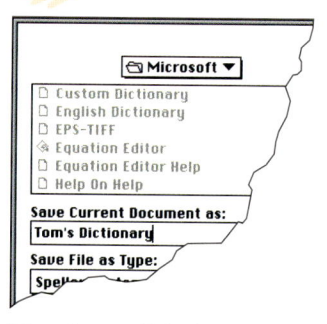

Naming a Dictionary
It is a good idea to use your own name when naming a custom dictionary.

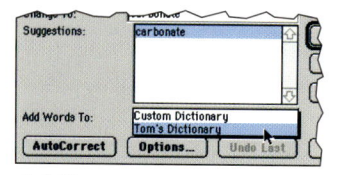

Adding a Word
Select the dictionary to which you want to add a word before clicking on Add. Double-check the spelling of a word before you add it. Be careful when adding uppercase words — the spelling checker will flag any occurrences that are not capitalized.

ADDITIONAL CUSTOM DICTIONARIES

To create an additional custom dictionary, choose *Options* from the *Tools* menu and click on the *Spelling* tab. (You can also reach this section of the *Options* dialog box while running a spelling check by clicking on the *Options* button in the *Spelling* dialog box.) Under *Custom Dictionaries,* click on the *New* button. In the dialog box that appears, type a name for the new dictionary in the *Save Current Document as* box. Then click on *Save*.

You see the new custom dictionary and any other custom dictionaries listed under *Custom Dictionaries* on the *Spelling* flipcard in the *Options* dialog box. If the box to the left of a custom dictionary is checked, the dictionary is open and can be consulted during a spell check. To close a custom dictionary, clear its check box. Click on *OK* to close the *Options* dialog box.

To add a queried word to a custom dictionary during a spelling check, select the dictionary from the *Add Words To* pop-up list (see left). Then click on *Add*.

How to Use the Thesaurus

Word provides a thesaurus that helps you find synonyms for selected words. The thesaurus also lists related words and antonyms when appropriate.

Substituting a Word

1 Select the word for which you want a synonym. Select **amazed** in the restaurant menu.

2 Choose *Thesaurus* from the *Tools* menu. The *Thesaurus* dialog box appears.

3 Amazed appears in the *Looked Up* text box, and the suggestion **blank** appears in the *Replace with Synonym* text box.

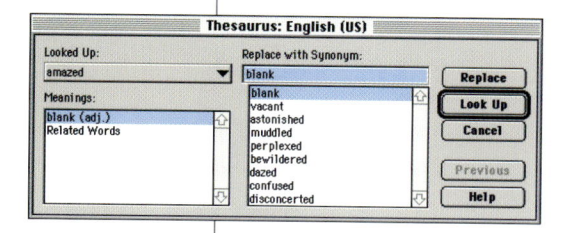

4 The word **blank** is unsuitable. Click on **astonished** in the *Replace with Synonym* list box. **Astonished** appears in place of **blank**. (You can also choose *Related Words* or *Antonyms*, if either appears, in the *Meanings* list box to display other choices.)

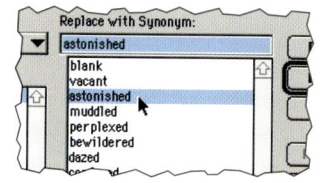

5 Click on the *Replace* button to substitute **astonished** for **amazed**.

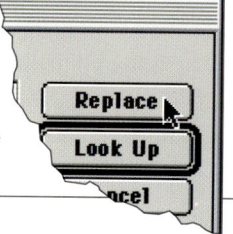

No Thesaurus?
If you can't find the *Thesaurus* command in the *Tools* menu, the thesaurus probably was not installed with Word. To gain access to the thesaurus, reinstall Word and include the thesaurus. The same applies to the grammar checker and spelling checker.

How to Use the Grammar Checker

If you want to check your document for grammatical errors, or if you want to know how readable your document is, you can use Word's built-in grammar checker. The grammar checker offers advice about sentence structure and punctuation. It also performs a spelling check, so you don't need to run the spelling checker before doing a grammar check. Remember that the grammar checker is only a guide — you won't always want to use its suggestions.

Running a Grammar Check

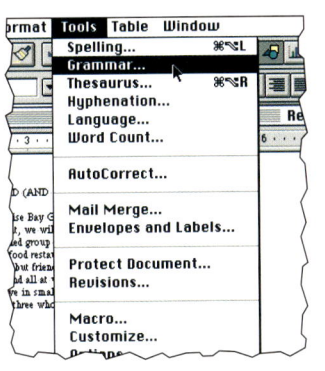

1 Position the insertion point at the beginning of your restaurant menu. Choose *Grammar* from the *Tools* menu.

2 The grammar checker queries the second sentence. Click on the *Explain* button to prompt the checker to explain its suggestion. After reading the explanation, click on the close box to close the *Explain* window. Click on *Ignore* to disregard the grammar checker's advice.

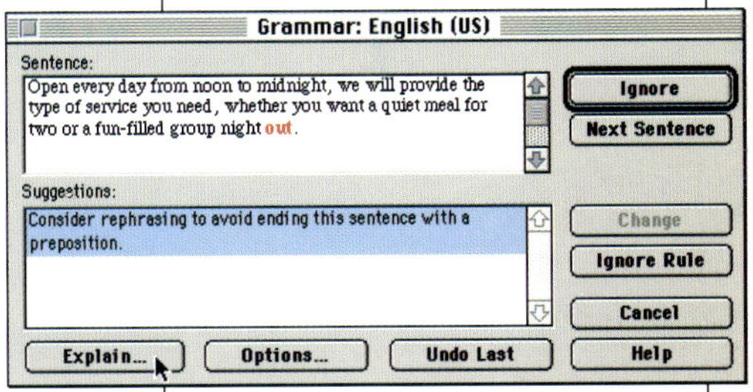

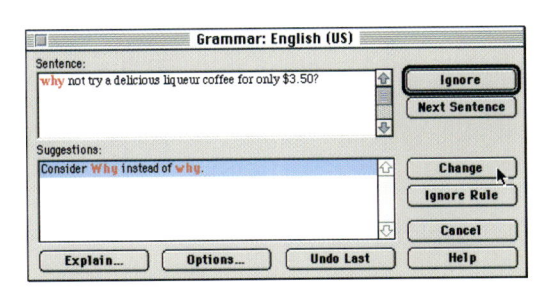

3 Continue checking the rest of your document. Ignore all the suggestions, including the spelling suggestions, except the last one that advises you to substitute **Why** for **why**. Click on *Change* to accept this suggestion. (The contents of the *Sentence* box can also be edited. After making your edit, click on *Change*.)

? Checker Too Strict for You?

You can control how strictly Word examines your grammar. Choose *Options* from the *Tools* menu and click on the *Grammar* tab. Here you can choose from three rule groups — strict, business, and casual — all of which you can customize to observe or ignore specific rules. You can also design your own rule groups.

Readability Statistics

When the grammar checker has finished looking through your document and has provided suggestions for grammar changes, a dialog box containing document statistics appears. The statistics under the headings *Counts* and *Averages* and the *Passive Sentences* score are self-explanatory. The meanings of the other statistics are briefly explained here. These statistics provide some indication of how easy your document is to read — but use them only as a guide.

■ The *Flesch Reading Ease* and *Flesch-Kincaid Grade Level* scores are both based on the average number of words per sentence and the average number of syllables per 100 words. A *Reading Ease* score of 60 to 70 is average; lower scores suggest that sentences are harder to read. A *Grade Level* of 7 or 8 is average; higher scores suggest that the text is more difficult.

■ The *Coleman-Liau Grade Level* and the *Bormuth Grade Level* use both the word length in characters and the sentence length in words to determine a grade level.

After reading the assessment of your document, click on *OK* to close the *Readability Statistics* dialog box.

Manipulating Windows

Y**OU MAY SOMETIMES** want to split the screen to see different parts of a document at the same time. This allows you to revise different parts of a document without scrolling back and forth continually. You may also want to change the size of a window or open a second document window to compare the two documents and move or copy text between them.

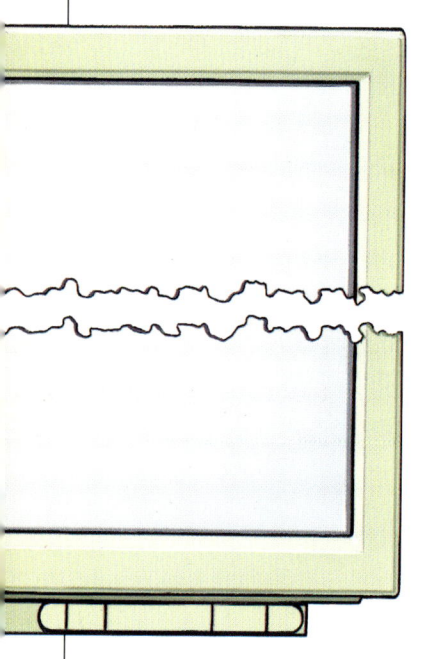

Split Screens

You can split a window into two horizontal parts. Each part of the split window is called a pane; and each pane scrolls independently. A change made to the text in one pane automatically affects the text in another pane.

OPENING AND CLOSING A SPLIT SCREEN

The black bar just above the up scroll arrow on the right side of the screen is called the split box. You use the split box to split and unsplit the screen. Let's practice these procedures on your restaurant menu:

1 Point to the split box above the vertical scroll bar. The mouse pointer changes to two split lines with an arrow above and below.

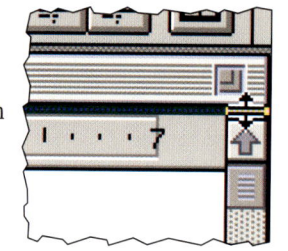

2 Hold down the mouse button and drag the pointer down the screen. You will see a horizontal guideline move downward along with the pointer as you drag the mouse.

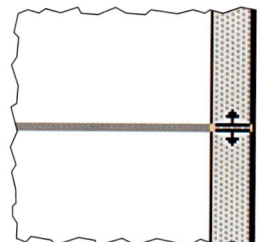

3 Release the mouse button when the guideline reaches the line just above the date. The screen splits into two panes.

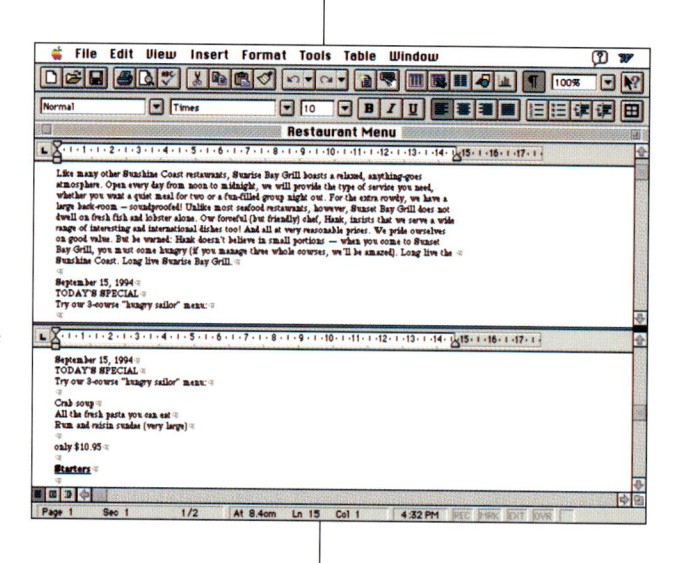

4 To close the split screen, position the pointer over the black bar between the two vertical scroll bars. Hold down the mouse button and drag the split symbol up to the top of the screen, above the top scroll-bar arrow.

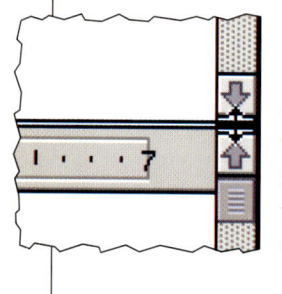

Across the Divide
Using a split screen makes it easy to cut or copy and paste sections of text in a long document. Split the screen into two panes and display the text you want to move or copy in one pane and the destination in the other; then perform the cut or copy and paste using the toolbar buttons.

Resizing

So far you have only worked with the Word document window maximized, so that Word's menu bar and toolbars and the document window appear to be a single element on your screen (see document window at right). However, you can change the size of your document window by dragging or clicking on it with the mouse. This is useful if you want to adjust your window size to view other documents or look at a single document in different views.

Word Size Box
If you want to resize your document window, drag the size box at the bottom right of the window (see illustration at right). By dragging the box in a diagonal direction, you can alter both the window's width and its depth.

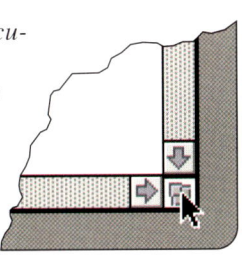

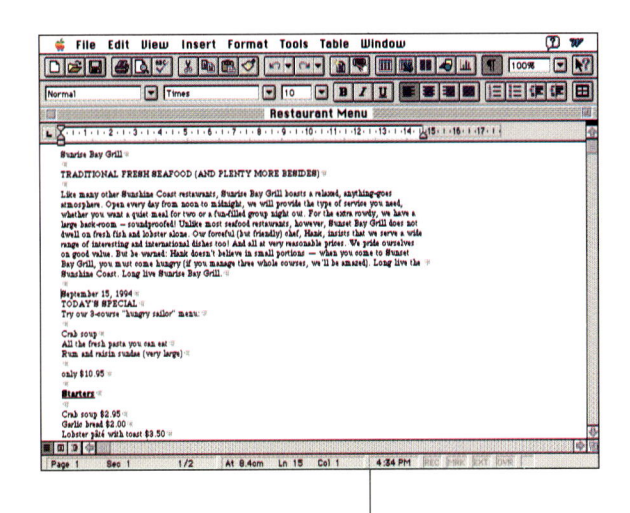

Word Zoom Box
If you have resized your Word document window and you click on the zoom box, your window is restored to its maximum size. If you click on the zoom box again, your window appears as you resized it.

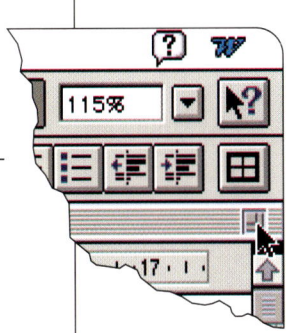

Magnifying Your Text

You can easily change the size of the text displayed in your document window. (Bear in mind that this won't affect the size of the text that is printed.) Try the following on your restaurant menu.

1 Choose *Zoom* from the *View* menu. In the *Zoom* dialog box, choose the magnification you want in the *Percent* box, or choose one of the options under *Zoom To*. Then click on *OK*. In this instance, choose *200%*.

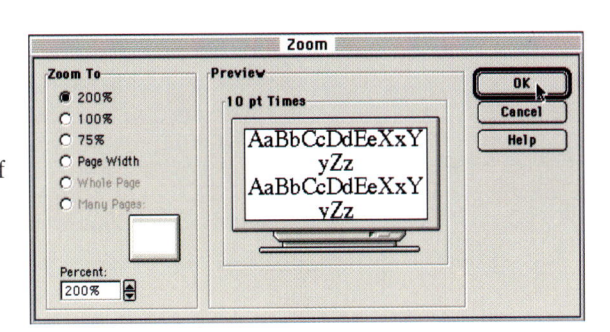

2 You will see your document magnified to 200% on screen. To return your document to normal magnification, use the Zoom Control box on the Standard toolbar (next to the Show/Hide ¶ button). With the mouse pointer over the down arrow, press on the mouse button and choose *100%* from the pop-up list.

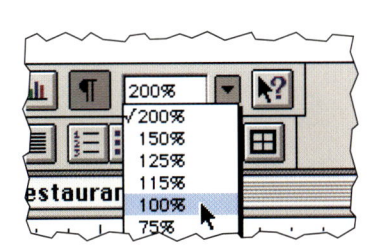

A Perfect Fit?
If you want the text of your document to fill the document window, choose *Page Width* in the *Zoom* dialog box or from the pop-up list that appears when you use the Zoom Control box on the Standard toolbar. Word will automatically resize your text to fit the window you're using.

MANIPULATING WINDOWS

Multiple Windows

Multiple windows are useful when you want to compare different documents or move text from one document to another document. With Word, you can have up to nine document windows open at one time. Multiple windows are different from a split screen in that they allow you to view several different documents at one time rather than two different views of the same document.

OPENING A SECOND DOCUMENT

When you open another document, it automatically becomes active. This means that it contains the insertion point, and any actions you carry out affect only this document. Here we show you how to open a second document on your screen. With your restaurant menu already open, choose *Open* from the *File* menu so that the dialog box below appears. Then follow these steps:

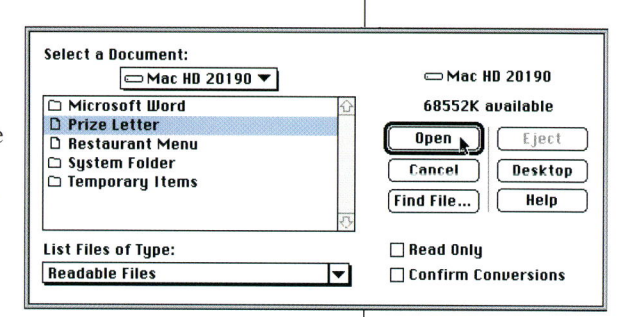

Opening a Recently Worked-On File?
To save time, Word displays the names of the four files you have worked on most recently at the bottom of the *File* menu. Open the *File* menu and choose the name of the file you want to open.

1 Choose *Prize Letter* from the file list, then click on *Open*. **Prize Letter** opens on the screen, hiding the *Restaurant Menu* window.

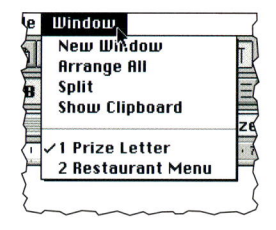

2 Each time you open a document, Word gives it a number that identifies it. To see the list of open documents, open the *Window* menu. A check next to a name indicates the active document. To bring a hidden window into view, choose its name.

Switching Between Windows

You can see all open windows on the screen at the same time by choosing *Arrange All* from the *Window* menu (left). When all windows are visible, you can switch between them by making an individual window the active window. You can click anywhere in a window to make it active, but it's good to make a habit of clicking on the title bar to activate a window. This way you won't accidentally select options or text you don't want. A window must be active before you can do anything to it, such as enter text or resize the window.   **Active Window**

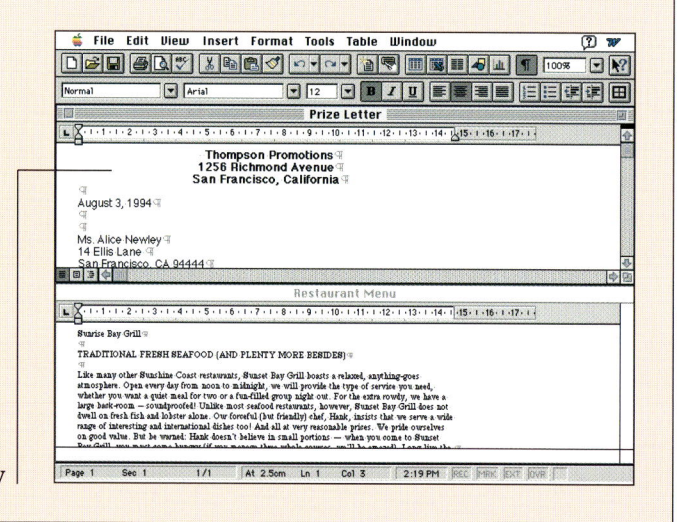

46

MOVING A WINDOW

You may want to move a window to see another window or an icon that is hidden behind it or to see several windows side-by-side. Your **Restaurant Menu** document should still be open. Follow the steps below:

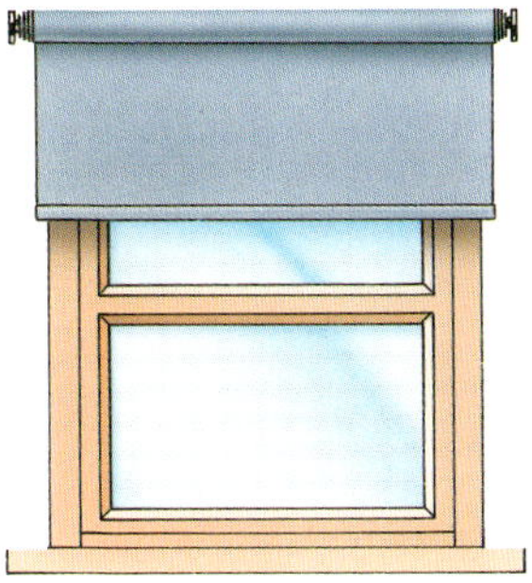

1 If you've recently chosen *Arrange All*, resize your windows as shown in the illustration at right. Then click on the title bar of the *Restaurant Menu* window and drag the window to a new position. You'll see its outline move on screen as you move the mouse.

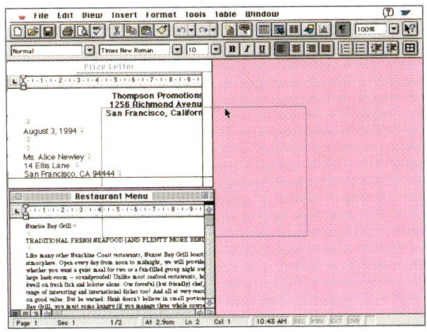

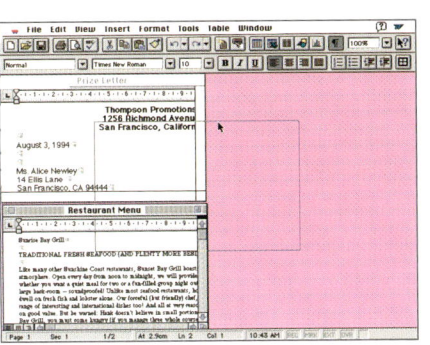

2 Release the mouse button to place the window next to the *Prize Letter* window.

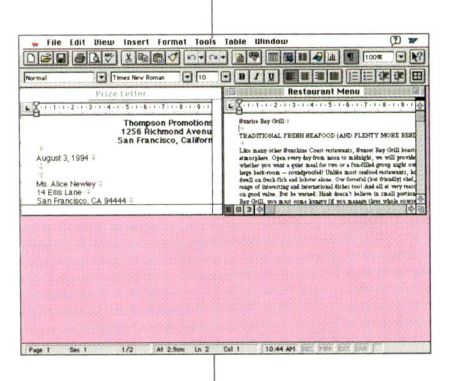

Keep Track!
Working with several windows at one time can be confusing. If you think you've lost a document, check the list of open windows on the *Window* menu – your document may only be hidden behind other windows.

TWO WINDOWS ON ONE DOCUMENT

You can open a document you're working on in two (or more) different windows, for example if you want to see it in different views (see page 66). For example, to open a second window on your **Restaurant Menu** document, first close the **Prize Letter** document and then do the following:

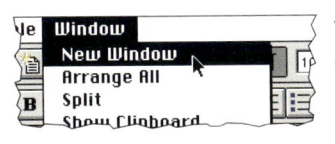

1 Choose *New Window* from the *Window* menu.

Multiple Choice
Remember that all the windows you currently have open are listed at the bottom of the Window menu.

2 A second **Restaurant Menu** window opens. Word adds a number in the title bar of the new window to distinguish it from the original. Both windows will reflect any changes regardless of which window you make them in.

3 Close the *Restaurant Menu :1* window by clicking on its close box. Repeat this action with the remaining *Restaurant Menu* window. (Alternatively, you could have chosen *Close* from the *File* menu, which would have closed both windows.)

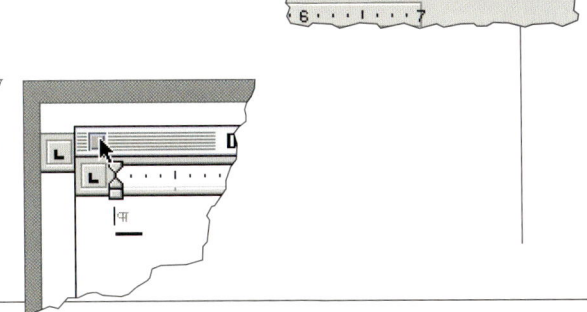

47

File Management

IF YOU ARE NEW TO THE APPLE MACINTOSH, the way in which the files are organized may seem a little confusing. It may help to think of your Macintosh hard disk as an electronic filing cabinet containing many folders. Each folder can contain files and other folders relevant to that folder. Folders and files can be placed on the Macintosh desktop — the area of the screen displayed behind any open windows — so you can see and manipulate them.

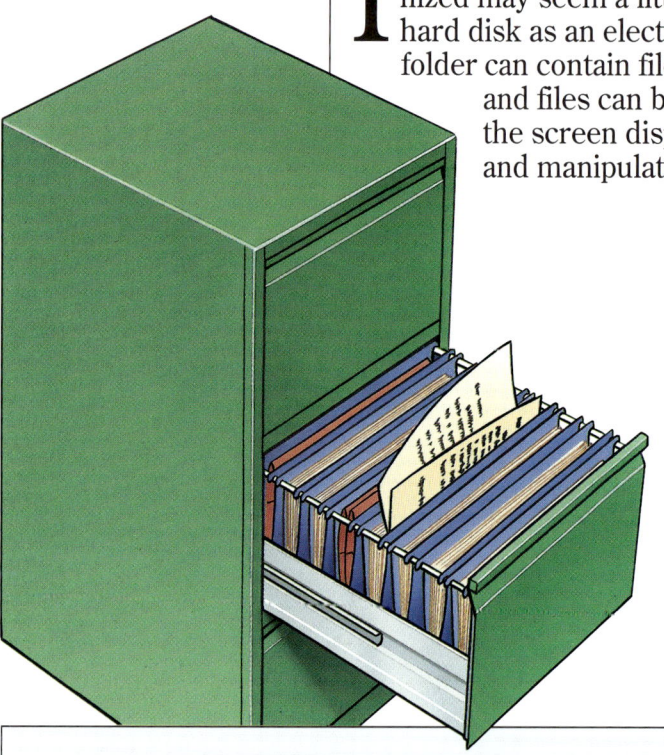

What's in a Name?

Just as you allocate names to specific folders and the documents within them in a filing cabinet, every folder and every file you create with your Macintosh must have a name that is easily recognizable to you and to anyone else who might use it. When you load Word, you'll find several folders and files already created and named on your hard disk. A folder name usually indicates its contents — for example, the start-up icon for Word 6 and related files are stored in a folder called **Microsoft Word**. Filenames are more specific — for example, **Restaurant Menu** for your restaurant menu.

The Macintosh File Structure

Your Macintosh has a file structure based on folders. A folder can contain files and other folders. A folder contained within another folder is called a subfolder.

For example, you could have a document called **Form Letter** in a subfolder called **Letters** in the **Microsoft Word** folder on your hard disk (see illustration at right).

The System Folder

The main folder for the Macintosh's operating system is normally called the **System Folder**. This folder holds the **System** file, **Finder**, initialization programs, fonts, and printer and network drivers the Macintosh uses to run applications and print files.

You should avoid putting your own files and folders into the **System Folder** to prevent confusion between your own work and your Macintosh's system files. Don't delete anything from your **System Folder** unless you're sure you won't need it.

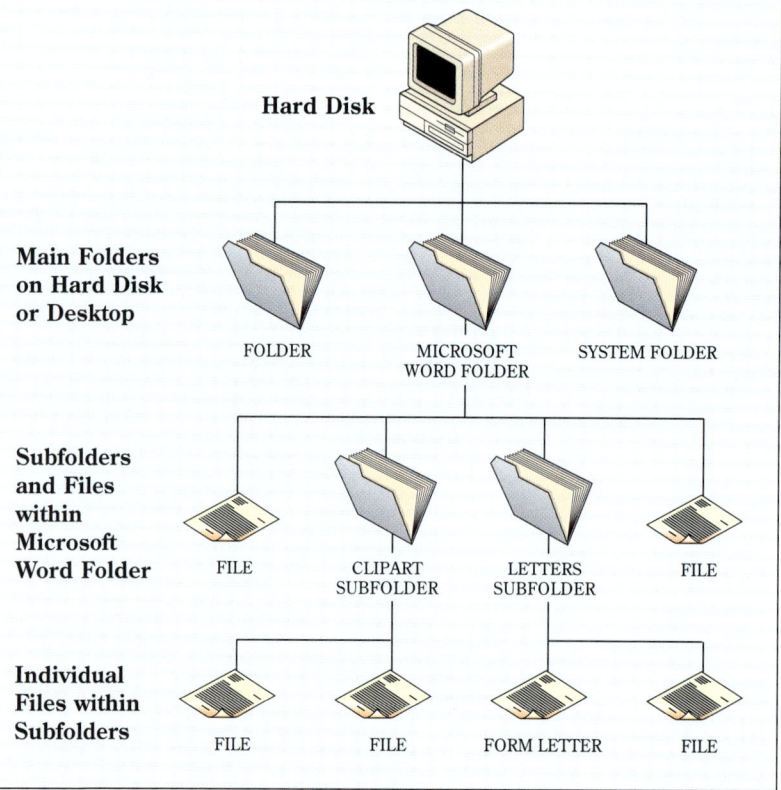

Hard Disk

Main Folders on Hard Disk or Desktop
FOLDER — MICROSOFT WORD FOLDER — SYSTEM FOLDER

Subfolders and Files within Microsoft Word Folder
FILE — CLIPART SUBFOLDER — LETTERS SUBFOLDER — FILE

Individual Files within Subfolders
FILE — FILE — FORM LETTER — FILE

How to Manage Your Files

To organize your folders and files in Word, you use the Macintosh Finder. The Finder gives you several options for storing, finding, and retrieving files.

USING THE FINDER

To use the Finder to inspect the folders and files on your hard disk, follow the steps below:

1 Point to the Application menu icon at the top right of your screen, press on the mouse button, and then choose *Finder* from the menu.

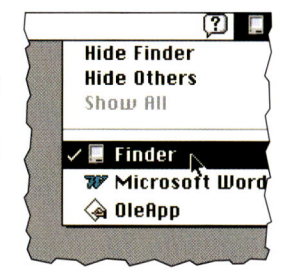

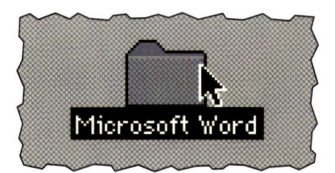

2 Double-click on the hard disk icon. Then double-click on the folder whose contents you want to see.

3 The folder opens. Double-click on any subfolders to see their contents. (Your folders may be different from this example.)

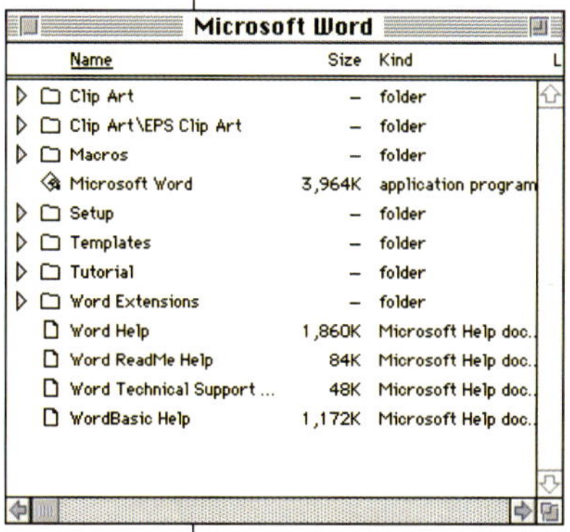

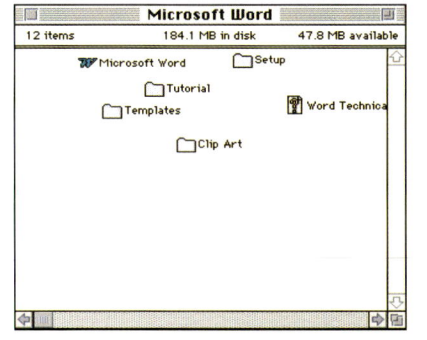

4 Choose different options from the *View* menu to view the contents of a folder in different ways — for example, as small icons or as names.

DISPLAYING A FOLDER'S CONTENTS WITHOUT OPENING IT

If you're displaying the contents of a folder by name, you can look at its sub-folders and files without actually opening it. Clicking on the triangle next to a folder turns the triangle downward and displays the files or subfolders that the folder contains. Clicking on the triangle again turns it upward and hides the folder's contents once more. Subfolders within folders also have triangles and behave in the same way.

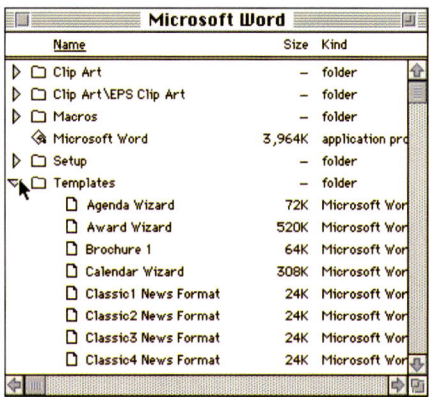

⚠ Closed Files!
Although you don't have to quit Word to use the Finder, you can't copy, move, delete, or rename an open Word document — you must first close that document.

❓ Want to Rename a File?
It's easy to rename files and folders on the Macintosh. Click on the current filename, just below or to the right of the file icon. The text appears in white in a black box. Now type in the new name. When you're done, click outside the filename text area to finish renaming the file.

49

FILE MANAGEMENT

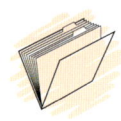

CREATING A NEW FOLDER

When you start using Word, it's a good idea to create one or more folders for storing various types of documents — for example, for memos, reports, or personal letters. Now that you know your way around the folders and subfolders, let's create an example folder on your hard disk.

1 Double-click on the Macintosh hard disk icon.

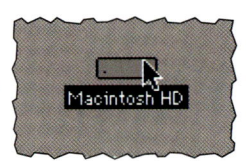

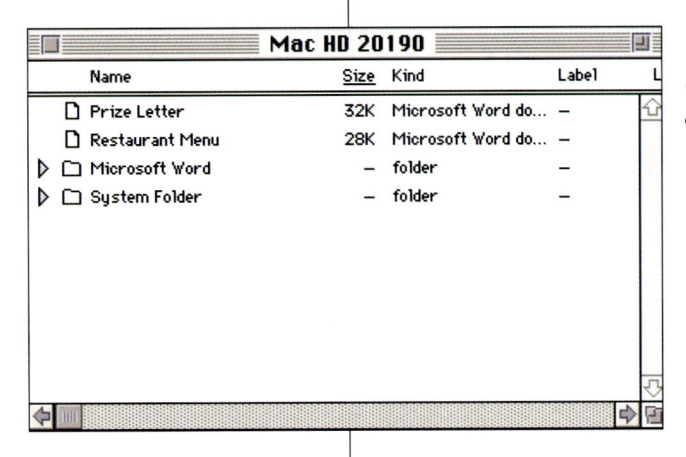

2 The Macintosh hard disk window opens.

3 Choose *New Folder* from the *File* menu.

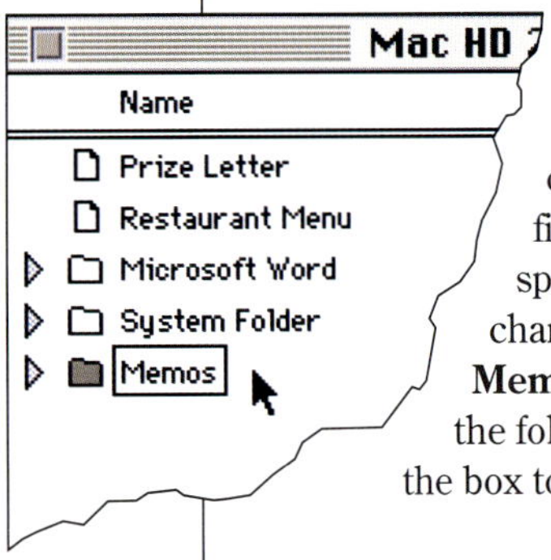

4 An untitled folder appears in the window. You can use either uppercase or lowercase letters for filenames; you can also include spaces. Names can be up to 32 characters long. Type the name **Memos** in the highlighted box by the folder. Click anywhere outside the box to finish naming the folder.

Saving to a Specified Folder

When you open Word, the default location for saving files is usually the Macintosh hard disk. If you want to save a file to a folder, you need to use the *Save* or *Save As* command and then specify that folder. Let's practice saving a document to the **Memos** folder. Return to Word, open a new document, and then follow the steps at the top of the next page to save the document to a particular folder.

Bad Management!
If you save document files "loose" to your desktop or hard disk, you'll have to trawl through many unrelated files to find the file you want. It's better to create specific folders and subfolders on your hard disk to hold the files you create.

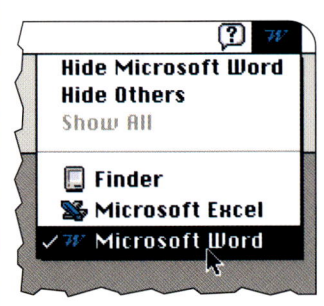

Getting Out of the Finder
You can't actually close the Finder because it's part of the Macintosh's system software. To switch to another application you've already launched, click on the Application icon at the top right of your screen and then choose the application you want from the Application menu.

How to Save a File to the Memos Folder

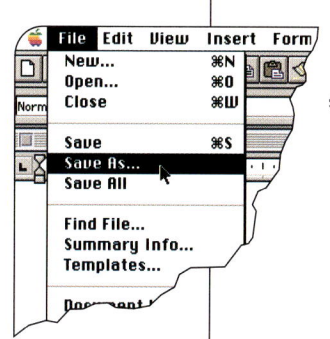

1 Choose *Save As* from the *File* menu. The dialog box shown at right appears.

2 In the location list box at the top, choose the **Memos** folder as your file's destination. Double-click in the *Save Current Document as* box and type **Practice**. Click on *Save.* The file is now saved to the **Memos** folder. Finally, close the **Practice** document.

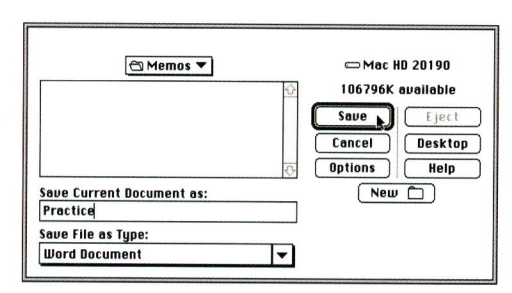

How to Use Find File

If you have recently started using Word, you've probably saved only a few files — but over time you'll create many documents and may have trouble remembering where each file is and what it contains. The *Find File* feature allows you to find a file and then view its contents without actually opening it.

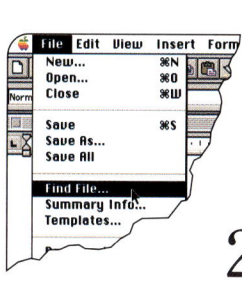

Finding a File

1 Choose *Find File* from the *File* Menu. The *Search* dialog box appears.

2 Type **Prize Letter** in the *File Name* box. Check *Rebuild File List*, and then click on *OK*. (If you've used *Find File* before, the *Find File* dialog box appears displaying the last search details.)

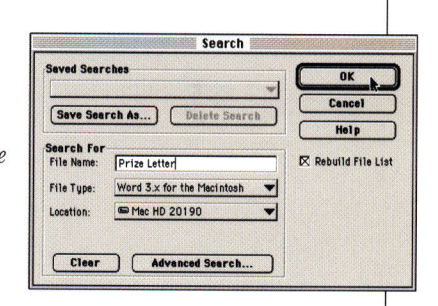

3 In the *Find File* dialog box, under *Listed Files*, **Prize Letter** and its location appear. The contents of the highlighted file appear in the *Preview of* box.

4 When you find the file you are looking for, you can open it directly by clicking on the *Open* button. For now, click on *Close* to close the dialog box.

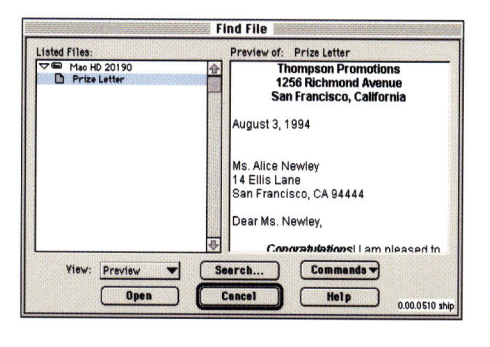

Keep Tidy!

From time to time, you might want to use *Find File* to browse through the files you've created in Word and clean up your folders. You can throw out any file you no longer need by pointing to the *Commands* button when the file is selected, pressing the mouse button, and then choosing *Delete* from the pop-up menu that appears.

3
CHAPTER THREE

*L*ooking Good

In this chapter, you'll learn how to improve the appearance and presentation of your Word documents, using the restaurant menu as an example. You'll find out how to format the text in a variety of ways and how to add more advanced items such as columns, frames, headers, and footers. You'll also learn how to use the WordArt and Drawing toolbars to create an attractive logo for your restaurant menu. Later in the chapter, you'll start work on another document that will allow you to practice creating tables and charts.

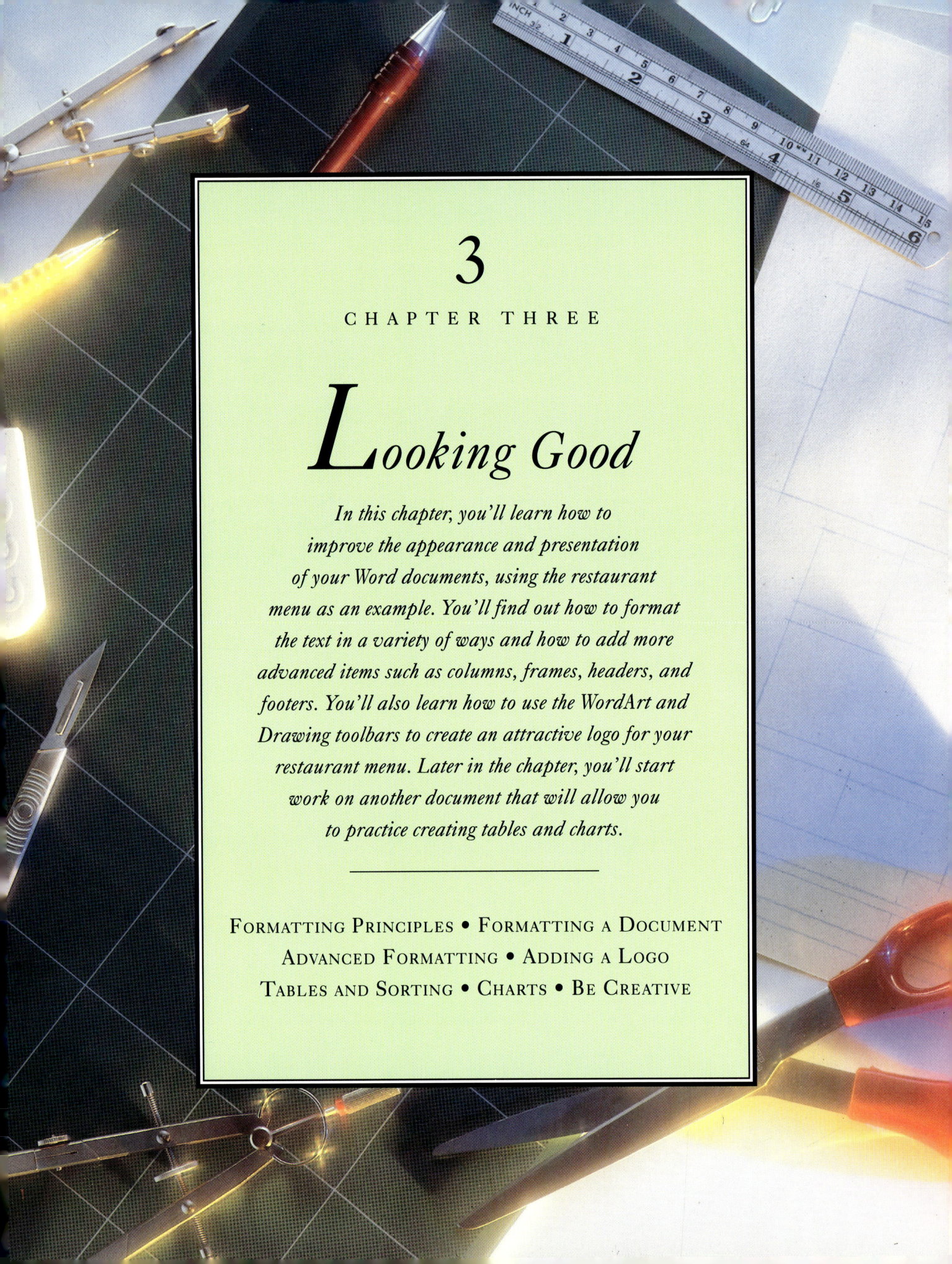

FORMATTING PRINCIPLES • FORMATTING A DOCUMENT
ADVANCED FORMATTING • ADDING A LOGO
TABLES AND SORTING • CHARTS • BE CREATIVE

Formatting Principles 54

An introduction to the various formatting elements that help you emphasize parts of a document and make it more attractive to read.

Formatting a Document 56

You'll be shown — from scratch — how to format your restaurant menu and through this you'll learn all basic formatting techniques.

Advanced Formatting 66

Jazz up your documents by using advanced formatting techniques like headers, footers, columns, borders, and frames.

Adding a Logo 72

There is an artist in everyone. Learn how you can create pictures and import graphics that will brighten up your documents.

Tables and Sorting 78

Let Word sort it out for you — improve your presentation of statistical data by using the table feature and the sorting tool.

Charts 82

Make your documents look really professional and give them a greater visual impact by adding graphs and charts.

Be Creative 86

More ideas for the many kinds of documents you can create using the features and tools available in Word.

FORMATTING PRINCIPLES

Formatting Principles

ONCE YOU'VE ENTERED AND CHECKED THE TEXT of your Word document, the next step is to format it. Through formatting, you can emphasize the most important parts of your document and help make it more attractive and enjoyable to read. Every time you create a document, ask yourself: "Does this document look right for its purpose?"

A Good Start

In many cases, you'll find that the templates and document-creation "Wizards" provided with Word (see pages 104 to 107) are sufficient to create professional-looking documents. But if you want to produce attractive, well-designed documents to suit your specific needs, you may want to use a template as a starting point and then format the document yourself.

There is no set order in which to format your Word document — it depends on the type of document you are trying to create. An efficient way is to start with the simplest formatting procedures and then move on to more advanced techniques. The illustration below suggests how you might organize the formatting of documents. You'll follow the steps in this illustration throughout the next pages as you format your menu.

YOUR DOCUMENT'S LAYOUT
The layout of your document is an important part of formatting. For example, if a heading needs to begin at the top of a page, you can insert a manual page break into the text above it. A long document may also look more interesting if it is broken up into *sections,* which allow you to create special effects, such as multiple columns, for different parts of the document. For more information on sections, see pages 68 to 69.

Character
- Font
- Type Size
- Font Styles (bold, italic, etc)
- Effects (superscript, small caps, etc)

Paragraph
- Alignment
- Indentation
- Line Spacing
- Bullets and Numbered Lists
- Borders
- Tabs

Section
- Page Numbers
- Columns
- Headers/Footers
- Margins
- Paper Size and Orientation (if the section is a whole page or a number of whole pages)

Document
- A document is made up of one or more sections.
- In single-section documents, the document and section level formatting are identical.
- In multiple-section documents, section-level formats can be applied to the whole document or selected sections.

Word's Formatting Levels

Each sheet represents a formatting level and describes the different attributes that can be changed at that level. Generally, you'll find it best to apply character and paragraph formatting first and then move on to the other levels.

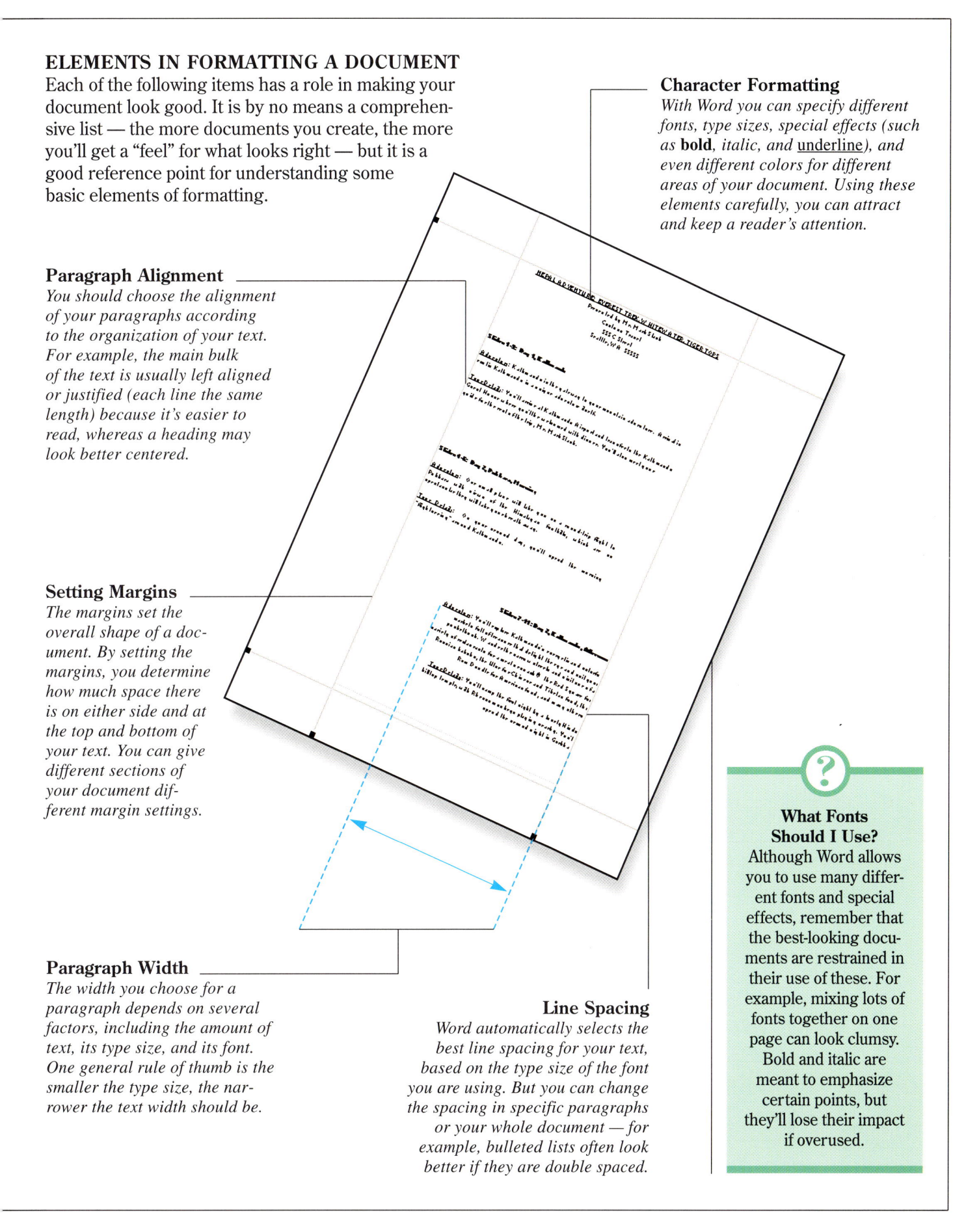

ELEMENTS IN FORMATTING A DOCUMENT

Each of the following items has a role in making your document look good. It is by no means a comprehensive list — the more documents you create, the more you'll get a "feel" for what looks right — but it is a good reference point for understanding some basic elements of formatting.

Character Formatting
*With Word you can specify different fonts, type sizes, special effects (such as **bold**, italic, and underline), and even different colors for different areas of your document. Using these elements carefully, you can attract and keep a reader's attention.*

Paragraph Alignment
You should choose the alignment of your paragraphs according to the organization of your text. For example, the main bulk of the text is usually left aligned or justified (each line the same length) because it's easier to read, whereas a heading may look better centered.

Setting Margins
The margins set the overall shape of a document. By setting the margins, you determine how much space there is on either side and at the top and bottom of your text. You can give different sections of your document different margin settings.

Paragraph Width
The width you choose for a paragraph depends on several factors, including the amount of text, its type size, and its font. One general rule of thumb is the smaller the type size, the narrower the text width should be.

Line Spacing
Word automatically selects the best line spacing for your text, based on the type size of the font you are using. But you can change the spacing in specific paragraphs or your whole document — for example, bulleted lists often look better if they are double spaced.

What Fonts Should I Use?
Although Word allows you to use many different fonts and special effects, remember that the best-looking documents are restrained in their use of these. For example, mixing lots of fonts together on one page can look clumsy. Bold and italic are meant to emphasize certain points, but they'll lose their impact if overused.

Formatting a Document

IN THE FIRST CHAPTER OF THIS BOOK, you learned how to apply some basic formatting to a simple letter. This section shows you how to format a document of greater complexity. As you work with different formatting elements — font, type size, alignment, margins, and so on — you'll realize how easy it is to improve the appearance of a document.

> **Missing a Toolbar?**
> To make a particular toolbar appear on your screen, choose *Toolbars* from the *View* menu. In the *Toolbars* dialog box, check the box next to the toolbar name. If a toolbar is already visible on the screen, you'll see a check next to its name in the *Toolbars* dialog box.

Getting in Shape

You can apply formatting quickly and easily by using the Formatting toolbar, which provides the most commonly used formatting options. Alternatively, you can apply formatting by choosing commands from the *Format* menu and specifying options in the dialog boxes that appear. This is a slower method, but more formatting options are available. For our sample document, using the Formatting toolbar will usually suffice, so we'll concentrate mainly on this method.

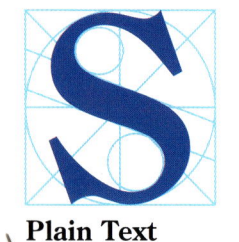

Plain Text

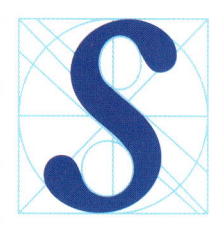

Italicized Text

How to Format Characters

Letters, numerals, symbols, punctuation, and spaces are all characters. To change the appearance of characters — and the words, sentences, or paragraphs they make up — you select the text and then apply one or more attributes. You may, for example, want to emphasize a word by making it bold, by underlining it, or by changing its type size or typeface.

Bold Text

Underlined Text

Using the Formatting Toolbar

The Formatting toolbar contains three pop-up list boxes and several groups of buttons. After selecting the text that you want to format, you choose the relevant item from the pop-up list or click on the button representing the desired format. A button appears depressed on the toolbar if the format it represents is already applied to selected text. Clicking on a button that appears depressed removes the formatting from selected text. Here are the names of the boxes and buttons that you'll find on the Formatting toolbar:

- Style (See More on Pages 108 to 109)
- Font (Typeface)
- Font Size (Points)
- Italic
- Bold
- Underline
- Align Left
- Center
- Align Right
- Justify
- Numbering
- Bullets
- Decrease Indent
- Increase Indent
- Borders

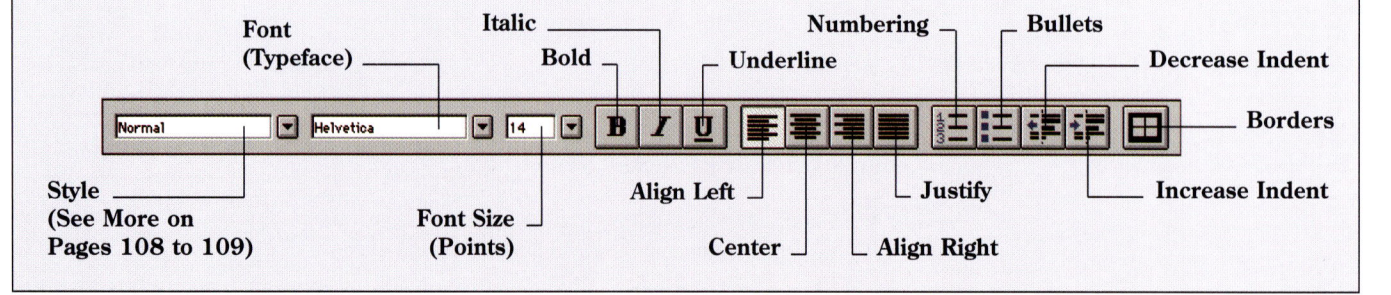

CHOOSING FONTS

When you change fonts, you alter the typeface that the text appears in. To change fonts you must first select the relevant text. Let's change the font in part of your restaurant menu. Open your **Restaurant Menu** document and follow the steps below. Your Macintosh may not have the same fonts in the Font list shown here. See page 119 for more information on fonts and their availability.

1 Select the heading **Starters** in your restaurant menu.

2 Point to the arrow to the right of the Font list box on the Formatting toolbar. Press on the mouse button. Choose *Arial*.

SETTING TYPE SIZE

You can alter the type size of any text using the Font Size list box on the Formatting toolbar. (The numbers in this list refer to points. A point is the fundamental unit of measure in typography — 72 points is roughly one inch.) Before you can change the type size, you must first select the text.

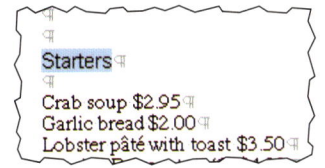

1 Select the heading **Starters** if it isn't still highlighted.

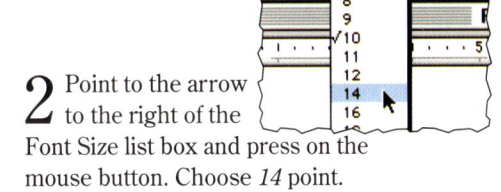

2 Point to the arrow to the right of the Font Size list box and press on the mouse button. Choose *14* point.

APPLYING FONT STYLES AND EFFECTS

Applying text attributes creates special typographical effects. To apply text attributes such as bold, italic, or underlining, first select the text you want to change.

1 The heading **Starters** should still be selected. Click on the Bold button on the Formatting toolbar.

2 Click on the Underline button on the Formatting toolbar.

Changing Size
You can change the type size of selected text quickly using your keyboard. To make selected text larger, hold down the Command key and Shift and press >. Each time you press >, the type size is increased to the next available size. To make selected text smaller, press the Command key and Shift and <. The type size is indicated in the Font Size list box on the Formatting toolbar.

The End Result
This is how your heading should appear after completing the formatting procedures.

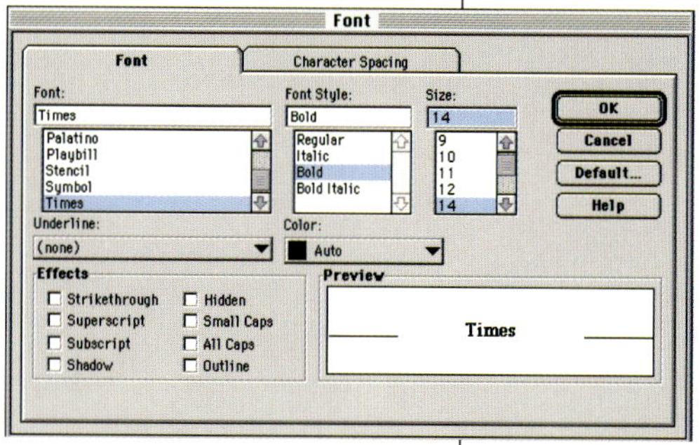

FORMATTING A DOCUMENT

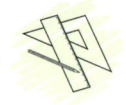

ALTERNATIVE PATHS

If you want to apply several text attributes at once, you may find it easier to use the *Font* dialog box. Select the text you want to change and choose *Font* from the *Format* menu. In the *Font* dialog box, you'll see all the character formatting options, including several other options, such as *Strikethrough* and *All Caps,* that do not appear on the Formatting toolbar. The *Preview* box in the *Font* dialog box displays how these choices affect the text.

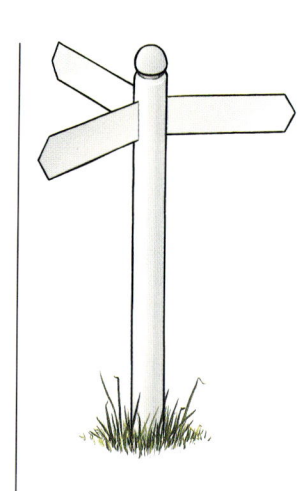

Font Dialog Box

COPYING CHARACTER FORMATS

You can copy character formats from one part of your document to another using the Format Painter. First select the text containing the formats you want to copy, then click on the Format Painter button on the Standard toolbar. The mouse pointer changes to a paintbrush with an I-beam pointer. Now select the text you want to format and release the mouse button. The new format is applied and the pointer returns to its normal shape. If you double-click on the Format Painter button after selecting text, you can continue to paste the copied format throughout your document.
To return to the normal pointer, click on the Format Painter button again.

Format Painter Button

Cut it Short
You can display a timesaving shortcut menu by selecting text you want to format, holding down Control, and pressing on the mouse button. The shortcut menu contains a list of commonly used commands, such as the *Font* command, related to selected text. To close the shortcut menu without choosing a command, release the mouse button.

Working on Your Restaurant Menu

Now that you have practiced the basic character formatting techniques, you can apply them to other parts of your document. The standard (default) setting for your text is probably Times New Roman, 10 point.

■ Select the heading **TRADITIONAL FRESH SEAFOOD....** Change the type size to 11 point and make it bold.

■ Select the largest paragraph (**Like many other...Grill**) in your restaurant menu. Change the type size to 11 point.

■ Select the heading **Main courses**. Change it to Arial, 14 point, bold, underlined. Repeat this for **Desserts** using the Format Painter.

■ Select all the dishes — including the prices — under **Starters** (**Crab Soup ...$4.00**). Make them italic. Repeat this for the dish titles under **Main courses** (including the line **All dishes...**) and the dish titles under **Desserts**.

■ Now select only the prices of the dishes you have just formatted and make them bold.

■ Select the entry for **TODAY'S SPECIAL**, beginning with **September 15, 1994** and ending with **only $10.95**. Make it 9 point.

■ Select the date and the line **TODAY'S SPECIAL**. Make them bold. Repeat this for **only $10.95**.

■ Select only the special dishes **Crab soup...(very large)**. Make them italic.

■ Select the last line of your restaurant menu — **Why not try...**. Change it to 12 point and make it bold.

58

What Is a Paragraph?
A paragraph is any amount of text — a single word, a single line, or a number of sentences — that appears between two paragraph marks. The paragraph formatting is contained within the paragraph mark at the end of the paragraph — if you delete the paragraph mark, the paragraph will take on the formatting of the paragraph immediately following it.

How to Set Paragraph Formats

Formatting a paragraph changes the way the whole paragraph is presented. Most paragraph formatting can be done quickly using the Formatting toolbar or the Ruler. You can also choose *Paragraph* from the *Format* menu and set options in the *Paragraph* dialog box. You can change text alignment, set degrees of indentation, determine spacing before and after the paragraph, and specify line spacing within the paragraph all at one time. The *Preview* box shows you how the paragraph looks with the options you've chosen.

Alignments

Text can be left aligned, right aligned, centered, or justified. Left aligned text has a flush left margin (straight and lined up against the left margin of the page) and a ragged right margin. Right aligned text has a flush right margin and a ragged left margin. Centered text lines up symmetrically down a center line and has ragged left and right margins. Justified text has both a flush left and a flush right margin and is often used for columnar text in magazines and newsletters. Let's practice changing the alignment of various parts of your **Restaurant Menu** document.

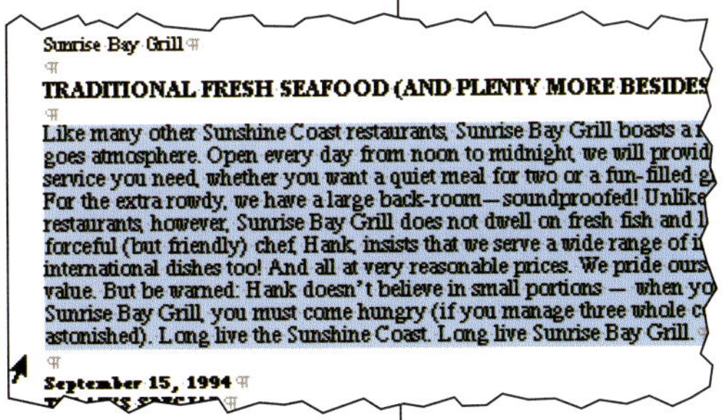

Setting Alignments

1 In your restaurant menu, select the paragraph **Like many other...Bay Grill**.

2 Click on the Justify button on the Formatting toolbar. Notice that the last line is not aligned at the right margin — this is an accepted typographic convention.

Justify Button

3 Select the line **TRADITIONAL FRESH SEAFOOD...** and click on the Center button on the Formatting toolbar. Follow the same procedure to center the line **Why not try...** at the bottom of the restaurant menu.

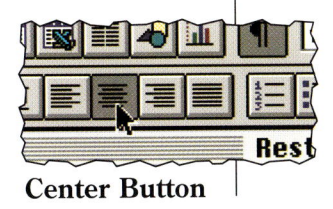

Center Button

Get in Line
Left alignment is the most commonly used setting. Centered alignment tends to emphasize text. Justified text takes on a uniform look. Right alignment is most often used for text accompanying illustrations on the right-hand side of a page.

Left Aligned Text

Centered Text

Right Aligned Text

Justified Text

59

FORMATTING A DOCUMENT

Adding Bullets and Numbers

To make a document more readable, you can emphasize lists by adding bullets or by numbering sequential paragraphs. But doing so manually can take a lot of time. Word allows you to bullet or number paragraphs by clicking on buttons on the Formatting toolbar.

ADDING BULLETS
In a bulleted list, a bullet symbol is displayed at the beginning of each paragraph. To add bullets to a list you must first select the desired paragraphs.

Unwanted Bullets?
You cannot delete a bullet with the Del or Delete keys. To remove bullets, select the paragraphs from which you want the bullets removed, and then click again on the Bullets button on the Formatting toolbar.

1 In your restaurant menu select the dish titles below **Starters (Crab soup...$4.00)**.

2 Click on the Bullets button on the Formatting toolbar. You'll see bullets appear to the left of the dish titles in the **Starters** section.

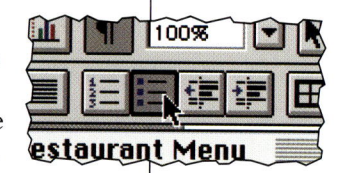

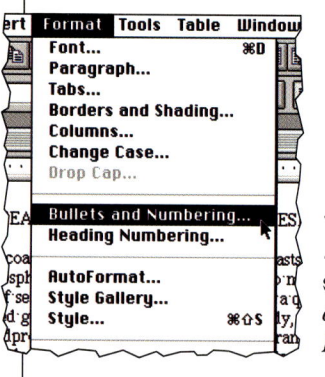

CHANGING THE BULLET CHARACTER
There are several different types of bullets available to you in Word. To change the appearance and the size of the bullets you have just created, follow these steps.

1 The dish titles below **Starters** should still be selected. Choose *Bullets and Numbering* from the *Format* menu.

2 The *Bullets and Numbering* dialog box appears. Under *Bulleted*, click on the diamond bullet style shown at right. Then click on *Modify*.

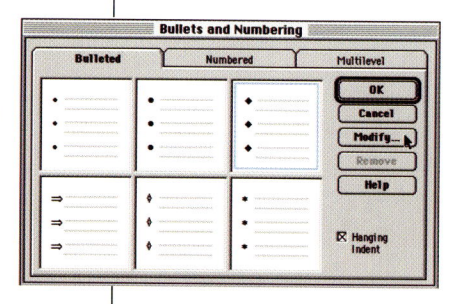

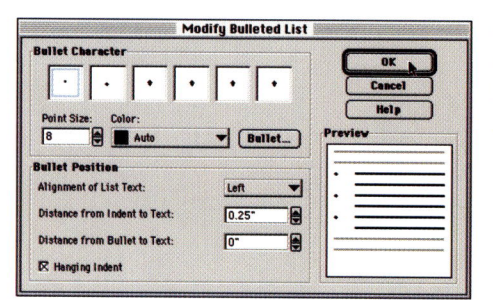

3 The *Modify Bulleted List* box appears. Under *Point Size*, change the value to *8*, and then click on *OK*.

4 The new bullets appear. Any more bullets you add will look like this until you change the bullet again. Use the Bullets button to add bullets to the dishes under **Main courses** and **Desserts**.

ADDING NUMBERS
In a numbered list, Word displays a number or letter at the beginning of each line or paragraph. To create a numbered list, select the relevant text, and then click on the Numbering button on the Formatting toolbar.

60

Indentation

Indents determine the width of a paragraph. In Word, a quick way to change indents is to use the Ruler, the numbered strip below the Formatting toolbar.

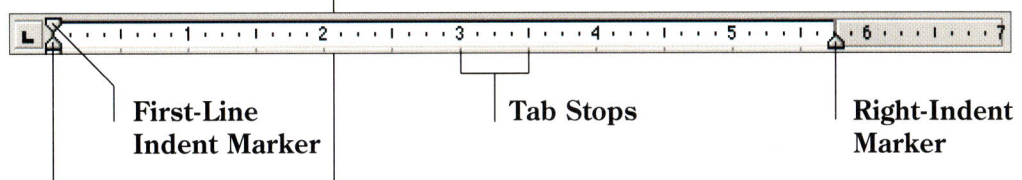

Ruler Display
The Ruler displays the indent settings and tab stops of each paragraph.

- **First-Line Indent Marker**
- **Left-Indent Marker**
- **Tab Stops**
- **Right-Indent Marker**

In your restaurant menu, click anywhere outside of the bulleted lists. At the left side of the Ruler, you'll see two triangles; these are the left-indent markers. The position of the top triangle determines the indent of the paragraph's first line. The position of the lower triangle sets the overall left indent of the paragraph. The triangle on the right side of the Ruler is the right-indent marker. It determines the right indent. To move an indent marker, you point at it, and then hold down the mouse button and drag the marker along the Ruler (see box at left).

Setting Indents

To change the width of one or more paragraphs using the Ruler, select the paragraphs and then drag the relevant indent marker along the scale to the new location.

To set	Drag
First-line indent	
Left indent	
First-line and left indents	
Right indent	

PRECISION INDENTING

Setting paragraph indents using the Ruler can be tricky. To set exact indents you should use the *Paragraph* dialog box. First you have to select the paragraph(s) you want to alter. Note that if you select text with different formats applied, some of the boxes in the Formatting toolbar and the *Paragraph* dialog box will be blank. Follow these steps to set indents for your restaurant menu.

Get to the Point
To change the formatting of a single paragraph, you can just position the insertion point anywhere within that paragraph. Only when formatting multiple paragraphs do you need to select at least a part of each paragraph you want to format.

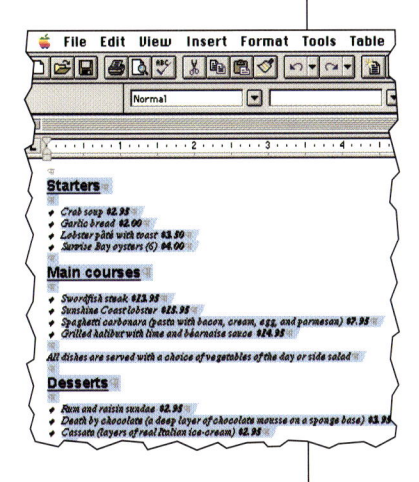

1 Select the text beginning with the heading **Starters** down to the last dish in the **Desserts** list, **Cassata ... $2.95**.

2 Choose *Paragraph* from the *Format* menu to open the *Paragraph* dialog box.

3 Under *Indentation* on the *Indents and Spacing* flipcard, go to the *Left* box and click on the up arrow until you reach the value *0.7* inches. The highlighted text in the *Preview* window shifts to the right to indicate the result of your choice. Finally, click on *OK*. In your document, you'll see the selected text move to the right.

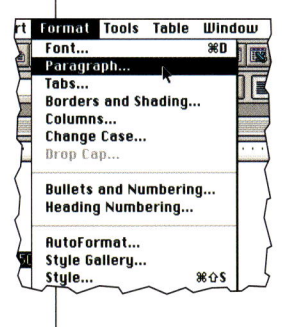

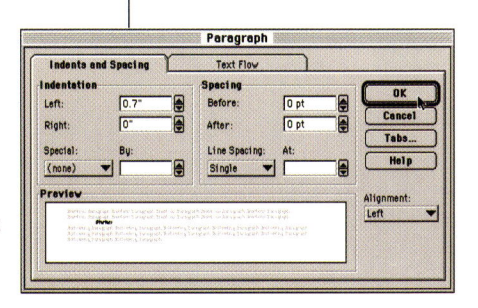

61

FORMATTING A DOCUMENT

SPECIALIZED INDENTING

You can also use the *Indentation* section of the *Indents and Spacing* flipcard in the *Paragraph* dialog box to change indents from the left or right, specify an indent for the first line of each paragraph (*First Line*), or format a paragraph in which the first line begins farther to the left than the rest of the paragraph (*Hanging*). To avoid changing the **Restaurant Menu** document, create a practice document if you want to practice these techniques. Clicking on the down arrow under *Special* in the *Paragraph* dialog box reveals the pop-up list from which you can choose the option you want. If you choose *Hanging* or *First Line*, Word sets the indent at 0.5 inches. You can change this value by typing or selecting the new value in the *By* box.

You can also use the Ruler to set a hanging indent. Select the paragraph that you want to format with a hanging indent. Then drag the bottom left-indent marker to the right to create the hanging indent. (You can see how a hanging indent is displayed on the Ruler by clicking in the bulleted list in your restaurant menu.)

Special Indents

First-Line Indent

Hanging Indent

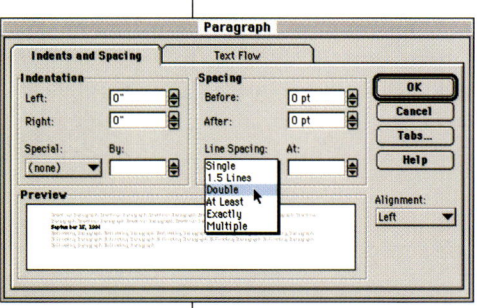

Creating a First-Line Indent

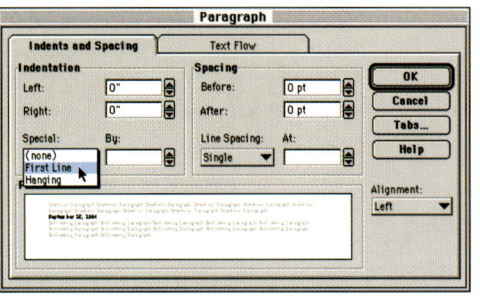

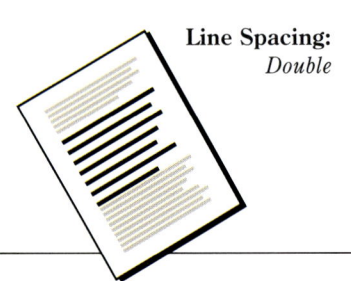

Setting Line Spacing

If you want to change the spacing between the lines in a paragraph, you use the *Indents and Spacing* flipcard in the *Paragraph* dialog box (after choosing *Paragraph* from the *Format* menu). For the most part, the default line spacing, *Single*, gives you perfect results for your documents because Word automatically adjusts the spacing according to the type size you use. But there are also other set spacings you can choose. Under *Spacing*, you can click on the down arrow next to the *Line Spacing* box to reveal a pop-up list. To select another spacing option, such as double or 1.5-line spacing, choose the option you want from the list and then click on *OK*. You can set the line spacing manually by choosing an option from the *At* box next to the *Line Spacing* box. You can also type the measurement in points in the box (for example, **12 pt**).

You can also adjust the spacing between paragraphs. To do this, you highlight the relevant paragraphs, open the *Paragraph* dialog box, type or choose the measurements you want in the *Before* and *After* boxes in the *Spacing* section, and then click on *OK*.

Examples of Different Line Spacings

Line Spacing: *Single*

Line Spacing: *1.5 lines*

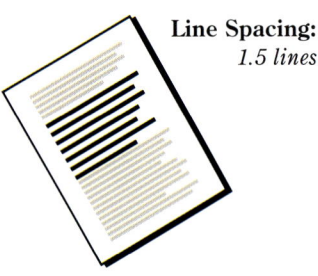

Line Spacing: *Double*

Setting Double-Line Spacing

Quick Paragraph? The quickest way to open the *Paragraph* dialog box is to double-click on the left- or right-indent markers.

Tab Stops

Tab stops are set positions marked on the Ruler at which you can align text or numbers in columns. Tabs are useful for presenting lists of information such as products and their prices. However, if you want to organize data in several rows and columns, you should create a table (see page 78).

Text or numbers can be aligned left or right against a tab stop, or centered across the tab stop. A decimal tab stop is used to align a column of decimal numbers such as the dish prices in your restaurant menu; the tab stop aligns the numbers on the decimal points.

Tabs are paragraph-level formats. To set them you must first select the paragraph or paragraphs you want to tab, and then set your tab stop(s). The button used to create tab stops, the Tab Alignment button, is on the left side of the Ruler. To set or change the tab stop, you must first click on this button until it displays the type of tab stop you want to create. The different appearances of the Tab Alignment button are shown at right.

Left-Aligned Tab

Centered Tab

Right-Aligned Tab

Decimal Tab

Want to Remove a Tab Stop?
To clear a tab stop quickly, select the paragraphs in which you want to remove the tab stop and drag the tab marker from its position on the Ruler to a position below the Ruler. The tab marker and tab stop position disappear.

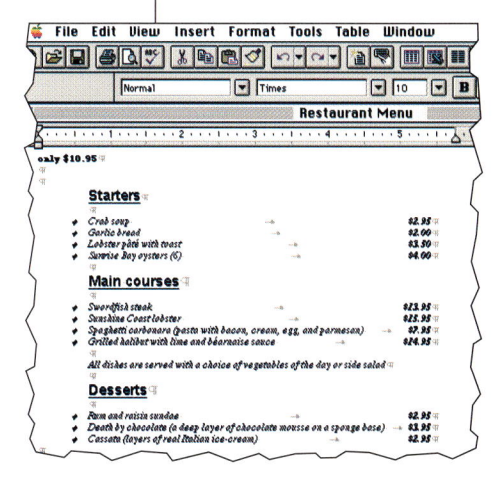

SETTING TAB STOPS

Word provides preset left-aligned tab stops at every half-inch along the Ruler. You can add a tab stop by choosing the relevant Tab Alignment button (right, left, centered, or decimal) and then clicking on the Ruler at the position you want the new tab stop to appear. Word clears the Ruler of the preset tab stops to the left of the new tab stop. The position of tab stops can also be altered by clicking on a tab-stop marker and dragging it to the left or right.

How to Set a Tab Stop

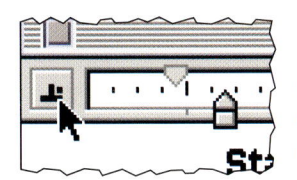

1 Select the text beginning with **Crab soup** under **Starters** down to the last dessert dish, **Cassata …$2.95**. Click on the Tab Alignment button until the decimal tab appears as shown here.

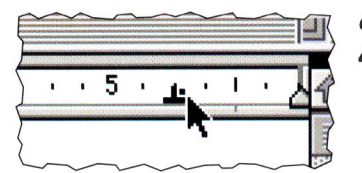

2 Click on the 5.25 inches mark on the Ruler.

3 Place your insertion point to the left of the price (**$2.95**) for **Crab soup** in the **Starters** section and press the Tab key. Word aligns the decimal point at the 5.25-inch tab stop. Do this for all the dishes in all three courses as shown here.

FORMATTING A DOCUMENT

USING THE DIALOG BOX
To set a tab stop with more precision, choose *Tabs* from the *Format* menu to open the *Tabs* dialog box. To set the tab, you type its value in the *Tab Stop Position* box, choose an option in the *Alignment* box, click on *Set*, and then click on *OK*. To remove tabs using the *Tabs* dialog box, select the relevant tabs in the *Tab Stop Position* box, click on *Clear*, and then click on *OK*.

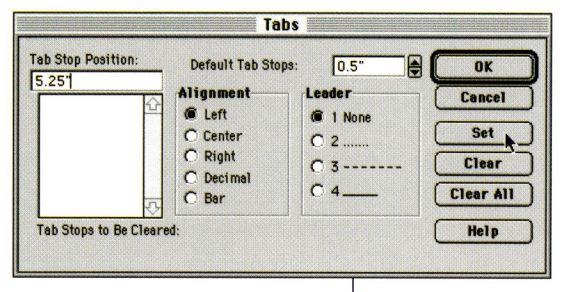

***Tabs* Dialog Box**

How to Add Page Numbers

You don't need to add page numbers to your restaurant menu, but you may want to number the pages of other documents you create. You can number the pages of your document quickly and easily using the *Page Numbers* command from the *Insert* menu. Word inserts numbers on every page and automatically renumbers the pages for you if you move text. You can't see page numbers in Normal view; you have to change to Page Layout view for this (see page 66).

Page numbers are section-level formats. This means that you can apply different page number formats to different sections. Page numbers are inserted into either a header or footer that appears at the top or bottom of the page. See pages 67 to 69 for more information on headers, footers, and sections.

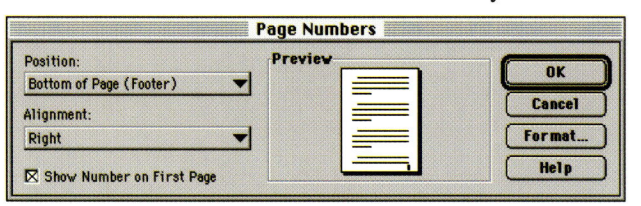

Adding Page Numbers
To number the pages of a document, choose Page Numbers *from the* Insert *menu to open the* Page Numbers *dialog box. Select a location in the* Position *box and an alignment in the* Alignment *box, and see the results in the* Preview *box. Click on* OK *to insert the numbers into the document.*

Your Format Options
If you want to change the format of your page numbers, click on Format *in the* Page Numbers *dialog box. The* Page Number Format *dialog box will appear showing the options that are available.*

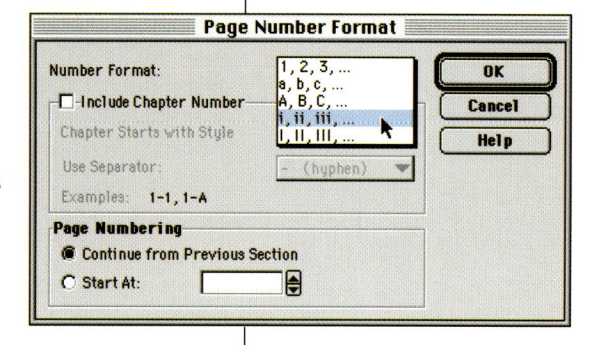

Top Margin
Right Margin

Using Your Margins

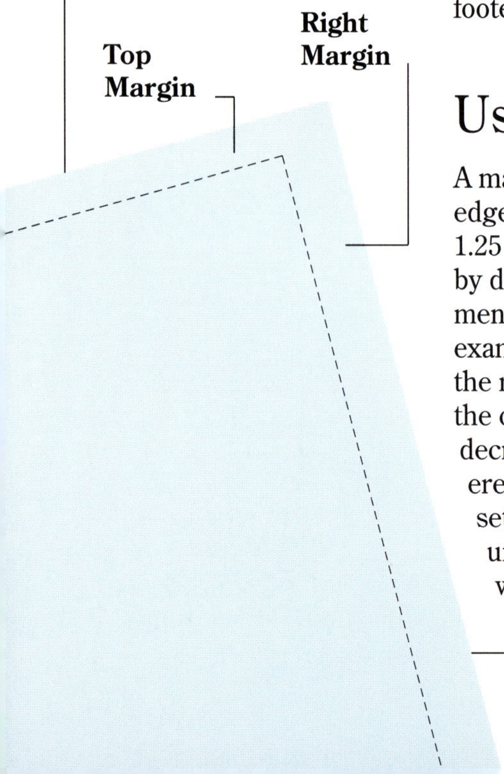

A margin can be defined as the distance between paper edge and text. Word sets the left and right margins at 1.25 inches and the top and bottom margins at 1 inch by default. These margins are adequate for most documents, but you can easily change these settings. For example, for a short letter you may want to increase the margins so that the text sits more comfortably. On the other hand, you may want to gain space for text by decreasing the margins. Margins are usually considered document-level formats — if you change margin settings you usually change them for the whole document. But you can also change margin settings within different sections (see page 68).

Marginal Problems!
Most printers cannot print right to the edge of your paper — bear this in mind when you set your margins. A rough rule of thumb is to allow at least half an inch either side and around one inch top and bottom. Setting margins too narrow may also make a document look cramped.

Setting Margins Using the Rulers

With Word, you can drag your margins to different positions using the horizontal or vertical ruler. If your document consists of only one section, the margins are changed for the whole document. However, you can't use this method in Normal view. You must first change to a different view that displays both a vertical ruler and a horizontal ruler. You can either use Page Layout view (see page 66) or Print Preview. Print Preview is often easier to use because you can see the whole page on the screen, but the method you use for setting margins is the same in both cases.

If you click on the Print Preview button on the Standard toolbar, the Print Preview window opens, displaying the two different rulers as shown here. If the rulers are not displayed, click on the View Ruler button on the Print Preview toolbar. The gray areas on the rulers indicate the current page margins. To change margins, place the mouse pointer over a margin boundary so that the pointer changes to a two-headed arrow, and then drag the boundary to its new position. The page display gets updated as you move the boundaries.

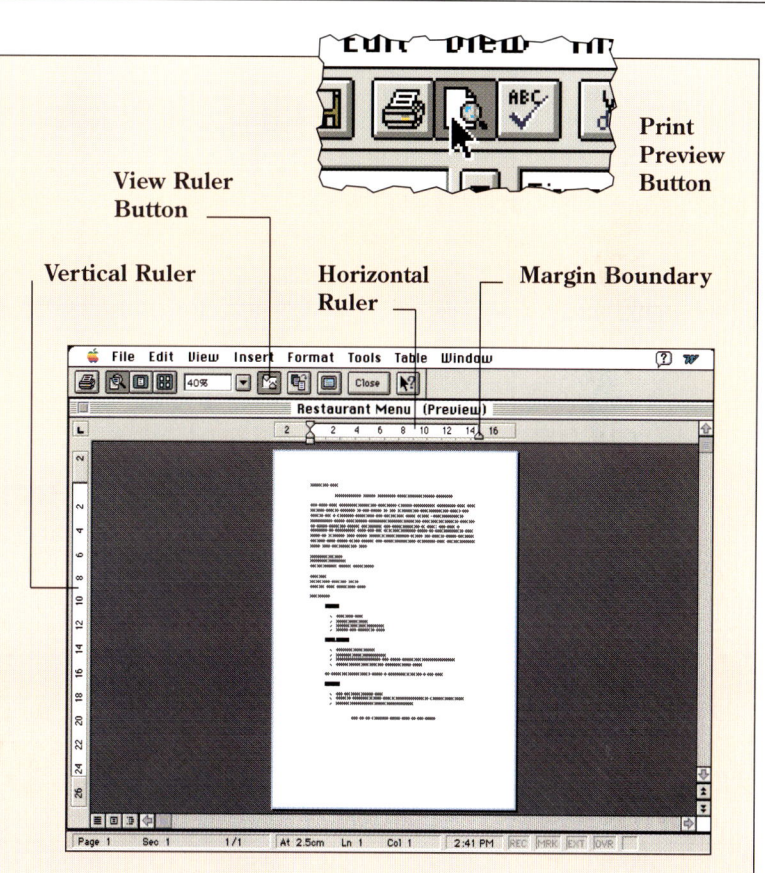

Print Preview Button

View Ruler Button

Vertical Ruler

Horizontal Ruler

Margin Boundary

Going Metric?

To change the measurements on the horizontal and vertical rulers from inches to centimeters, select *Options* from the *Tools* menu. Click on the *General* tab, and then choose *Centimeters* from the *Measurement Units* list box. Click on *OK*.

ANOTHER WAY TO SET MARGINS

Alternatively, you can use the *Document Layout* dialog box to change your margin settings. Let's practice using this method to narrow the margins of your restaurant menu. When you complete your document later in this chapter, you'll see that the narrower margins allow you to fit everything on one page.

Adjusting Your Margins

1 Choose *Document Layout* from the *File* menu to open the *Document Layout* dialog box.

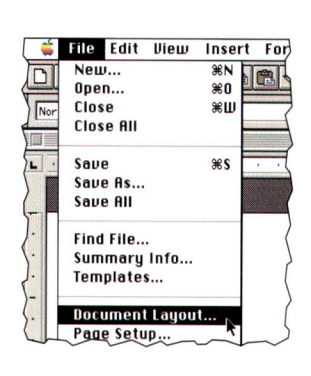

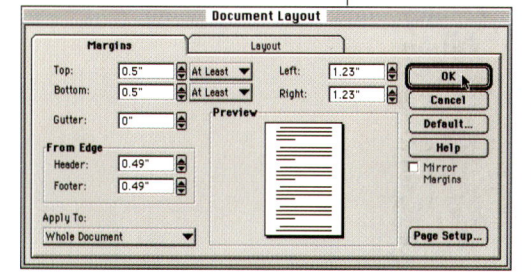

2 Click on the *Margins* tab if the *Margins* flipcard is not already displayed. In the *Top* and *Bottom* boxes, change the value to 0.5 inches. In the *Left* and *Right* boxes, change the value to 1.23 inches. Finally, click on *OK*.

65

Advanced Formatting

WITH WORD YOU CAN MAKE YOUR DOCUMENT look more attractive using some advanced formatting techniques. These include adding headers or footers, creating columns, and adding frames and borders. In this section, you'll apply these advanced techniques to your restaurant menu. But before you perform these tasks, it's helpful to know how to change the view of your document.

Changing Your View

You can view a document on the screen in a number of ways. Each viewing option helps you focus on a different aspect of your work. The three options you are likely to use are Normal, Page Layout, and Outline. You can switch views by clicking on the relevant button above the status bar (see left) or by choosing an option from the *View* menu. The standard view, and the one that is convenient for most tasks, is Normal. It reveals all text formatting but doesn't show the full layout of the document. Page Layout view is best for viewing the document as it will appear when printed.

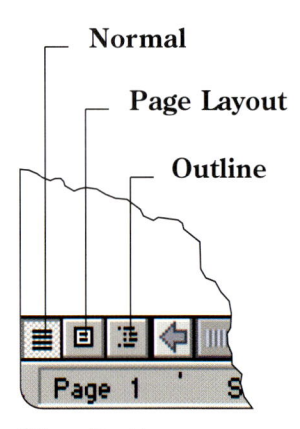

Normal
Page Layout
Outline

View Buttons

The Right Scale?
Remember that you can magnify or reduce the size of your document in any view using the down arrow next to the Zoom Control box on the Standard toolbar (see page 45). But bear in mind that zoomed views do not give accurate views of how the printed document will look.

A View from the Keyboard?
If you prefer, you can select a document view or switch between views by using the keyboard. Press down the Option key, the Command key, and N for Normal view, O for Outline view, or P for Page Layout view.

Your Viewing Options

Later in this section, you'll look at your restaurant menu using different views. Here are the three main views:

■ **Normal** view shows the document filling the entire document window. Although you see the correct fonts, the text appears in one continuous stream, with only dotted lines indicating page or section breaks. You can't see items such as columns (see page 69) or frames (see page 70) in Normal view.

■ **Page Layout** view is the closest to true WYSIWYG and shows your document as it will appear when it is printed. You can edit and format the text in this view and see the results on the screen. Page Layout view is useful for a final glance at your document to make sure any section breaks and page breaks you have made are in the right place.

■ **Outline** view helps you structure a document, using a hierarchy of headings in predetermined styles. Outlining allows you to collapse a document and view only the headings — the body text gets hidden temporarily. The overall structure of a document becomes more apparent and the outline tools make reorganizing your document very easy. For more information, see page 117.

Different First Page?
To omit the header or footer on the first page of a document, click on the Document Layout button on the Header and Footer toolbar. Under *Headers and Footers* in the *Layout* flipcard of the *Document Layout* dialog box, check *Different First Page*. Click on *OK*.

Headers and Footers

A header or footer is text, such as a title or an explanatory note, that appears at the top or bottom of each page of a document section. Headers and footers are section-level formats. By default, a header or footer is printed 0.5 inches from the top or bottom paper edge. If you divide a document into sections, you can use different headers or footers for each section (see page 68). Because you can see a header or footer only in Page Layout view, begin by clicking on the Page Layout button on the status bar. Then follow these steps to insert a footer into your restaurant menu.

Inserting a Footer

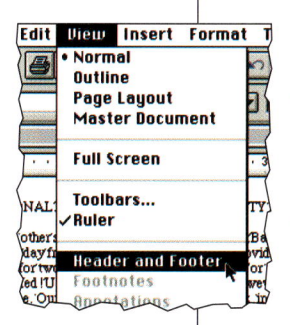

1 Choose *Header and Footer* from the *View* menu. Your document appears dimmed and the insertion point appears in the header area. The Header and Footer toolbar also appears.

2 Now click on the Switch Between Header and Footer button on the Header and Footer toolbar to go to the footer area.

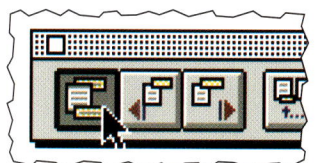

3 In the footer area, type **See our drinks menu for coffees, soft drinks, cocktails, wines, beers, and spirits.** Select the footer text and make it bold and italic with centered alignment. Do this in the same way you format other text. Don't close the Header and Footer toolbar just yet —you'll add a border to your footer on the next page.

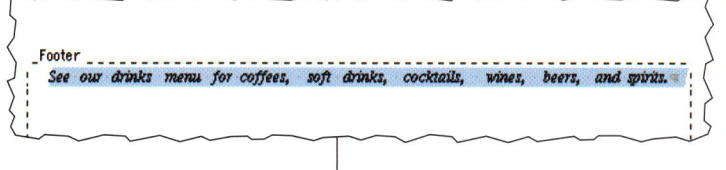

The Header and Footer Toolbar

Here is a brief explanation of the buttons you'll find on the Header and Footer toolbar.

Switch Between Header and Footer
To move between headers and footers.

Show Previous
To move to the previous header or footer, if there are different headers and footers in a document.

Show Next
To move to the next header or footer, if there are different headers and footers in a document.

Page Numbers
To automatically insert page numbers on each page.

Date
To automatically insert the current date.

Time
To automatically insert the current time.

Same as Previous
To apply a header or footer from a previous section to the current section.

Show/Hide Document Text
To show or hide the dimmed text in the main document.

Document Layout
To change the page setup of the document or selected sections.

ADVANCED FORMATTING

ADDING A BORDER

A border is a box surrounding a block of text that makes it stand out from the main flow of text. You can add a border to any paragraph or group of paragraphs in your document. To add a simple border, you click on the Borders button on the Formatting toolbar to display the Borders toolbar. Then you can choose a border style and apply it. You can add more complex border effects by using the *Paragraph Borders and Shading* dialog box. Let's use this method to emphasize your footer by adding a border and a shadow.

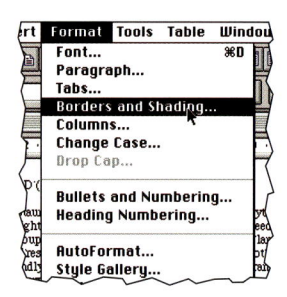

Removing a Border?
To remove a border, select the item surrounded by the border, then click on the Borders button on the Formatting toolbar. On the Borders toolbar that appears, click on the No Border button (the last button on the right). Click on the Borders button again to hide the toolbar.

1 With your footer still selected, choose *Borders and Shading* from the *Format* menu.

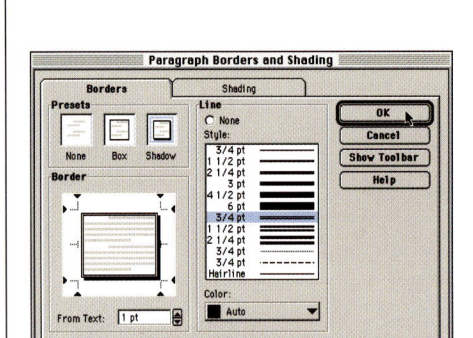

2 The *Paragraph Borders and Shading* dialog box appears. In the *Borders* flipcard under *Line*, select the ¾ pt double-line border in the *Style* box. Click on the *Shadow* icon in the *Presets* section. Finally, click on *OK*.

3 A double-line border with a shadow appears around the text of the footer. Now click on *Close* on the Header and Footer toolbar to return to your restaurant menu. Remember that you can see your footer only in Page Layout view.

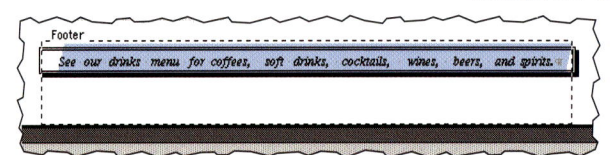

How to Create Sections

When you open a new document, there are no section breaks — the document consists of one section. With Word, it's easy to divide a document into different sections. You need to create sections if you want to apply certain formatting changes to a section that you don't want to apply to the rest of your document. If you only want to format characters or format paragraphs — for example, making text bold and aligning it right — you don't need to create separate sections. But you do need to create sections if you want different parts of your document to have different margin settings or different numbers of columns. The importance of sections becomes clear when you follow the steps on the opposite page to insert a separate section in the restaurant menu to create columns.

Different Margins?
If your document is broken up into sections, you can change the margin settings in one section without affecting the rest of the document. Position the insertion point in the relevant section, then choose *Document Layout* from the *File* menu. Type the new margin values in the *Margins* flipcard, and choose *This Section* in the *Apply To* box. Click on *OK*.

68

Creating Separate Sections

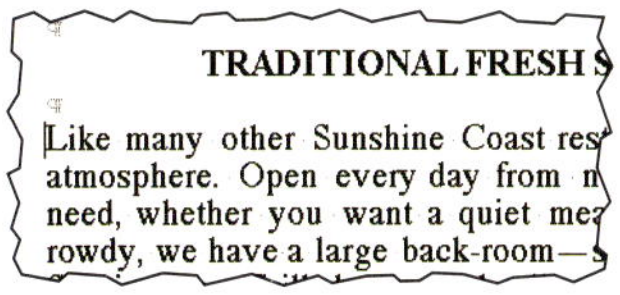

1 Position the insertion point at the beginning of the largest paragraph.

2 Now choose *Break* from the *Insert* menu.

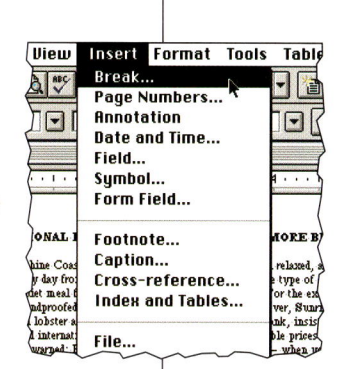

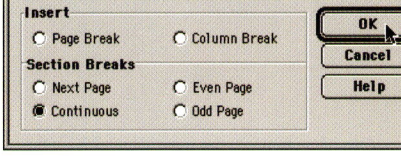

3 The *Break* dialog box appears. Under *Section Breaks*, choose *Continuous* to create a section without starting a new page. Then click on *OK*. In your document the section break appears as a double dotted line. Position the insertion point at the end of the paragraph and press Return. Then repeat the procedure to mark the end of the section.

Breaking Point
You can use the Break *dialog box to insert a manual page break — to make sure, for example, that a particular heading is at the top of a page. Place the insertion point where you want the break to occur, then choose* Break *from the* Insert *menu. In the* Break *dialog box, choose* Page Break, *and then click on* OK.

How to Create Columns

With Word, you can format all or part of your document as newspaper-style columns in which text flows from the bottom of one column to the top of the next. You can specify however many columns you need, but as a general rule, two or three columns per page looks best. To create two columns for the largest paragraph of your restaurant menu, follow these steps:

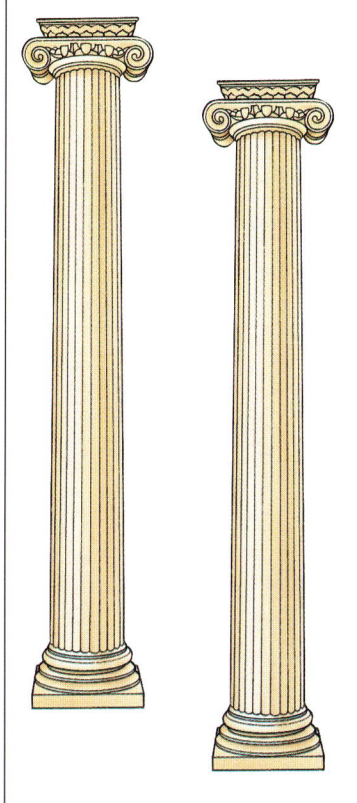

Forming the Columns

1 Reposition the insertion point at the beginning of the largest paragraph.

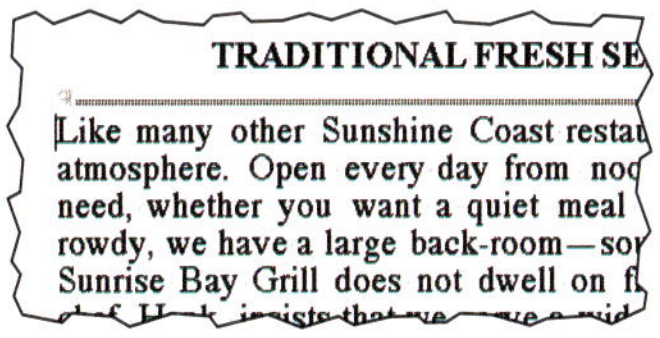

2 Click on the Columns button on the Standard toolbar. Hold down the mouse button and drag to select two columns.

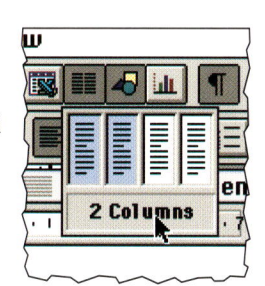

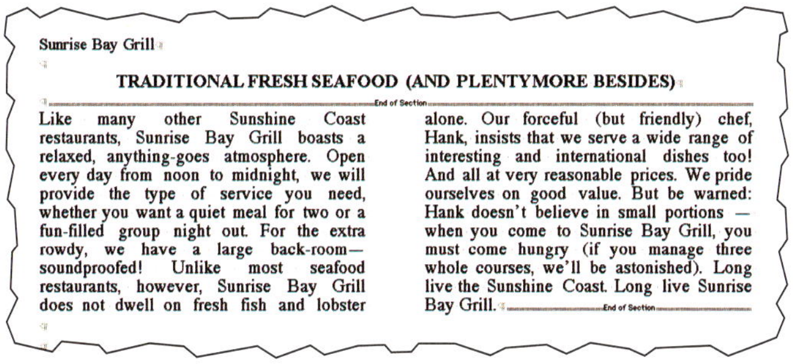

3 In your restaurant menu, the largest paragraph now appears as two columns.

My Columns Are Missing!
Even if you have created separate columns, you will only see one column if you are in Normal view. To see your columns, you must make sure you are in Page Layout view.

ADVANCED FORMATTING

How to Create a Frame

A frame is a box of text, graphics, or a mixture of these elements that is separate from the body text and can be moved around the document independently. By default, any text outside the frame wraps around a frame. Placing items within a frame is a good way to separate them from the main text. To define a frame for your restaurant menu, make sure you are in Page Layout view, then follow these steps.

Adding a Frame

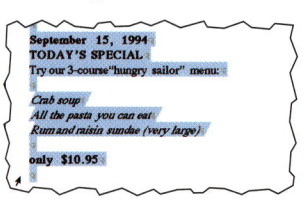

1 Position the insertion point on the blank line above the date. Select the blank line and the following lines of text down to and including the blank line after **only $10.95**.

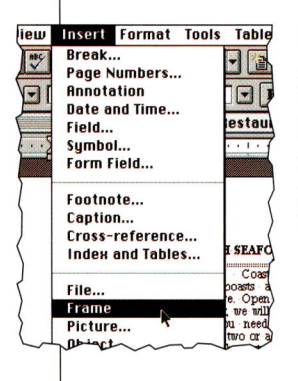

2 Choose *Frame* from the *Insert* menu. Word encloses the selected text in a box and an anchor appears in the margin, indicating that the paragraph contains a frame. Because the frame is selected, you'll also see a shaded border with black handles.

3 To resize the frame so that it closely surrounds the text, move the mouse pointer to the handle at the center of the right hand border. The pointer changes to a two-headed arrow. Drag the border to the left to decrease the frame's width to just less than half its original width. As soon as you start dragging the border, the two-headed arrow changes to a cross hair.

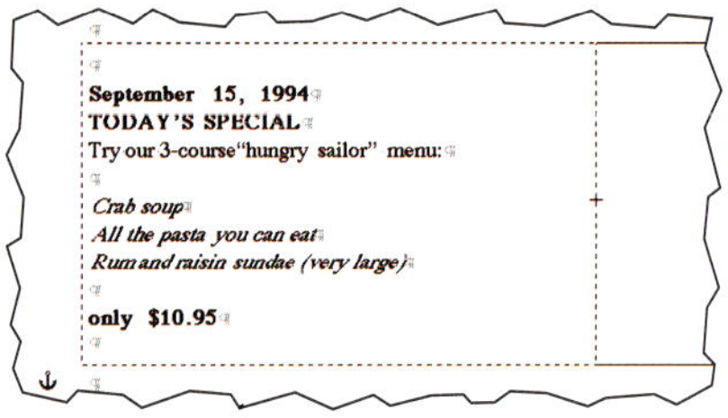

4 Click inside the frame and select all the text, including the two blank lines at the top and bottom. Then click on the Center button on the Formatting toolbar to center the text within the frame. Finally, deselect the text by clicking anywhere outside the frame.

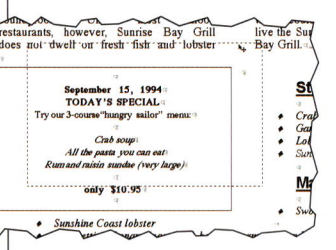

5 Click on the frame to select it. Move the mouse pointer over any part of the frame's border so that the pointer changes to a four-headed arrow, then hold down the mouse button and drag the frame up and to the right.

6 Position the frame between the two columns so that its top border falls roughly over the third line, then release the mouse button. The frame should sit in the text roughly as shown at right. (It may take a moment for the new layout to appear on your screen.)

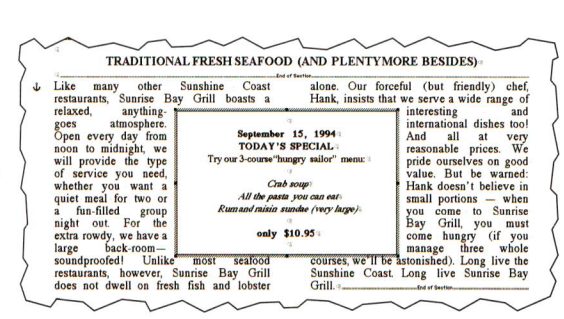

On the Borderline

The standard border for a frame is a single-line box border. To change the border, click on the frame border to select the frame, choose *Borders and Shading* from the *Format* menu, and select the options you want in the dialog box.

⚠ Don't Press Del!

While your frame is selected, be careful not to press the Del or Delete keys. Doing so deletes the entire frame and its contents.

70

ADJUSTING YOUR FRAME

Now that you have inserted your frame, you may need to adjust its dimensions and position so that the text flows neatly around it. You can adjust the frame's width and height by dragging the handles with the mouse and its position by dragging the whole frame. Use these methods so that the flow of the text around your frame is as close as possible to that shown at right.

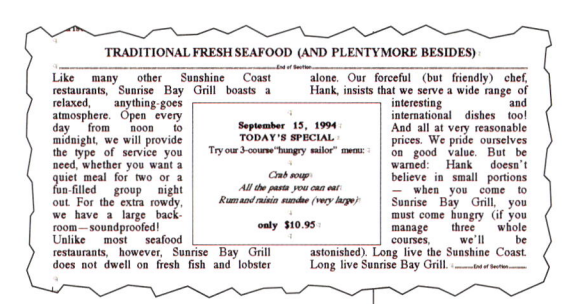

The Frame Dialog Box

For precise control over the adjustment of a frame, it's best to choose options in the *Frame* dialog box (right). To open the dialog box, you select your frame by clicking on its border, and then choose *Frame* from the *Format* menu. The various options you can choose are explained below.

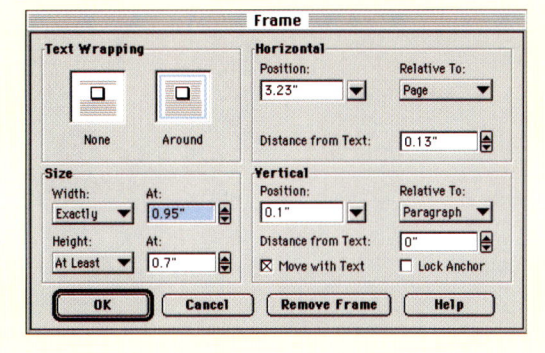

■ *Text Wrapping* — Choose whether you want the text to wrap around the frame or simply flow above and below it.

■ *Position* — In these boxes, type or select the horizontal and vertical positions you want for the frame.

■ *Relative To* — Select *Margin*, *Page*, *Column*, or *Paragraph* to indicate the item to which you want the positions in the *Position* boxes to relate.

■ *Move with Text* — When this option is checked, Word moves the frame up or down the page automatically as you add or remove text above or below it.

■ *Distance from Text* — Type or select values in these boxes to set the spacing between the frame and the surrounding text.

■ *Lock Anchor* — Click on this option if you want your frame to remain locked in the specified position, regardless of any text changes you make.

■ *Size* — Use this section to choose a width and height for your frame. If you choose *Auto,* Word sizes the frame according to the text inside it. If you want to specify your own measurements, type or select the required values in the *At* boxes.

How to Hyphenate Your Text

To avoid raggedness in left or right aligned text or to reduce gaps between words in justified text, you can hyphenate text. In the restaurant menu, highlight the justified text in columns, and then follow these steps:

1 Choose *Hyphenation* from the *Tools* menu.

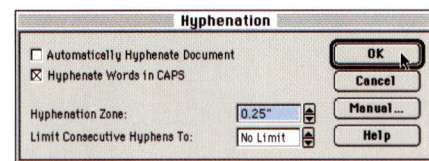

2 In the *Hyphenation* dialog box, click on *Manual*.

3 Word finds the first word, in our example **international**, and asks if you want it hyphenated. Click on *No*. When Word suggests hyphenating **restaurant**, click on *Yes*.

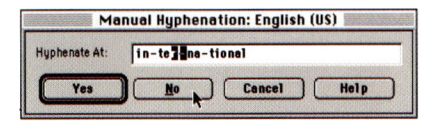

4 Click on *No* when you see the message at right. Word then informs you that the hyphenation is complete. Click on *OK*.

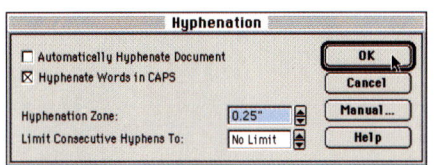

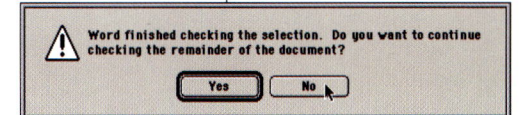

Auto Hyphenation?
Word can hyphenate text as you type. In the *Hyphenation* dialog box, check the *Automatically Hyphenate Document* box. The smaller the measurement in the *Hyphenation Zone* box, the more words will be hyphenated.

71

ADDING A LOGO

Adding a Logo

Graphics can brighten up the appearance of any document. With Word it's easy to create such special effects — you can use WordArt for creating special typographical effects such as logos and the Drawing toolbar for designing your own pictures. In this section, you'll add the finishing touch — an attractive logo — to your restaurant menu. You'll also learn how to import ready-made pictures from Word's own "picture library."

Jazz Up Your Text

WordArt allows you to create special effects with words — for example, you can make words form a circle or an arch, make them slope diagonally, or even flip them upside down. Let's create a special effect for the name of the restaurant at the top of your document. In Page Layout view, follow the steps below.

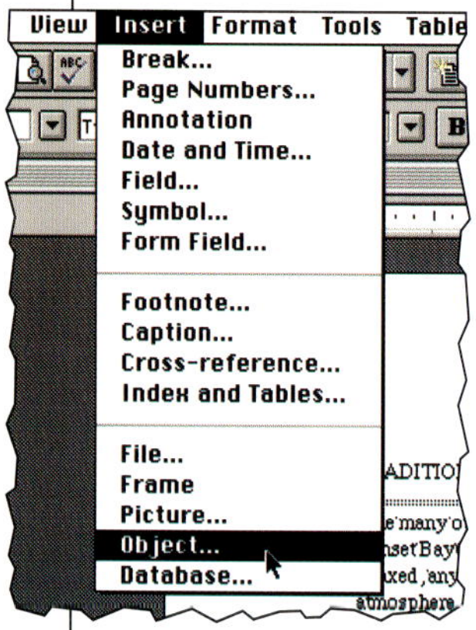

Styling the Name

1 Delete the name **Sunrise Bay Grill** at the top of the document, leaving the insertion point at the top left-hand corner of the window. Then choose *Object* from the *Insert* menu.

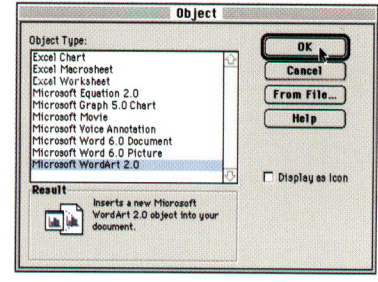

2 In the *Object* dialog box, choose *Microsoft WordArt 2.0* and then click on *OK*.

3 The *WordArt 2.0* dialog box appears. Type the words **Sunrise Bay Grill** in the *Enter Your Text Here* box.

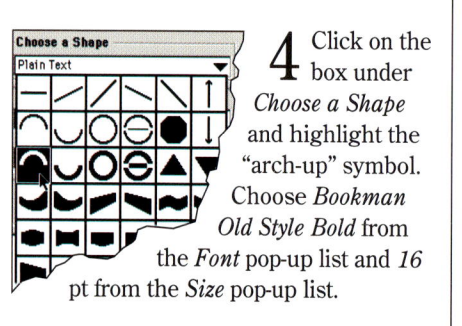

4 Click on the box under *Choose a Shape* and highlight the "arch-up" symbol. Choose *Bookman Old Style Bold* from the *Font* pop-up list and *16* pt from the *Size* pop-up list.

5 To return to Word, click on *OK*. The text is inserted into your document. Select the WordArt text by clicking on it, and then click on the Center button on the Formatting toolbar to center the name.

WordArt Explorer
After selecting a shape for your text in WordArt, play with the buttons on the WordArt toolbar at the bottom of the *WordArt 2.0* dialog box. For example, flip or stretch the letters by clicking on the Flip Letters or Stretch Letters buttons (third and fourth buttons from the right). Undo an effect by clicking on the same button again.

Changed Your Mind?
If you want to change WordArt text that you have already inserted into your document, simply double-click on the WordArt object to activate WordArt. Then change the text or change any of the formatting options.

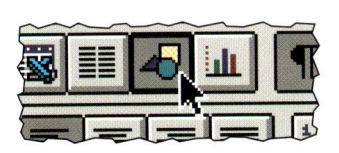

A Budding Artist

Using the Drawing toolbar, you can put together attractive pictures for your document. When you click on the Drawing button on the Standard toolbar, Word switches you to Page Layout view and the Drawing toolbar appears at the bottom of the screen. On the toolbar, you'll see a number of tools that you can use to create various shapes — lines, squares, rectangles, circles, ovals, and so on. You click on the relevant button to activate a particular drawing tool. You can also create text boxes and callouts, color single lines or the outline of an image, and fill your images with different colors. After drawing an image, you can manipulate it in several ways — for example, rotate the image or insert a frame around it. Over the next few pages, you'll assemble an image and add it to your restaurant menu. Below is a brief description of the buttons on the Drawing toolbar.

Drawing Button

Rise and Shine
The image you'll create for your logo will consist of the sun rising above the sea.

Calling Out?
A callout is a text box with a line extending from it. The line links text with a particular detail of an image — a useful feature for any informative illustration. Click on the Format Callout button to open the *Callout Defaults* dialog box if you want to add a border around the text, change the type or angle of a callout line, or the way the line is attached to the text box.

The Drawing Toolbar

By combining shapes formed with the Drawing toolbar, you can create images such as logos, maps, flow charts, organization charts, and so on.

Line Tool
Draws a straight line; hold down Shift to constrain the line to a preset angle.

Rectangle Tool
Draws a rectangle; hold down Shift for a square.

Ellipse Tool
Draws an ellipse (oval); hold down Shift to produce a circle.

Arc Tool
Draws an arc; hold down Shift for a circular arc.

Freeform Tool
Draws any shape (polyline) you want to draw. Double-click to end the shape.

Text Box Tool
Creates a text box. You can format the text in the same way you format any other Word text.

Callout Tool
Draws a text box with an attached line.

Format Callout
Specifies the appearance of a callout.

Fill Color
Fills a drawing with a selected color.

Line Color
Outlines a drawing with a selected color.

Line Style
Specifies a line style.

Select Drawing Objects
Drag pointer to select one or several drawings at once.

Bring to Front
Brings a selected drawing in front of other drawings.

Send to Back
Sends a selected drawing behind other drawings.

Bring in Front of Text
Brings a selected drawing in front of text layer.

Send Behind Text
Sends a selected drawing behind text layer.

Group
Connects two or more drawings so they can be moved or sized as a group.

Ungroup
Ungroups drawings.

Flip Horizontal
Flips a selected drawing from right to left.

Flip Vertical
Flips a selected drawing from top to bottom.

Rotate Right
Rotates a selected drawing 90° to the right.

Reshape
Reshapes a selected Freeform drawing.

Snap to Grid
Sets up snapping grids to help position both text and drawings.

Align Drawing Objects
Aligns drawings to each other on the page.

Create Picture
Inserts an empty drawing container.

Insert Frame
Frames a selected drawing or text.

ADDING A LOGO

MAKING WAVES
The first part of the image you'll draw are the waves. To create them, you draw an arc, copy it, and overlap the arcs. If the Drawing toolbar isn't displayed, click on the Drawing button on the Standard toolbar. Position the insertion point immediately after **Sunrise Bay Grill** and press Return six times to make space for the drawing. (You should have a total of seven "empty" lines.)

1 Click on the Arc tool on the Drawing toolbar. When moved into your document, the mouse pointer changes to a cross-hair shape.

2 Move the pointer to the area above **TRADITIONAL FRESH SEAFOOD....** Hold down the mouse button and drag the pointer up and to the right to create a "wave," and then release the mouse button. Roughly follow the position and proportions shown at right.

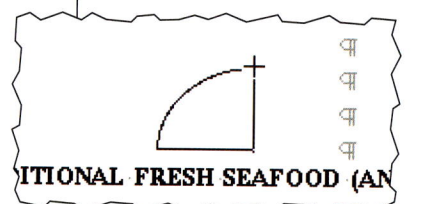

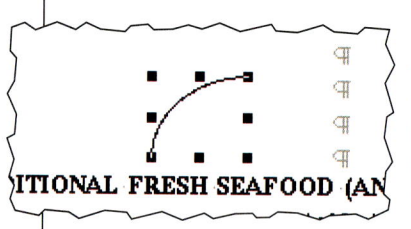

3 The wave you have drawn should be selected. (You can tell it's selected because black handles appear; if it isn't, click on the wave.) You can now copy this wave to produce several others of the same proportions.

4 Place the mouse pointer over the wave so that it is accompanied by a four-headed arrow.

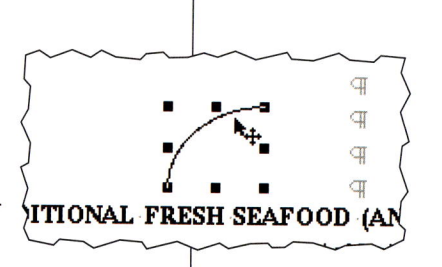

5 To copy the wave, hold down the Option key and drag the mouse pointer to the right as shown here. You'll see an outline of the wave move as you move the mouse. Release the mouse button and the Option key to drop the copy of the wave into its new position.

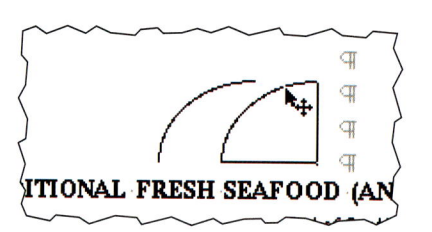

6 Repeat the procedure to produce two more waves, and then click outside the waves to deselect the last wave. You should now have four waves lined up in one row as shown at right.

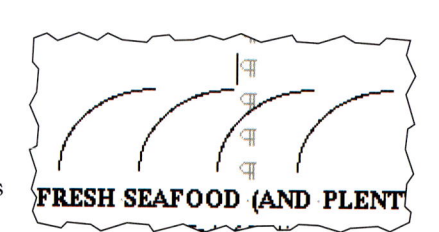

Drawn the Wrong Thing?
To delete a drawn object, first select the item by clicking on it. (If the object is not filled, click on one of the object's edges.) When an object is selected, a box with black handles appears around it. Now press Del.

Wrong Size!
You can easily resize a drawn object. Simply click on the object to select it, and then drag any handle to resize it. To enlarge or shrink an object and keep its original proportions, hold down Shift and drag any corner handle.

LET THE SUN SHINE
Follow these steps to create the second part of your image — the sun and its rays. When you create an object, it appears in front of any text or other object in the document. (You'll be shown how to layer drawings in "Making the Final Adjustments" on page 76.)

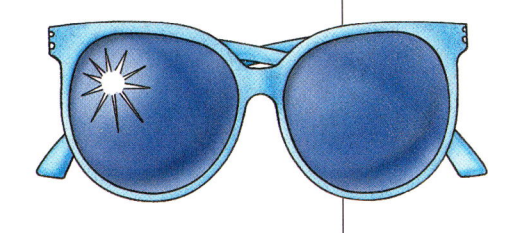

1 Click on the Ellipse tool.

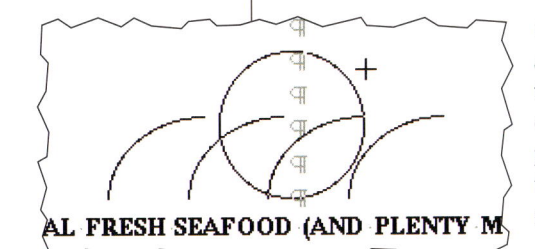

2 Hold down Shift and position the pointer at the foot of and between the second and third waves. Hold down the mouse button and drag the pointer to the right to create a circle two thirds of an inch in diameter. Then release the mouse button and Shift.

3 Double-click on the Line button to select it. (Double-clicking on a Drawing button allows you to draw several objects of the same type without having to return to the toolbar.)

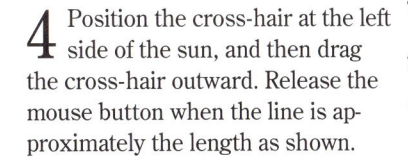

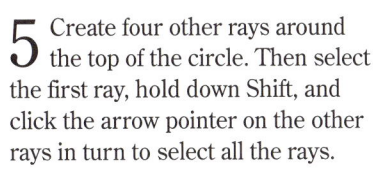

4 Position the cross-hair at the left side of the sun, and then drag the cross-hair outward. Release the mouse button when the line is approximately the length as shown.

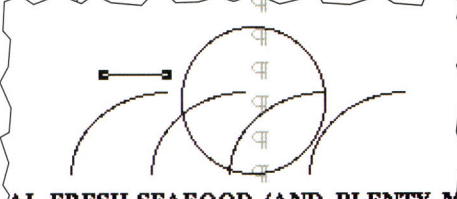

5 Create four other rays around the top of the circle. Then select the first ray, hold down Shift, and click the arrow pointer on the other rays in turn to select all the rays.

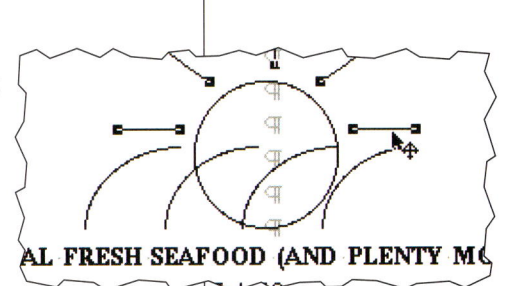

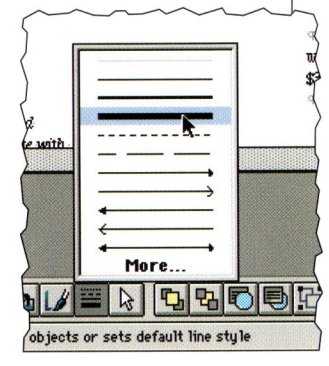

6 Click on the Line Style button and select the thickest line from the pop-up list. When you release the mouse button, the rays will be formatted with a thick line. Leave the five rays selected.

Big Selection
To select several objects at the same time, you can either hold down Shift and then click on each object in turn, or you can click on the Select Drawing Objects button (the arrow button) on the Drawing toolbar, and drag the pointer to create a rectangle that encloses the objects you want to select.

ADDING A LOGO

COLORING OBJECTS AND LINES
Now that you have drawn the separate parts of your image, you can color them. But bear in mind that unless you have a color printer, the colors show only on your screen — the image will be printed in black. Follow these steps to color your image.

1 The rays should still be selected. Click on the Line Color button and select the yellow square from the pop-up palette — the rays turn yellow. Click in a blank spot to deselect the rays.

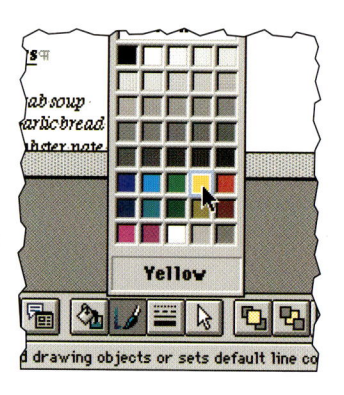

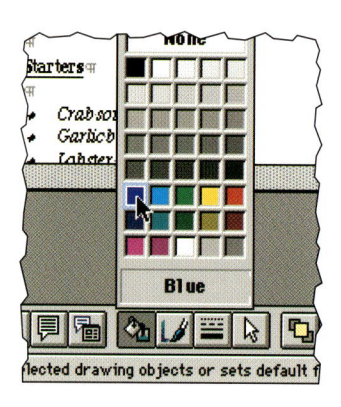

2 Click on the first wave, hold down Shift, and click on the other waves to select them all. Click on the Fill Color button and select bright blue from the pop-up palette. While the waves are still selected, choose the same blue from the Line Color palette. Finally, deselect the waves.

3 Select the circle and choose yellow from both the Fill Color and the Line Color palettes.

MAKING THE FINAL ADJUSTMENTS
Your image is now complete except for its layering. For a better fit, you may also want to alter the size and shape of your WordArt text (see box at left).

1 Some of the waves are hidden behind the sun. With the sun still selected, click on the Send to Back button to move the sun behind the waves. Click in a blank spot to deselect the sun.

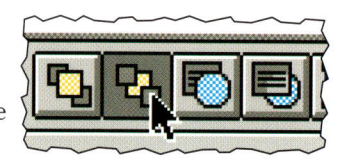

2 Your image is now complete and you've finished formatting your restaurant menu. Save your document and then print it. The printed version should look like the one shown here.

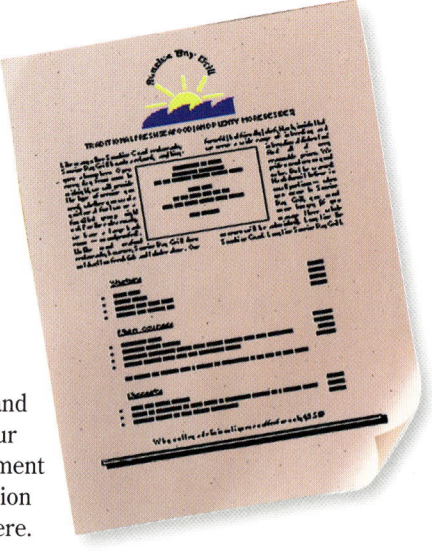

Cut It to Size
You may want to manipulate the size of the WordArt text to improve the overall fit of your logo. Click on the WordArt object to select it. Then drag any of the corner handles to enlarge or shrink the image without distorting it. Dragging a center handle will distort the image slightly to fit the resized frame.

Ready-Made Pictures

You can also include pictures from the **Clip Art** or **Clip Art\EPS Clip Art** folders. All the files in these folders contain images that have already been created — you just choose the image you want, and then import it into the document. After you've imported an image, you can resize it in your Word document. Let's add an image to the **Prize Letter** document that you created earlier in Chapter One. Make sure you have closed your **Restaurant Menu** document, and then open **Prize Letter**.

A Quick Preview?

Before you import a Clip Art image, it's a good idea to see what it looks like. To do this, check *Preview Picture* within the dialog box that appears after choosing *Picture* from the *Insert* menu. When you select a file in a Clip Art folder, the image appears in the *Preview* window. If you like the image, click on *Insert* to import it into your document.

Inserting the Picture

1 Place the insertion point in front of the word **Thompson** in the return address, and then choose *Picture* from the *Insert* menu.

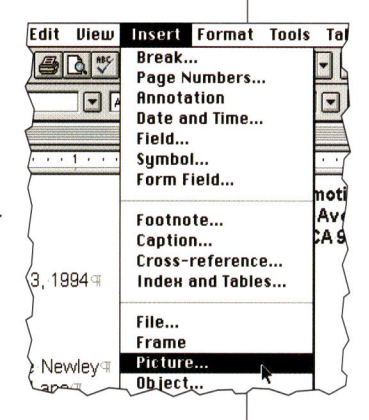

2 The dialog box shown at left appears. Display the **Clip Art\EPS Clip Art** folder (which is within the **Microsoft Word** folder) in the pop-up list box under *Select a Picture to Insert*. In the file list, you'll see a list of names for different Clip Art images. Scroll through the list and choose *Compass.eps*. Click on *Insert* to insert the image into your document.

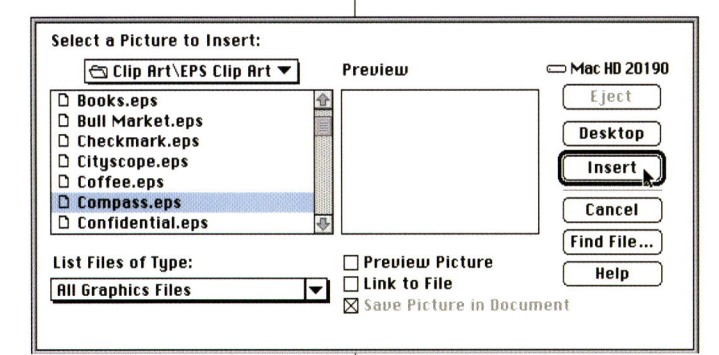

3 The picture appears at the top of the document, in front of the line **Thompson Promotions**, where the insertion point was placed. Press Return once to insert a new line so that the picture is above the return address as shown here. Then save the document and close it.

Want to Modify Your Image?

It's easy to modify the pictures that you import from the Clip Art folders. Double-clicking on the image displays the Drawing toolbar. You can use tools on the Drawing toolbar (see page 73) to modify the image. For example, you can give a background color to the compass you've just imported by double-clicking, highlighting the compass, and then choosing a color from the Fill Color palette.

Tables and Sorting

YOU MAY SOMETIMES WANT TO ORGANIZE and present text or data in a table. Word has several features that make working with tables easy. You can apply character and paragraph formatting to the items in a table; you can produce a chart directly from a table without entering any of the figures again; and you can instruct Word to sort data in various ways, such as alphabetically or chronologically. Word can even add up data in a table for you.

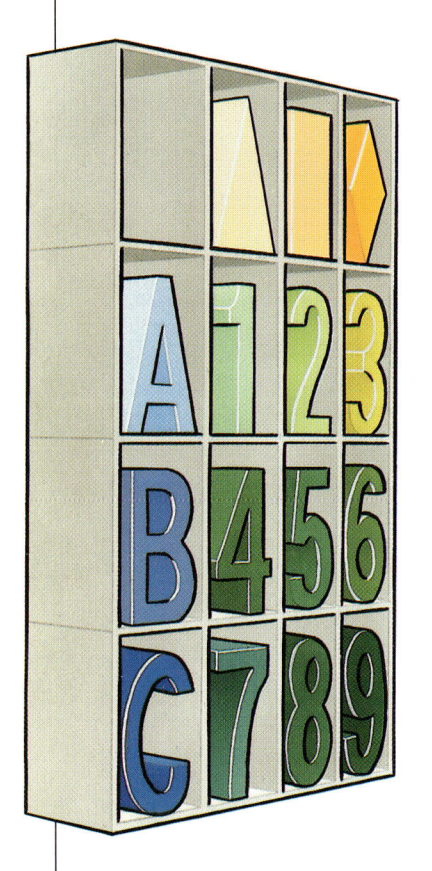

How to Create a Table

In a table, you enter text, data, or graphics into boxes, called cells, which are arranged in columns and rows. On the screen, nonprinting gridlines show the boundaries of individual cells and the entire table. The gridlines are guides that make it easier to work with a table. If they don't appear, choose *Gridlines* from the *Table* menu. For gridlines that will print, click in the table, choose *Borders and Shading* from the *Format* menu, click on *Grid* under *Presets*, and click on *OK*.

Before you build a table, decide how many columns and rows you'll need. Remember to add a row or column for the headings. You can also add extra rows and columns after you have created a table, if necessary.

AN ELECTION IN SMALLTOWN

In this section, you'll create an example table within a letter from a polling organization. You can create the letter by clicking on the New button on the Standard toolbar. Save the document as **Poll Letter** on your hard disk, and then type in the text below. Make the first line after the date, **Precision Polls Inc.**, 18 point, bold, and centered.

> **Want to Change Your Table Manners?**
> In this section, you'll learn how to insert a table using the Standard toolbar, but you can also create a table by choosing *Insert Table* from the *Table* menu. In the *Insert Table* dialog box, type the number of rows and columns you want in the relevant text boxes, and then click on *OK*.

> **Wrapping Around**
> A table also provides a convenient way to present side-by-side paragraphs. Within each cell in a table, text wraps just as it does between the margins of a document; the cell expands vertically to fit the amount of text you type.

July 20, 1994 <Return>

Precision Polls Inc. <Return>

The Editor <Return>

Smalltown Gazette <Return>

Smalltown <Return> <Return>

Dear Sir, <Return> <Return>

Please find below the results of our latest survey (mid-July) of voting intentions for the forthcoming (August 10) election for Mayor of Smalltown. As before, we contacted the same sample of 835 Smalltown residents by telephone and asked them "Which candidate do you expect to vote for on August 10?" The answers were as follows (the results from our two previous surveys also appear): <Return> <Return>

SETTING UP THE TABLE

Position the insertion point two lines beneath the last paragraph. This is where you'll insert the table. Now follow these steps:

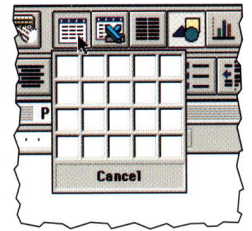

1 Point to the Table button on the Standard toolbar and hold down the mouse button. A small grid drops down.

2 Drag over the grid to select five rows and four columns. The line at the bottom of the table displays how many rows and columns you have selected. Then release the mouse button.

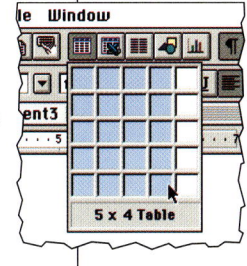

3 A blank table is inserted into your document. The small squares are end-of-cell and end-of-row marks. You can hide or display them by clicking on the Show/Hide button. Display them for now to make the table easier to work with.

Gridline

End-of-Row Mark

End-of-Cell Mark

ENTERING AND FORMATTING DATA

Now type the following poll results into the table, row by row. Begin by positioning your insertion point in the second cell in the top row. After typing the contents of a cell, press Tab to move to the next cell in a row. At the end of a row, press Tab to move the insertion point to the first cell in the next row. Alternatively, use the direction keys.

Formatting Data in a Table

1 Select the column of candidates' names by clicking on the top gridline of the column — where the pointer changes to a black arrow.

2 Click on the Bold button on the Formatting toolbar to make the candidates' names bold.

3 Select the top row of the table by clicking in the selection bar next to it, then click on the Bold button to emphasize the months.

How Can I Select Table Entries?
To select a single cell, position the I-beam pointer between the left edge of the cell and the first character in the cell, where the pointer changes to an arrow. Then click the mouse button. To select any rectangular block of cells, hold down the mouse button and drag over the area you want to select.

79

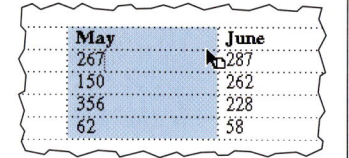

TABLES AND SORTING

ADDING ROWS AND COLUMNS
If you want to include more data in a table, you'll need to add extra columns or rows. The quickest method is to select in your existing table the number of columns or rows that you want to add, and then click on the Table button on the Standard toolbar. Word inserts new columns to the left of selected columns and new rows above selected rows.

To insert a new row at the bottom of a table, follow the procedure described at the bottom of this page. To add a new column at the right of a table, position the insertion point just to the right of the last column, choose *Select Column* from the *Table* menu so that the end-of-row marks are selected, and then choose *Insert Columns* from the *Table* menu.

INSERTING AND DELETING CELLS
To insert one or more new, blank cells (but not a whole row or column) in a table, select the cell or cells where you want the new cells to appear. Click on the Table button on the Standard toolbar. In the *Insert Cells* dialog box, choose *Shift Cells Right* or *Shift Cells Down* to specify whether the existing cells move to the right or down when the new cells are added. Click on *OK*.

To delete cells in a table, select the cell or cells you want to delete, and then choose *Delete Cells* from the *Table* menu. Choose one of the four options displayed in the *Delete Cells* dialog box, and then click on *OK*.

The *Insert Cells* Dialog Box

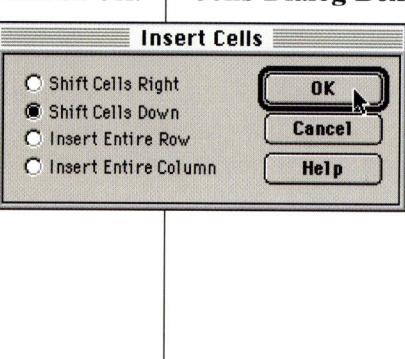

Adding a New Row to Your Table

1 Position the insertion point in the rightmost cell of the last row of your table. Then press the Tab key.

2 A new row of blank cells appears at the bottom of your table. Type **Total** in the first column of the new row.

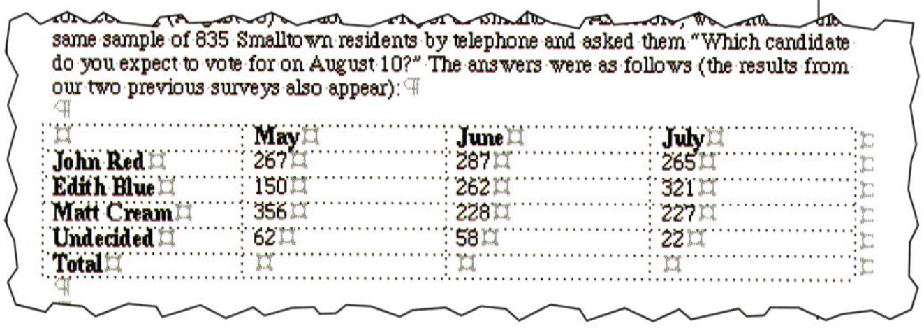

What a Drag!
You can easily change the order of columns or rows. Just like text, you can drag selected cells, columns, or rows to different positions within a table to reorganize your data.

Keep Tabs on It!
Make sure you press the Tab key when you want to add a new row. Pressing Return by mistake adds a new line to the last row.

A Tight Fit?
If you want to change the width of a column in a table, first select the column and then position the mouse pointer over the column's right gridline, where it changes to a split vertical bar with side arrows. Drag the gridline to the right or left until the column is the desired width.

80

HOW TO TOTAL NUMBERS IN A TABLE

When you have set up a table, you can easily add up numbers in a column or a row. Let's total the contents of each column in your table.

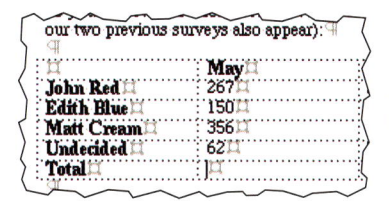

1 Position the insertion point in the empty cell next to **Total** in the **May** column.

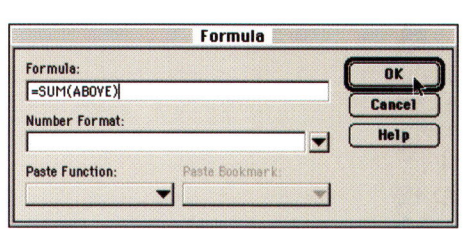

2 Choose *Formula* from the *Table* menu.

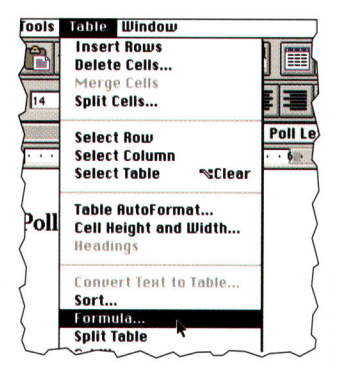

3 The *Formula* dialog box appears. The *Formula* box contains the formula *=SUM(ABOVE)*. Click on *OK*.

4 You'll see the total of the column displayed in the bottom cell of the column. Repeat the procedure for the **June** and **July** columns. The total for each column should be 835.

HOW TO SORT DATA IN A TABLE

You may want to reorganize the rows of your table so that the contents of cells in a specific column are listed in a particular order — alphabetically, for instance, or by size. To do so, you use the *Sort* command.

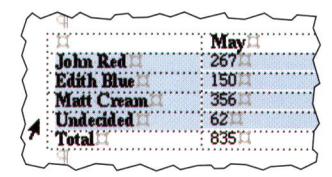

1 Select the four rows containing the polling data, as shown. Don't include the top or bottom row.

2 Choose *Sort* from the *Table* menu to open the *Sort* dialog box.

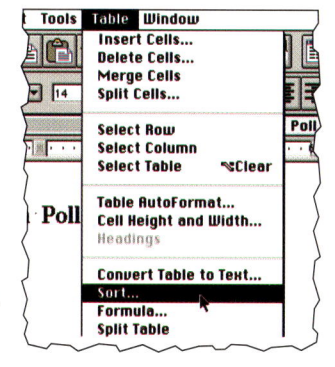

3 Under *Sort By,* click on the down arrow next to the first pop-up list box and set it to *Column 4* so that the table is sorted according to the candidates' popularity in July. The *Type* list box, under *Sort By*, should then display *Number*. Select the *Descending* option to put the most popular candidate first. Then click on *OK*.

Be Calculating
You can direct Word to perform simple calculations and paste the result where you've placed the insertion point. Choose *Field* from the *Insert* menu. Type the numbers with the relevant mathematical symbols (+ for add, - for subtract, / for divide, * for multiply) after the equal sign in the *Field Codes* box. When you click on *OK*, the results appear in your document.

Lost in the *Sort* Box?
Some of the options in the *Sort* dialog box may need explaining. *Sort By* identifies the column by which to sort the data. Under *Type* you choose to sort data alphabetically, numerically, or by date. *Ascending* means sorts go from A to Z, or from 1 to larger numbers, *Descending* the other way around.

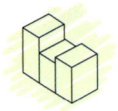

Charts

ADDING CHARTS TO YOUR DOCUMENTS gives them a more professional look and greater visual impact. Studies suggest that people take in visual information far more quickly than written information. Illustrating data using the Graph feature that comes with Word not only makes your document look professional, it can be the best way to get your message home.

Creating Charts

To convert the data within a table into a chart, select all or part of the table and click on the Insert Chart button on the Standard toolbar. This opens Microsoft Graph, an application included with Word. A chart appears in your document (surrounded by a gray border) and a window entitled *Graph in Poll Letter – Datasheet* also appears together with the first of a series of *ChartWizard* dialog boxes, which help you design your chart. Let's create a chart from the table you made earlier. First add the text below to **Poll Letter**, beneath the table. Then follow the steps at right.

> As you can see from the chart below, there appears to have been a late switch to Ms. Blue, mainly from previously undecided voters. <Return> <Return>

How to Create a Column Chart

1 Click the pointer in the selection bar at the top left of your table and drag the pointer down to select the first five rows.

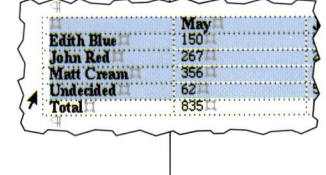

2 Click on the Insert Chart button on the Standard toolbar.

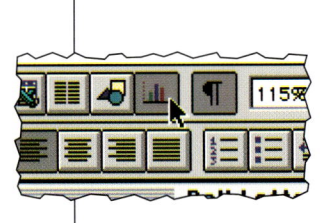

3 Microsoft Graph opens. A chart appears below your table of data. Then the *Graph in Poll Letter - Datasheet* window opens, and finally the first *ChartWizard* dialog box appears. In the *ChartWizard* dialog box, you choose the type of chart for displaying your information. Choose *Column* for your chart and then click on the *Next* button.

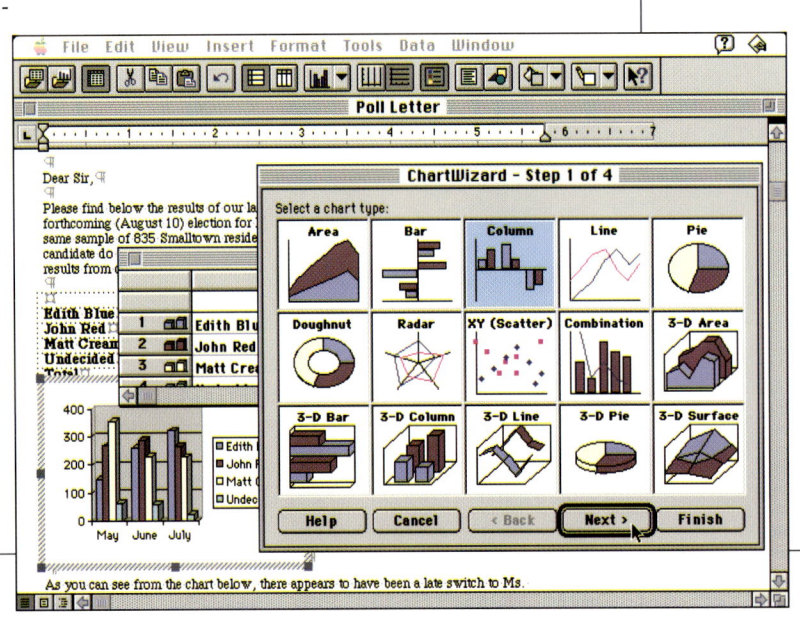

? No Table?
If you don't have a table to work with, you can click on the Insert Chart button and type the information directly into the datasheet. The first row and column are reserved for category names and data series names. In our example, the category names are May, June, and July, and the data series names are the election candidates. Don't put any data into the first cell (row 1, column 1).

4 In the second *ChartWizard* dialog box, choose option *1* and then click on *Next*. Also click on *Next* in the third *ChartWizard* dialog box.

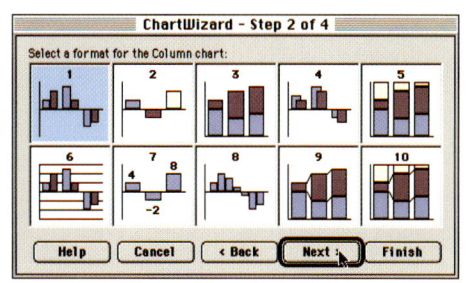

5 In the final *ChartWizard* dialog box, you can give your chart a title, decide whether you want a legend, and add labels to the X and Y axes. Enter **Precision Poll Results** in the *Chart Title* box, make sure *Yes* is checked under *Add a legend?*, and then click on *Finish*. Close the *Graph in Poll Letter - Datasheet* window by clicking on its close box. Click outside the gray border surrounding the chart. Microsoft Graph closes.

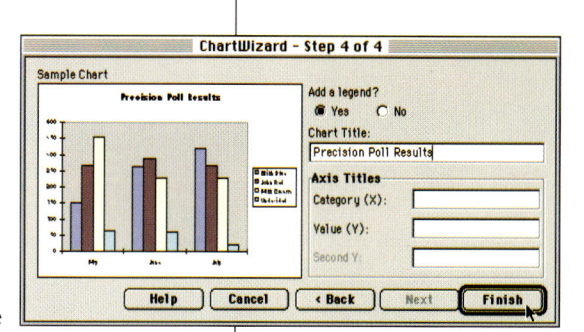

6 The chart is now an embedded object in your **Poll Letter** document and appears as shown at right. The chart remains selected, as indicated by the border and black handles surrounding the chart. With the chart selected, use the *Cut* and then the *Paste* commands on the *Edit* menu to move the chart just below the last paragraph of text in your letter. Alternatively, switch to Page Layout view, choose *Frame* from the *Insert* menu to insert a frame around the chart, and then drag the frame to its new position.

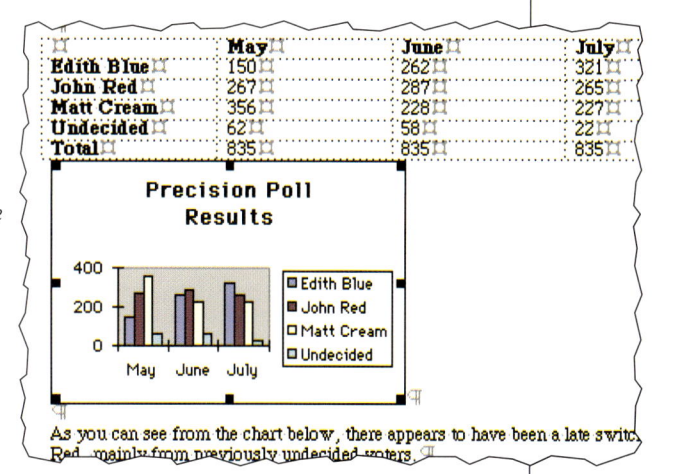

7 You can easily resize a chart. Click on the chart to select it and then drag the black handle at lower right down and to the right to make the chart a little wider and deeper. Click outside the chart to deselect it, and then click the Save button on the Standard toolbar.

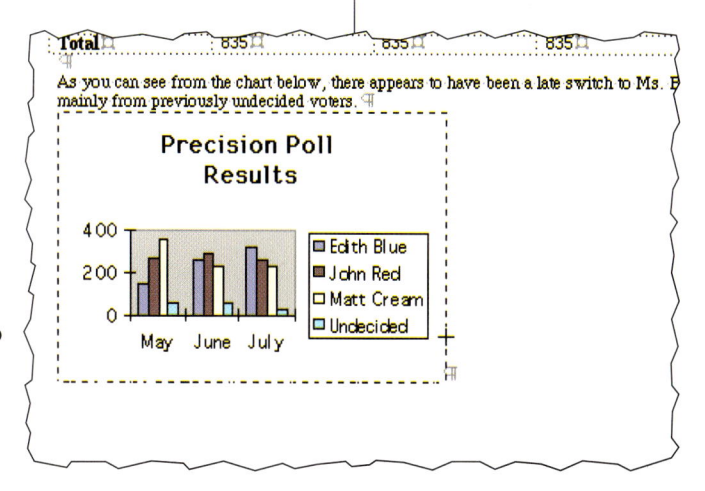

CHARTS

HOW TO CREATE A PIE CHART

Now let's add a second chart — a pie chart — to your document to show how voting intentions in the Smalltown election are distributed according to the latest (July) survey. Before creating the pie chart, add the text at left underneath the column chart. Then follow the steps described below.

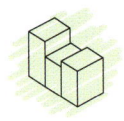

The chart below shows how voting intentions are split by percentage according to our latest survey: <Return>

1 Move the pointer into the selection bar and drag it down to select the first five rows in your opinion poll table. (Again, the **Total** row is not needed for this chart).

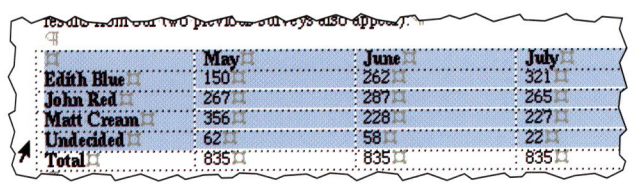

2 Click on the Insert Chart button on the Standard toolbar to open Microsoft Graph. Click on *Cancel* in the *ChartWizard* dialog box.

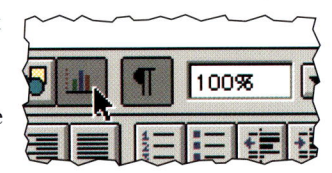

3 Since you want to chart only the July data, you need to exclude the May and June data. In the *Graph in Poll Letter – Datasheet* window, click on the bar above **May** and drag to the right to select the columns **May** and **June**.

4 Choose *Exclude Row/Col* from the *Data* menu.

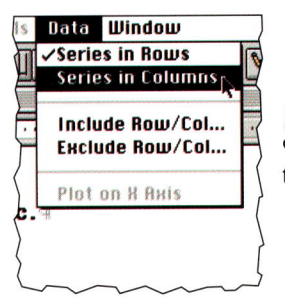

5 Choose *Series in Columns* from the *Data* menu.

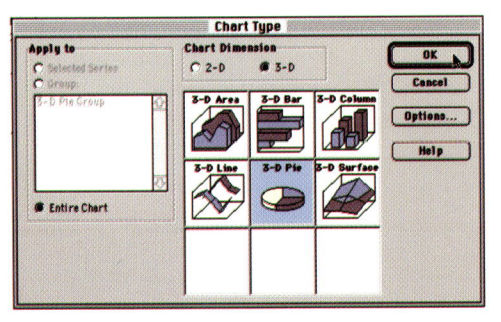

6 Choose *Chart Type* from the *Format* menu.

7 Choose *3-D Pie* from the *Chart Type* dialog box, and then click on *OK*. Close the *Datasheet* window by clicking on its close box. The pie chart appears, surrounded by a gray border.

Get Chart Smart!

Take care when choosing the type of chart to use when plotting data. Column charts and line graphs are especially suitable for indicating trends over time. Pie charts are best used to show how something breaks down into its parts — for example, how much income a company derives from various product lines.

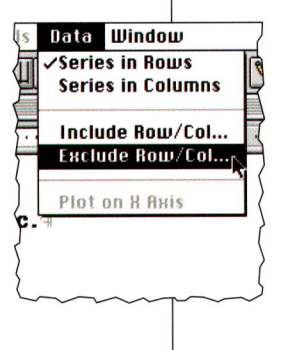

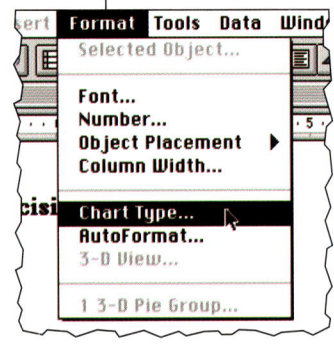

THE FINISHING TOUCH

You have now created an attractive pie chart. Let's add a few finishing touches to the chart and finalize your **Poll Letter** document:

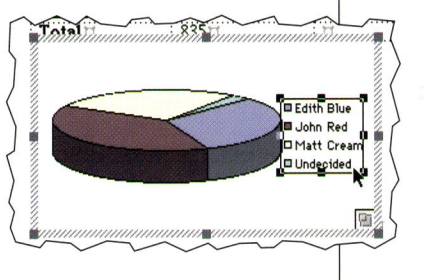

1 Click on the legend to select it. Press Delete to remove it from the chart.

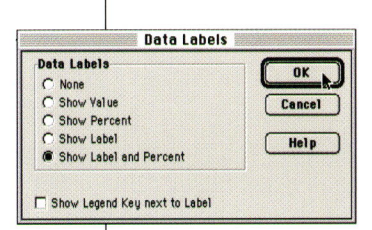

2 To show the labels and percentages for each section of the chart, choose *Data Labels* from the *Insert* menu, then choose *Show Label and Percent* in the *Data Labels* dialog box. Click outside the gray border. Microsoft Graph closes. Then click on *OK*.

3 The pie chart appears immediately beneath the table. Click on the chart to select it, and then cut and paste it to its correct position beneath the last paragraph. Alternatively, you can insert the chart into a frame and drag it to its correct position.

Don't Distort!
In Microsoft Graph, you can drag any of the borders or corners of a chart to resize it. But watch the effects on the size of titles and legends — there may no longer be sufficient room for them if you reduce the size of the chart. Back in Word, you can resize a chart by clicking on it once, and then dragging the border handles with the mouse. Again, you must be careful because resizing may distort your chart.

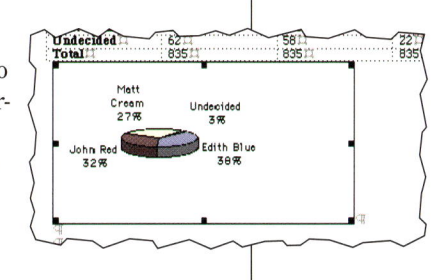

Chart Charter

To create effective charts, you should stick to a few basic rules:

■ Don't make charts too complicated — they should be easily understood.

■ Don't put too much data into a chart. For example, five series of data per column in a column chart is a sensible maximum.

■ Remember to specify the units and categories that are in your chart. Charts without labels mean nothing to people reading them.

■ Bear in mind that charts may lose some impact when printed in black and white.

4 Type the text at right underneath the pie chart to finish your **Poll Letter** document.

Looks like the final results could be close! <Return> <Return>

Sincerely yours, <Return> <Return>

Melvin T. Pollster

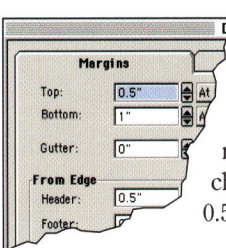

5 To fit the entire document on one page, you need to change the margins. Choose *Document Layout* from the *File* menu. In the *Margins* flipcard, change the value in the top box to 0.5 inches. Then click on *OK*.

6 Finally, save your letter and print it. The finished document should look like the example shown here.

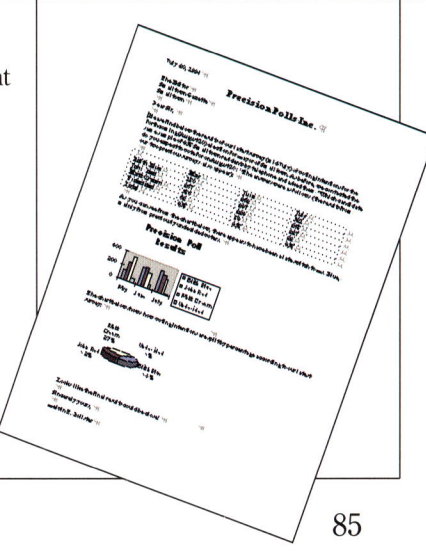

85

Be Creative

IN THIS SECTION, you'll find some more ideas for the different types of documents you can create using Word. Here we show you four different examples, but with lots of practice and plenty of imagination, you'll see just how easy it is to create virtually any type of document to suit your personal or business needs — or even just for fun.

Helpful Hints

You can create the example documents on these pages using the skills you've learned earlier in this book. The labels provide formatting information to help you along the way. Of course, these are just a few ideas; you can modify the documents in any way you wish using your newly-acquired skills, or you can create your own documents from scratch. So go ahead — be creative, and see how many different things you can do using Word.

Want to Crop?
With Word, it's easy to crop an image so that only part of it appears in your document. Select the image by clicking on it, then hold down Shift and drag one of the handles inward or outward, depending on how much of the image you want to see.

Travel Brochure Cover

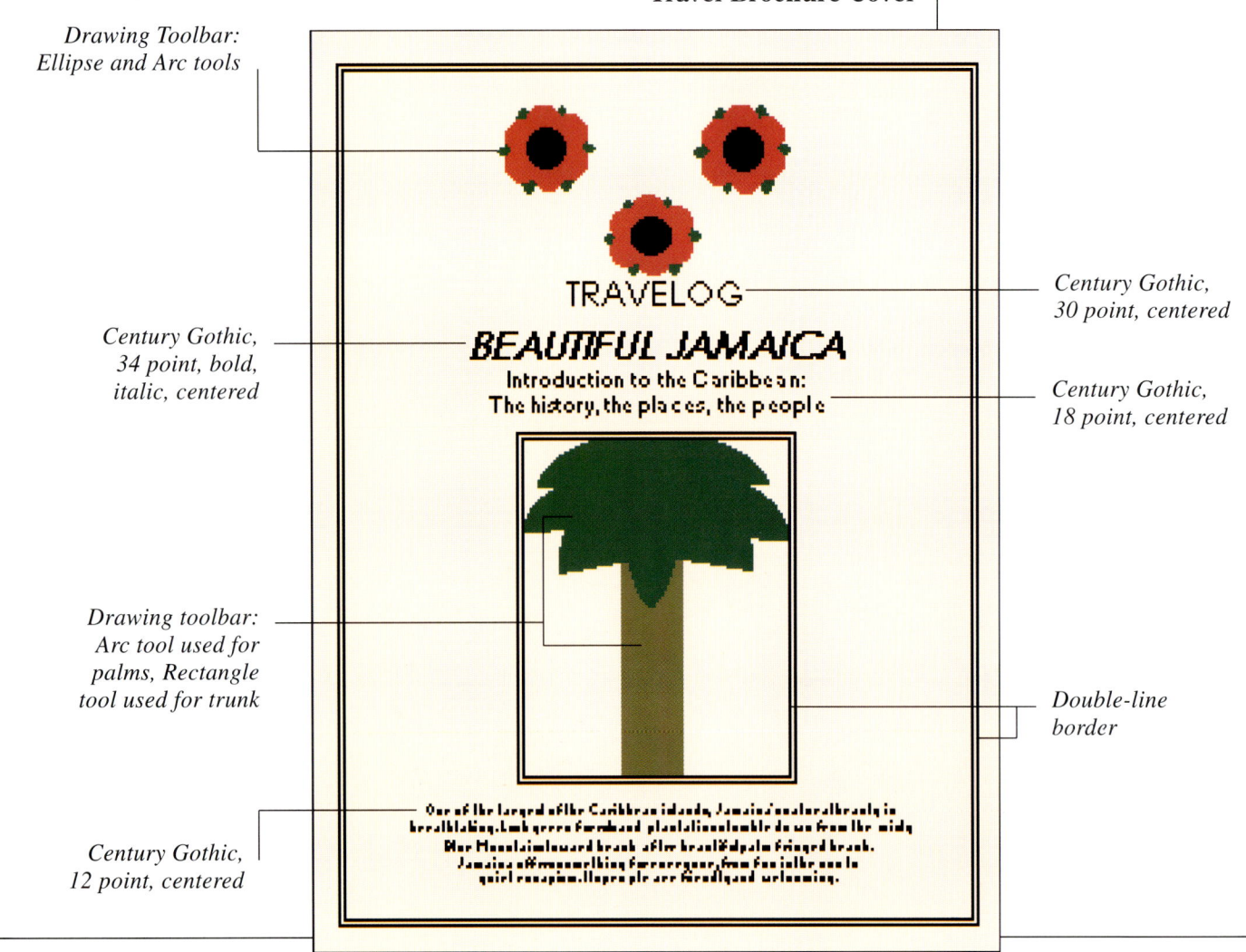

Drawing Toolbar: Ellipse and Arc tools

Century Gothic, 34 point, bold, italic, centered

Drawing toolbar: Arc tool used for palms, Rectangle tool used for trunk

Century Gothic, 12 point, centered

Century Gothic, 30 point, centered

Century Gothic, 18 point, centered

Double-line border

Promotional Leaflet

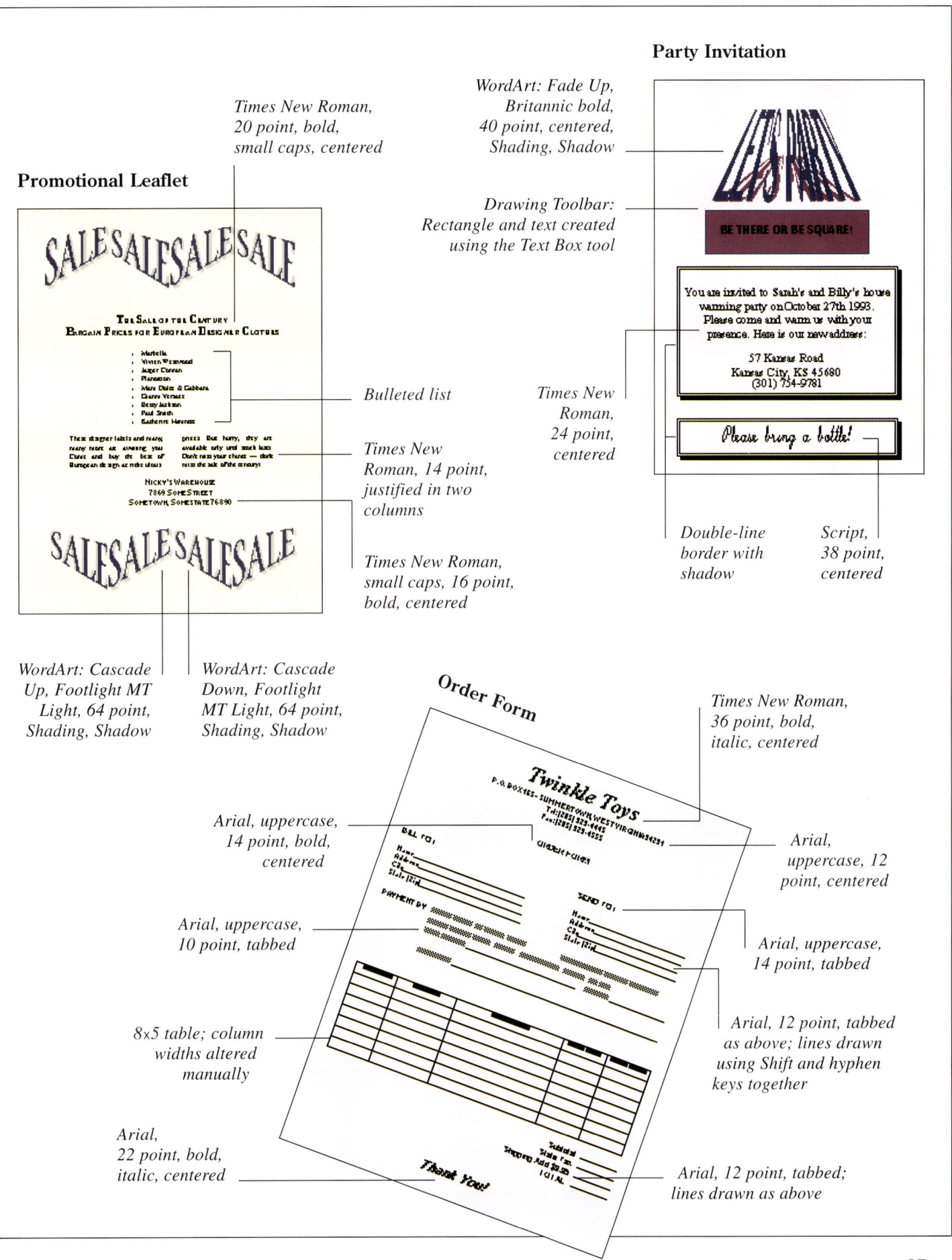

Party Invitation

Times New Roman, 20 point, bold, small caps, centered

WordArt: Fade Up, Britannic bold, 40 point, centered, Shading, Shadow

Drawing Toolbar: Rectangle and text created using the Text Box tool

Bulleted list

Times New Roman, 14 point, justified in two columns

Times New Roman, 24 point, centered

Times New Roman, small caps, 16 point, bold, centered

Double-line border with shadow

Script, 38 point, centered

WordArt: Cascade Up, Footlight MT Light, 64 point, Shading, Shadow

WordArt: Cascade Down, Footlight MT Light, 64 point, Shading, Shadow

Order Form

Arial, uppercase, 14 point, bold, centered

Times New Roman, 36 point, bold, italic, centered

Arial, uppercase, 12 point, centered

Arial, uppercase, 10 point, tabbed

Arial, uppercase, 14 point, tabbed

Arial, 12 point, tabbed as above; lines drawn using Shift and hyphen keys together

8x5 table; column widths altered manually

Arial, 22 point, bold, italic, centered

Arial, 12 point, tabbed; lines drawn as above

4
CHAPTER FOUR

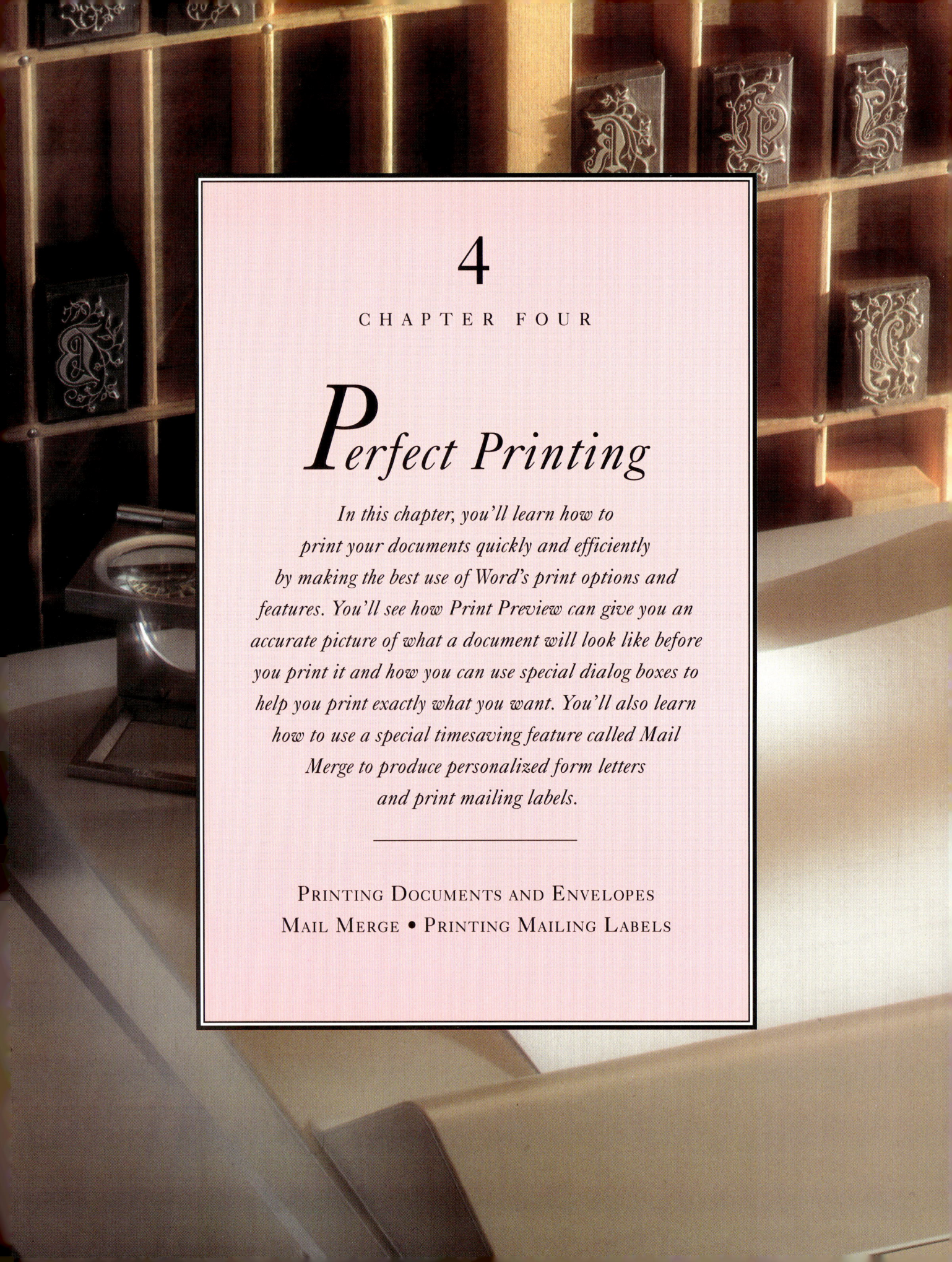

Perfect Printing

In this chapter, you'll learn how to print your documents quickly and efficiently by making the best use of Word's print options and features. You'll see how Print Preview can give you an accurate picture of what a document will look like before you print it and how you can use special dialog boxes to help you print exactly what you want. You'll also learn how to use a special timesaving feature called Mail Merge to produce personalized form letters and print mailing labels.

PRINTING DOCUMENTS AND ENVELOPES
MAIL MERGE • PRINTING MAILING LABELS

PRINTING DOCUMENTS AND ENVELOPES 90

A basic guide to printing — find out how to print your Word documents and how to specify various options to control the way they are printed.

MAIL MERGE 96

With Word's Mail Merge feature, you can automate the production of individualized form letters to send to many different people. Learn how to perform a mail merge using an example document.

PRINTING MAILING LABELS 100

You can use a specialized form of the Mail Merge feature to print names and addresses on different types of mailing labels. Discover how this feature can save you time and effort.

PRINTING DOCUMENTS AND ENVELOPES

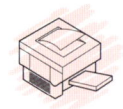

Printing Documents and Envelopes

WITH WORD, PRINTING IS SIMPLE — to print using Word's standard settings, just click on the Print button on the Standard toolbar. If you want to specify certain options, you can use dialog boxes obtainable by choosing the *Print* and *Page Setup* commands from the *File* menu and the *Options* command from the *Tools* menu. This section shows you how to print a document and how to use the options in these dialog boxes.

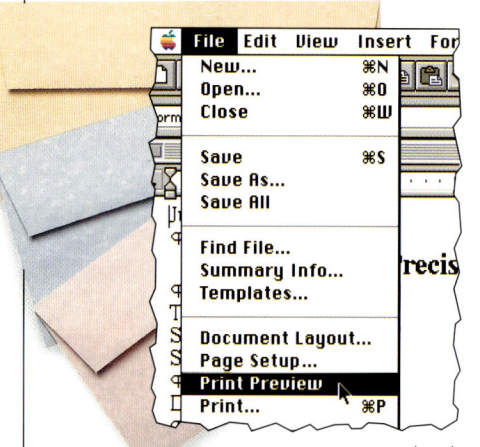

How to Use Print Preview

The Print Preview feature reveals all elements of your document, allowing you to check that your document looks just right before you print. You can also edit in this view if you want to change something at the last minute.

In the Print Preview window, the document is reduced in size so that you can see one or more pages on the screen. Let's display a document in Print Preview. First create a multiple page document: Type in some text, add a table, select the text and table, and then use the *Copy* command from the *Edit* menu and then the *Paste* command repeatedly. Now choose *Print Preview* from the *File* menu or click on the Print Preview button on the Standard toolbar. An example document is shown in Print Preview on the opposite page, along with a description of the functions of the various buttons on the Print Preview toolbar.

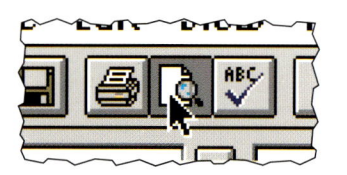

Print Preview Button

Making Moves!
In the Print Preview window, you can easily change the margins of a document. If you can't see the rulers, click on the View Ruler button on the Print Preview toolbar. Move the pointer to the relevant margin boundary on the vertical or horizontal ruler, where the pointer changes to a double-headed arrow, and then drag it to the new position.

Preview Unavailable?
If the *Print Preview* command is unavailable, it may be because no printer has been installed yet; or no default printer has been selected in the Chooser; or the default printer isn't connected to a port. See page 118 for information on how to install a printer.

Moving Through Your Document

There are a number of ways to display different pages of your Word document in the Print Preview window:

■ To move forward or backward through your document one page at a time, click on the bottom or top single arrows in the vertical scroll bar.

■ To scroll several pages forward or backward through your document, drag the box in the vertical scroll bar downward or upward.

■ Press Page Down to see the next page of the document. Continue to press Page Down to move forward through your document one page at a time.

■ Press Page Up to see the previous page. Continue to press Page Up to move backward through the document one page at a time.

90

The Print Preview Window

Print
If you're satisfied with the way your document looks in the Print Preview window, click on the Print button to print your document.

Magnifier
Click on this button to edit your document. The pointer changes to a magnifying glass when moved onto the document. Click on the area you want to edit, and when the document is magnified, click on the Magnifier button to restore the normal I-beam pointer. Once you've finished with your changes, click on the Magnifier button again and then click on the document to return to the original view.

One Page
Click on this button to view only one page at a time.

Multiple Pages
Click here and drag the pointer over the grid to select the number of pages you want to view.

Zoom Control
Click on the down arrow to the right of this box to choose the percentage by which you want to scale your document's view.

View Ruler
Click to hide or show rulers. With the rulers displayed, you can adjust a document's margins (see "Making Moves!" opposite).

Shrink to Fit
If only a little text remains on the last page of a document, Word tries to fit it onto the previous page when you click on this button.

Full Screen
Click to maximize the Print Preview window. Click again to return to the original view.

Close
Click to close the Print Preview window and return to the previous view of your document.

Help
Click to get help on a specific command or screen item, or information on text formatting.

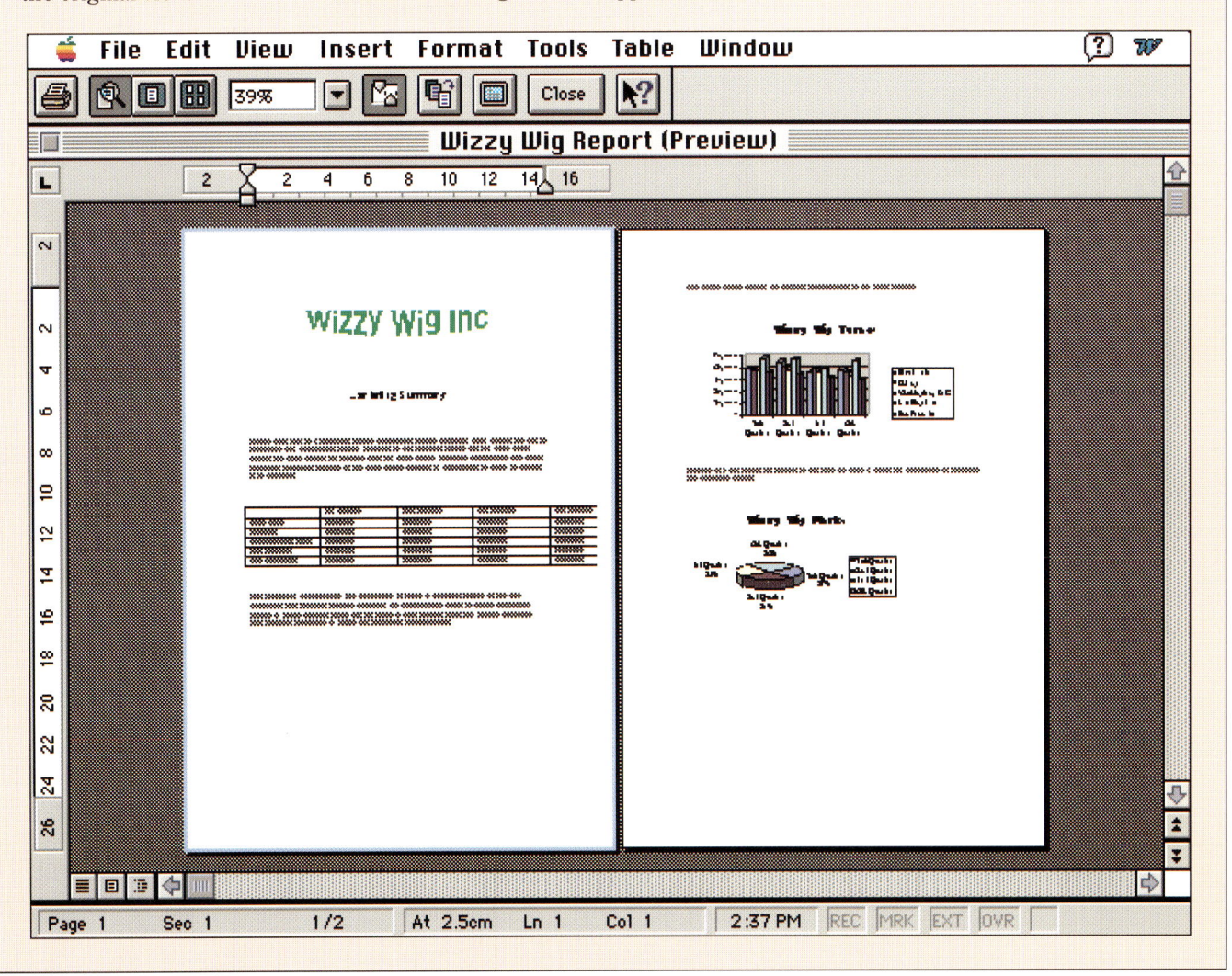

PRINTING DOCUMENTS AND ENVELOPES

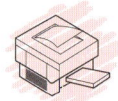

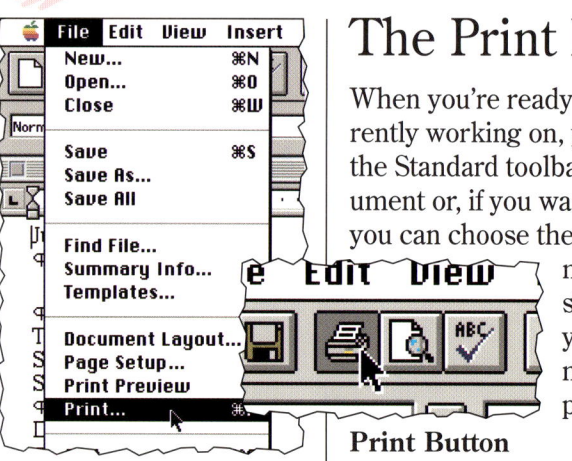

The Print Dialog Box

When you're ready to print the document you're currently working on, you can click on the Print button on the Standard toolbar to print one copy of the whole document or, if you want to specify certain print options, you can choose the *Print* command from the *File* menu. Word displays the dialog box shown below. Remember to save your document before you print to make sure that no work is lost if a printer problem occurs.

Print Button

Be Selective!
To print just a selected part of your document, select the text or graphics you want to print, choose *Print* from the *File* menu, check *Print Selection Only* at the bottom left in the dialog box, and then click on *Print*. This technique is useful for printing a selection that spans a soft page break (a break created automatically by the program) because you don't have to print both pages.

Your Printing Options

Using the dialog box shown below, you can specify a number of different options that affect the way your document is printed. Once you have chosen your options, you just click on *Print* to print. Here are a few examples of the print options that are available:

- To print items related to your document, such as *Styles* (see page 108), choose the relevant item from the pop-up list below the word *Print*.

- For more than one copy, type the desired number in the *Copies* box.

- To print the page containing the insertion point, click on the *Range* button, choose *Current Page* in the dialog box that opens, and then click on *OK*.

- To print a consecutive range of pages, click on the *Range* button and then type the page numbers, separated by a hyphen, in the *Pages* box. To print discontinuous pages, type the page numbers separated by commas.

- To print only odd or even pages, choose *Odd Pages* or *Even Pages* from the pop-up list above the *Range* button.

- If you're printing more than one copy, make sure you check the *Collate Copies* box so that Word will print a complete copy of your document before printing the next copy.

Don't Be a Loser!
Get into the habit of saving your document before you print it — if a printer error or other problem occurs while printing, Word may shut down. If you've saved your document, you won't lose any work.

92

The Options Dialog Box

For additional printing options, you can access the *Options* dialog box by clicking on the *Word Options* button in the dialog box that appears after *Print* is chosen from the *File* menu. Alternatively, choose *Options* from the *Tools* menu and then click on the *Print* tab. Once you set a print option in the *Options* dialog box, it remains in effect for all your documents, until you change it again. Some useful print options are explained here:

A Landscape View?
Most pages are printed in portrait (vertical) orientation. If your document is wider than it is long, you can print it in landscape (horizontal) orientation. Choose *Page Setup* from the *File* menu. In the dialog box that appears, click on the landscape icon next to the word *Orientation*, and then click on *OK*.

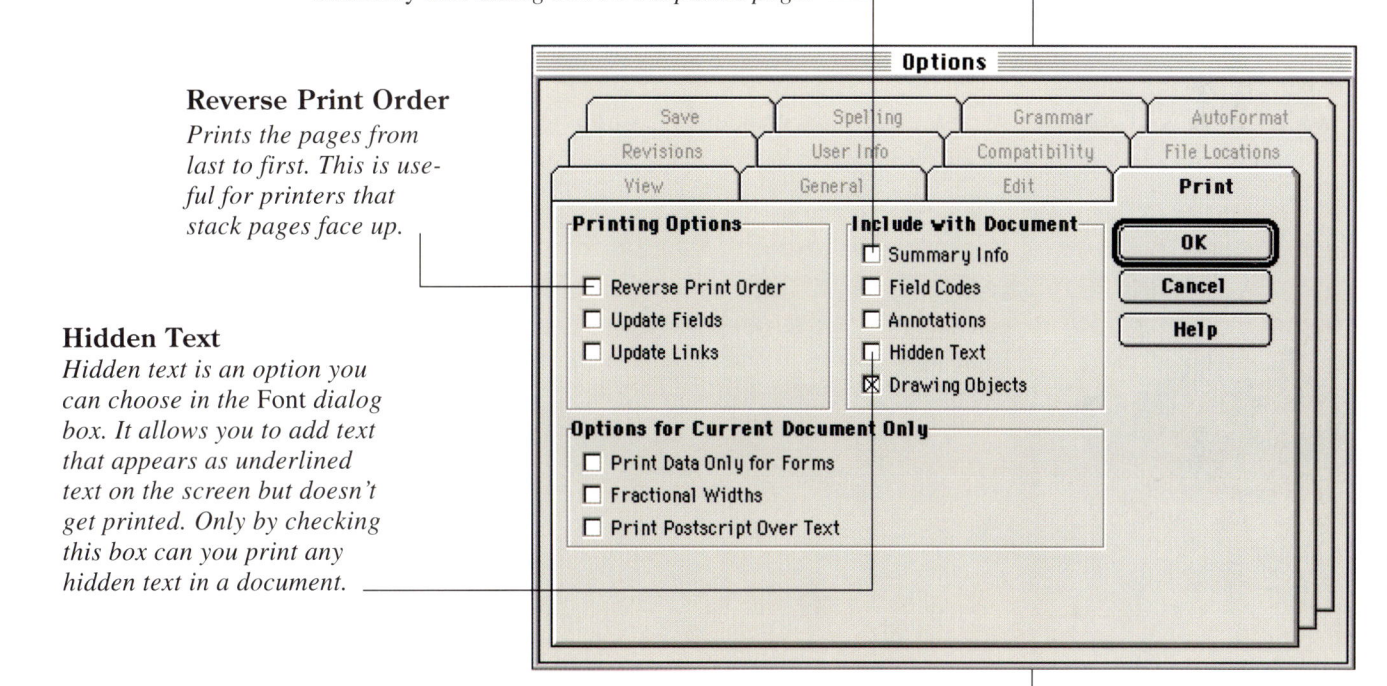

Summary Info
Summary Info *stores information about a document such as the author's name, subject, and keywords. You can also choose this command from the* File *menu. If you check this box, Word prints any information you've stored in the* Summary Info *dialog box on a separate page.*

Reverse Print Order
Prints the pages from last to first. This is useful for printers that stack pages face up.

Hidden Text
Hidden text is an option you can choose in the Font *dialog box. It allows you to add text that appears as underlined text on the screen but doesn't get printed. Only by checking this box can you print any hidden text in a document.*

The Nonprinting Area

Most printers are unable to print all the way to the outside edges of the paper. Any text or graphic that extends into the nonprinting area will not be printed. However, the exact dimensions of the nonprinting area depend on the printer you're using. In general, the size of the nonprinting area increases as the paper size increases. If you find you are missing parts of your document, you may have to reset the document's margins.

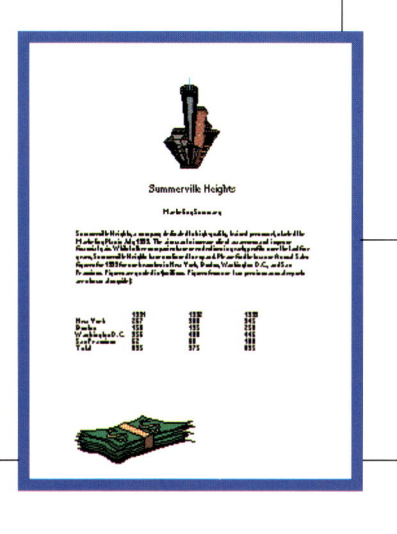

The Non-Printing Area

PRINTING DOCUMENTS AND ENVELOPES

Preparing to Print

It is possible to connect more than one printer or different types of printers to your Macintosh. For example, you may have two printers in your office and want to swap printers, using the one that is least busy or that provides better printing quality. To change the printer you're printing from, you must select options in the *Chooser* dialog box. To do this, open the Apple menu and choose *Chooser*.

In the *Chooser* dialog box, click on the printer icon. A list of available printers appears in the list box, with the printer you're currently using highlighted. To change to another printer, select it from the list and click on the close box. If no other printers are listed, there are no other printers installed. For more information on installing a printer, see page 118.

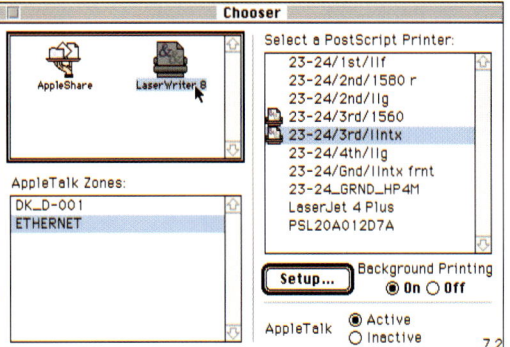

SETUP OPTIONS
Each type of printer has different printing capabilities, so you should check your printer manual for specific information. Most printers can accommodate different paper sizes and orientations, and you can change the settings for these in a special dialog box that varies depending on the printer that is selected. To change printer settings, choose *Page Setup* from the *File* menu. The options for one printer model are described below.

The *Chooser* Dialog Box

Feeling Disoriented?
You should use the *Page Setup* command from the *File* menu to set the paper size, orientation, and any reduction or enlargement for your document. You should use the *Print* command from the *File* menu to set the number of copies you want to print, the range of pages you want to print, and the paper source you want to use.

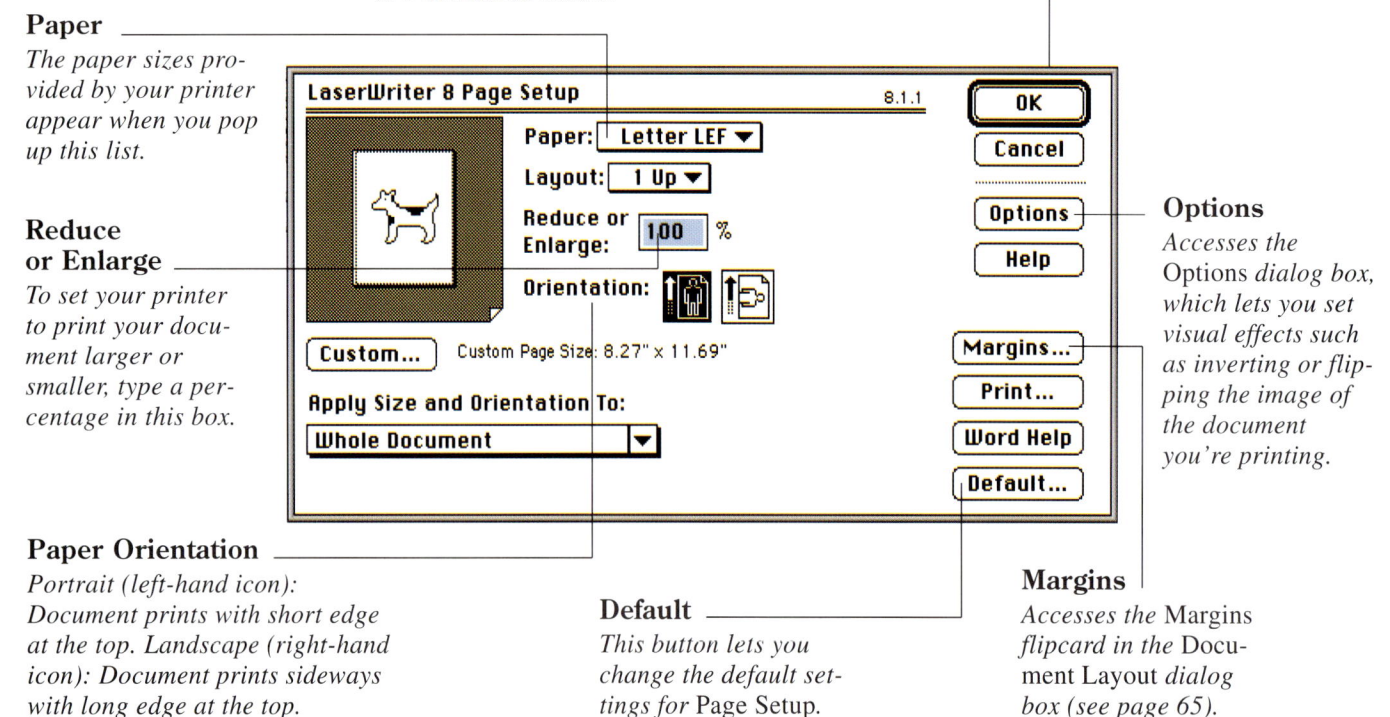

Paper
The paper sizes provided by your printer appear when you pop up this list.

Reduce or Enlarge
To set your printer to print your document larger or smaller, type a percentage in this box.

Paper Orientation
Portrait (left-hand icon): Document prints with short edge at the top. Landscape (right-hand icon): Document prints sideways with long edge at the top.

Default
This button lets you change the default settings for Page Setup.

Options
Accesses the Options *dialog box, which lets you set visual effects such as inverting or flipping the image of the document you're printing.*

Margins
Accesses the Margins *flipcard in the Document Layout dialog box (see page 65).*

Printer Fonts

The fonts available for the documents you print in Word depend on your printer's make and model. However, you also have access to a number of other fonts called "TrueType." TrueType fonts can be printed on any type of printer. To check which fonts are installed on your Macintosh, choose *Font* from the *Format* menu. Then browse through the scrolling list under *Font* to see the fonts available to you. See page 119 for more information on the different types of fonts that you can use in your Word documents.

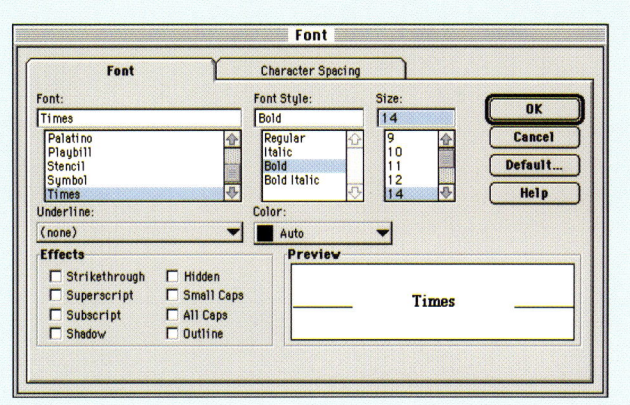

Font Samples
When you select a font by clicking on it in the Font *box, a sample of the font appears in the* Preview *window.*

Meltdown!
If you're printing envelopes with a laser printer, make sure the envelopes are specifically designed for use with one. Be particularly careful with self-sealing envelopes. If envelopes are not designed for use with a laser printer, which uses very high temperatures inside as part of the printing process, the gum could melt and cause internal damage to your printer.

HOW TO PRINT AN ENVELOPE

Word can print an envelope using an address stored in a document or one that you type in. Follow these steps to practice printing an envelope:

1. Open **Poll Letter** and select the address.

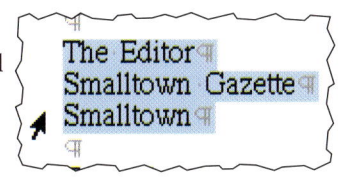

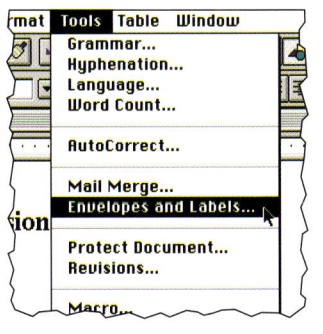

2. Choose *Envelopes and Labels* from the *Tools* menu to open the *Envelopes and Labels* dialog box.

3. On the *Envelopes* flipcard, the selected address appears in the *Delivery Address* text box. Under *Return Address,* either accept the proposed address, type in a new one, or check the *Omit* box. Click on *Options* and make sure that the *Envelope Size* box is set to *Size 10 (4 1/8 x 9 1/2 in)*. Click on *OK* to close the *Envelope Options* dialog box.

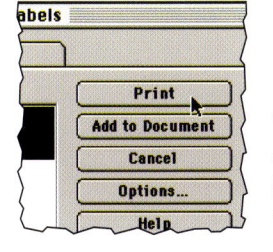

4. Insert a size 10 (standard business size) envelope into your printer's envelope feeder or manual feed slot, placing the envelope according to the *Feed* diagram in the *Envelopes and Labels* dialog box. Then click on the *Print* button in the *Envelopes and Labels* dialog box.

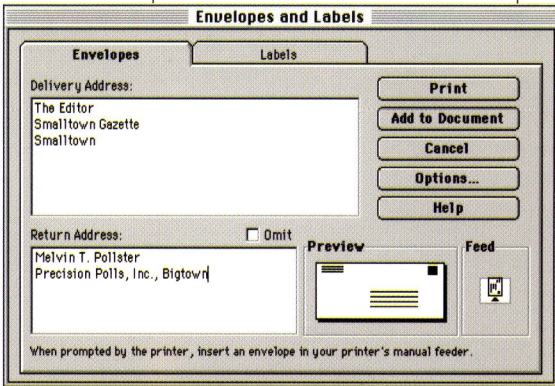

Mail Merge

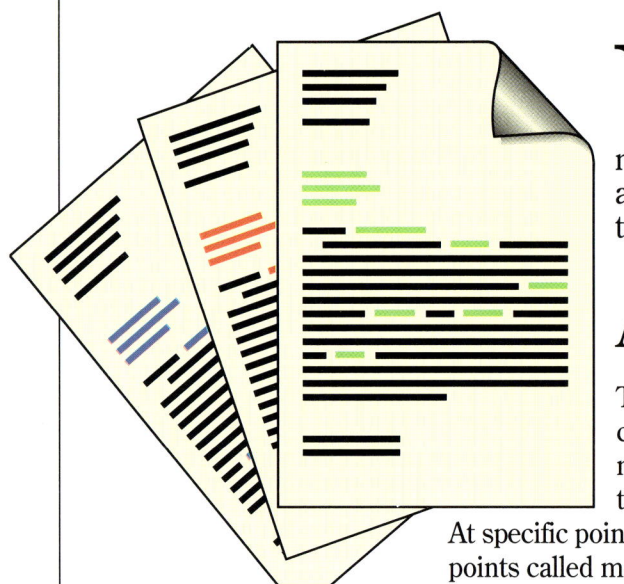

WORD'S MAIL MERGE FEATURE allows you to combine a standard form document with a list of data in another document to produce a set of individualized documents. For example, if you want to send the same basic letter to a number of different people but you want each letter to be customized for each individual, you can use Mail Merge.

A Clever Combination

To carry out a mail merge, you have to create two separate documents. The main document contains the basic text that you want to include in each letter. At specific points in this document, you place reference points called merge field names. These represent the variable information that Word inserts into each copy of the document during the mail merge. You then create a data source containing the specific information to be inserted at the reference points in each personalized letter. Creating the two documents is easy — a dialog box called the *Mail Merge Helper* guides you through the whole process. When you have created the documents, you then instruct Word to combine them.

Create Main Document

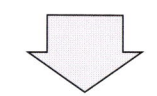

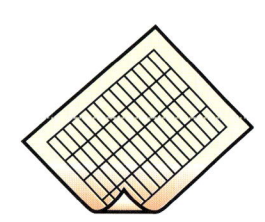

Create Data Source

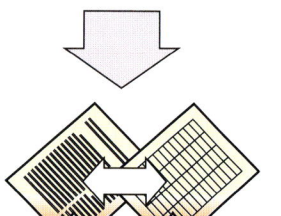

Merge Information in Both Documents

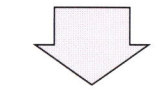

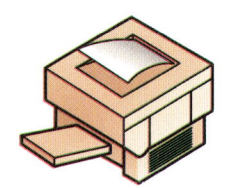

Print Individualized Documents

THE MAIN DOCUMENT
Your main document will typically be a letter, invoice, or circular, although you can use any type of document. You format the document as you would any other; the only difference is that you must insert merge field names where you want the data items to be inserted. In this example, the main document is a letter from a fan club in the United States that mails orders to people all over the world. The example uses seven items of data, represented by the merge field names FirstName, LastName, Address1, Address2, Address3, Communication, and Order. In your letter you'll type the letters **A, B, C, D, E, F,** and **G** to represent each of these merge field names. To create your letter, open a new document and save it to your hard disk with the name **Fan Club Letter**. Then enter the text to the left, pressing Return only where you see <Return> in the text. Then follow the steps on the next page.

The Grunge Band Fan Club <Return>
18 Main Street <Return>
Seattle, WA 98473 <Return>
<Return> <Return>

A B <Return>
C <Return>
D <Return>
E <Return> <Return> <Return>

Dear A, <Return> <Return>

Thank you for your recent communication by F. Please find enclosed the G that you ordered. <Return> <Return>

We hope you'll be in touch with us again soon. <Return> <Return>

Sincerely, <Return> <Return> <Return>

Tom Rogers <Return>
Fan Club Secretary

Creating the Main Document

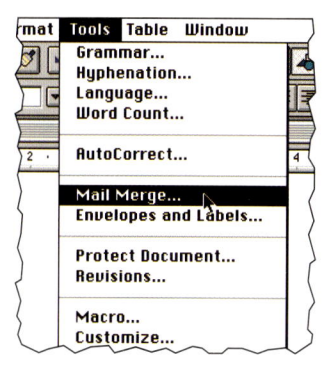

1 Choose *Mail Merge* from the *Tools* menu.

2 The *Mail Merge Helper* dialog box appears. Click on the *Create* button under *Main Document*, and then choose *Form Letters* in the pop-up list that appears. Choose *Active Window* in the message that follows.

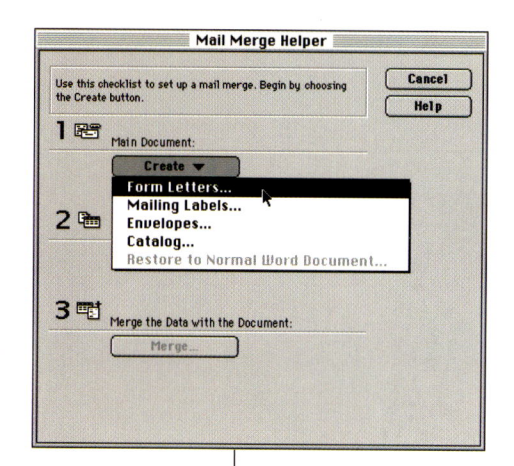

THE DATA SOURCE
Now you need to create your data source — the names, addresses, and other information that differs in each personalized letter.

1 In the *Mail Merge Helper* dialog box, click on the *Get Data* button under *Data Source*, and then choose *Create Data Source* from the pop-up list.

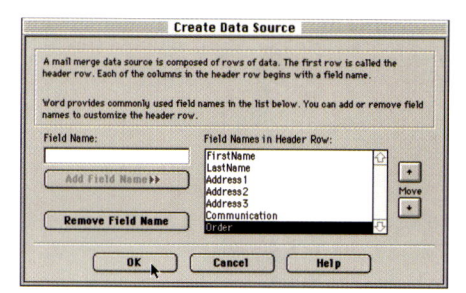

2 The *Create Data Source* dialog box appears, showing a list of commonly used merge field names. You can add a field name to the list by typing the name in the *Field Name* box and then clicking on the *Add Field Name* button. To remove a merge field name, highlight it and then click on the *Remove Field Name* button. Use these buttons to create the list shown in the dialog box at left. Then click on *OK*. The *Save* dialog box appears. Save your data source to your hard disk with the name **Orders**.

3 Click on *Edit Data Source* in the message that follows. The *Data Form* dialog box then appears, in which you enter the information for each addressee. Enter the information shown in the dialog box above, and then click on *Add New* to display a blank form for the next data record. Continue adding information so that you have the three entries shown at right. Then click on *OK* to return to the main document.

Spaced Out!
The field names you choose for the header list in your data source can contain up to 40 characters. Each name must start with a letter, and the following characters must be letters, numbers, or underscore characters. You must not use spaces in a merge field name.

Separate Entries
Because you cannot use paragraph marks in the Data Form *dialog box, you have to enter each line of the address as a separate entry. This ensures that each address is formatted correctly in the final letter.*

First Name	Last Name	Address	Communication	Order
Jonathan	Reed	5 Carlton Mansions James Avenue Seattle, WA 90232	carrier pigeon	two Grunge Band badges
Marie	Blanc	33 Rue de Gaulle Paris 7500 France	telephone	signed photograph of Eddie Grunge
Bruce	Davis	63 Golden Square Sydney Australia	letter	Greatest Hits Collection cassette

97

MAIL MERGE

The Mail Merge Toolbar

When you return to the main document after completing your data source, you'll see a new toolbar just above the Ruler called the Mail Merge toolbar (below). You use the buttons on this toolbar to control and perform your mail merge. To discover a button's function, move the mouse pointer over the button — an explanation of its action will then appear in the status bar.

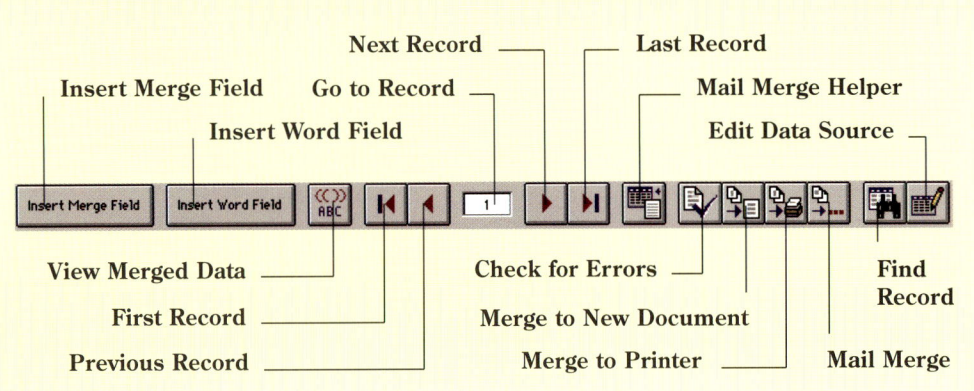

Buttons on the Mail Merge toolbar:
- Insert Merge Field
- Insert Word Field
- View Merged Data
- First Record
- Previous Record
- Go to Record
- Next Record
- Last Record
- Mail Merge Helper
- Edit Data Source
- Check for Errors
- Merge to New Document
- Merge to Printer
- Find Record
- Mail Merge

Changing Your Data?
You can add or change information in your data source at any time during a mail merge. Click on the Edit Data Source button on the Mail Merge toolbar. Then make the changes you want in the *Data Form* dialog box. When you have completed your changes, click on *OK* to return to your main document.

INSERTING MERGE FIELDS
You're now ready to complete your main document. Use the Mail Merge toolbar to insert the merge field names from your data source.

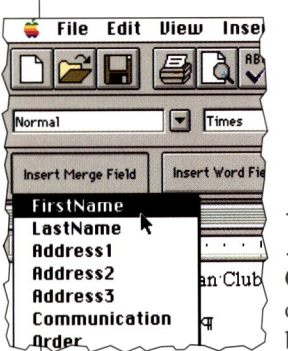

1 Highlight the first occurrence of A in your **Fan Club Letter** document. Then click on the Insert Merge Field button on the Mail Merge toolbar, and choose the merge field name that you want to insert from the list that pops up. In this case, choose *FirstName*.

2 In **Fan Club Letter**, the merge field name appears inside double-angle brackets.

3 Go through the rest of the document using the procedure described in steps 1 and 2 to insert the remaining merge field names in place of the letters representing them. Make sure that you type any spaces or punctuation that you want between the merge field names. When you have finished, your main document will look like the example shown at right.

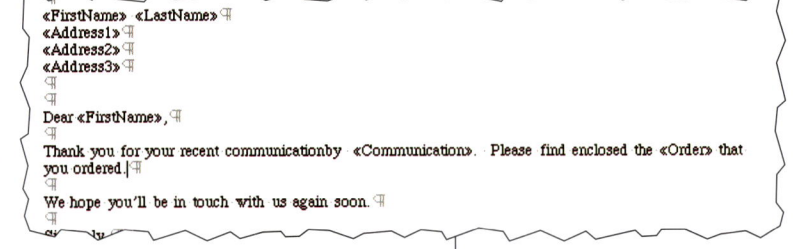

«FirstName» «LastName»
«Address1»
«Address2»
«Address3»

Dear «FirstName»,

Thank you for your recent communication by «Communication». Please find enclosed the «Order» that you ordered.

We hope you'll be in touch with us again soon.

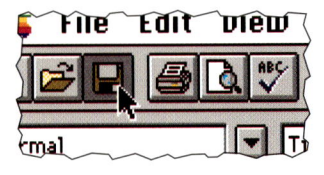

4 Click on the Save button on the Standard toolbar. **Fan Club Letter** is now saved as a Mail Merge document, attached to the data source called **Orders.**

98

TIME TO MERGE AND PRINT

Now you're ready to merge the information contained in your two documents, and print the resulting personalized letters. Word prints a different version of the letter for each record in the data source. So you'll get three letters, each with the merge field names replaced by the specific information contained in the data source. Follow the steps below to merge the data source and print the letters.

1 Click on the Merge to Printer button on the Mail Merge toolbar. Then click on the *Print* button in the dialog box that appears.

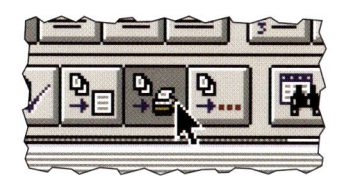

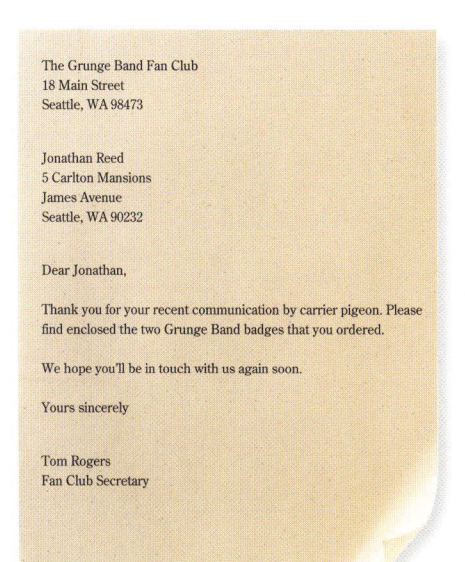

2 Word prints one copy of your mail merge document for each record in your data source. The example shown here shows the information contained in the first personalized letter. At the positions of the seven merge field names, you can see the data from the first record in the data source. When you have finished printing, close your merged **Fan Club Letter** document. Also save and close the data source **Orders**.

The Grunge Band Fan Club
18 Main Street
Seattle, WA 98473

Jonathan Reed
5 Carlton Mansions
James Avenue
Seattle, WA 90232

Dear Jonathan,

Thank you for your recent communication by carrier pigeon. Please find enclosed the two Grunge Band badges that you ordered.

We hope you'll be in touch with us again soon.

Yours sincerely

Tom Rogers
Fan Club Secretary

Want More Choice?
Before you merge your document, you can click on the Mail Merge button on the Mail Merge toolbar to open the *Merge* dialog box. This provides you with more options to control the way you merge your document. For example, you can choose to merge only certain data records.

Personal Preview

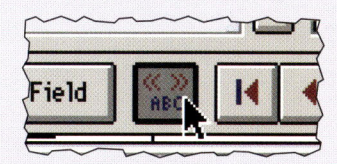

View Merged Data Button

If you want, you can see your personalized letters on screen before you print them. This allows you to check and further change each version of the letter. There are two ways of previewing your letters. If you click on the View Merged Data button on the Mail Merge toolbar, Word displays the information from the first data record in place of the merge field names in the main document text. To view the information from the other data records, you click on one of the arrow buttons next to the Go to Record box on the Mail Merge toolbar, or type the number of the data record you want to see in the Go to Record box.

If you click on the Merge to New Document button on the Mail Merge toolbar, Word merges the information in the main document and the data source and displays the merged documents as a single, new document, temporarily named *Form Letters1*. To view the different personalized letters, you scroll through the document using the vertical scroll bar.

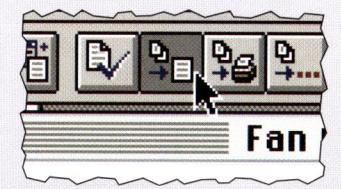

Merge to New Document Button

99

Printing Mailing Labels

WITH WORD, YOU CAN USE Mail Merge to print names and addresses on many types of commonly used mailing labels. Word creates the main document for you; you simply attach the necessary data source. You can use information from an existing data source, or you can create a new data source (see page 97).

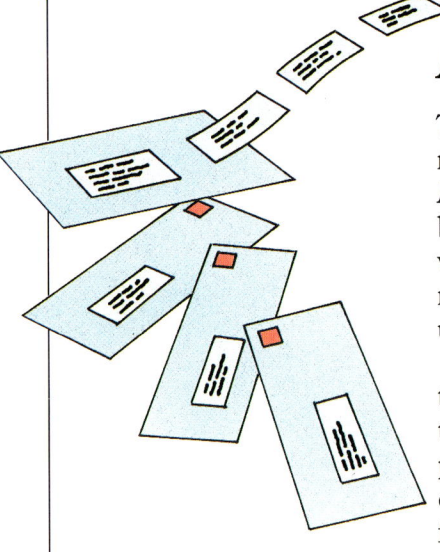

A Guided Tour

To print mailing labels, you must create a main document formatted for mailing labels. If you choose the *Mailing Labels* option in the *Mail Merge Helper* dialog box, Word will create the main document for you and will guide you through the process of producing your mailing labels. Using this method, you can set up a document for most types of Avery brand labels.

Before you can set up your mailing labels, you have to know what type of printer you're using. There are two kinds of mailing labels for the two main types of printers — continuous-feed labels for dot-matrix printers and label sheets for laser printers. Make sure you feed your printer with the correct type of label.

SETTING UP
Let's produce some mailing labels using information from the **Orders** file you created in the previous section. Load your printer with the correct labels, open a new document, and then choose *Mail Merge* from the *Tools* menu so that the *Mail Merge Helper* dialog box appears. Then follow the steps below:

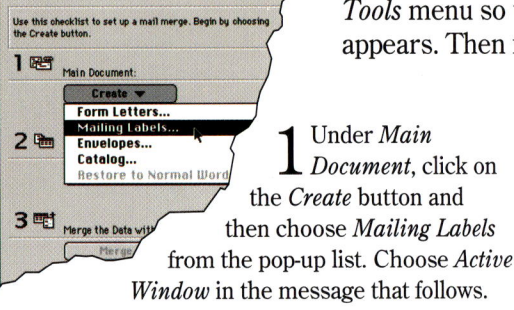

1 Under *Main Document*, click on the *Create* button and then choose *Mailing Labels* from the pop-up list. Choose *Active Window* in the message that follows.

2 Under *Data Source*, click on the *Get Data* button, and then choose *Open Data Source* from the pop-up list. In the *Open Data Source* dialog box, choose **Orders** from the *File Name* list, and then click on *OK*. Click on the *Setup Main Document* button in the message that follows.

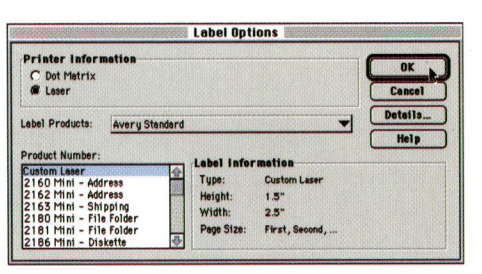

3 The *Label Options* dialog box appears. Under *Printer Information*, select the type of printer you're using, and then choose the type of label you want. For now, just click on *OK* to use *Custom Laser*.

Size Problem?
If you want to use a brand of labels other than Avery, select an Avery Standard label of the same size in the *Label Options* dialog box and then click on the *Details* button to open the relevant *Information* dialog box. If the labels you are using do not exactly match the dimensions of the Avery label, enter the exact dimensions in the relevant text boxes. Finally, click on *OK* to create a main document based on this new label size.

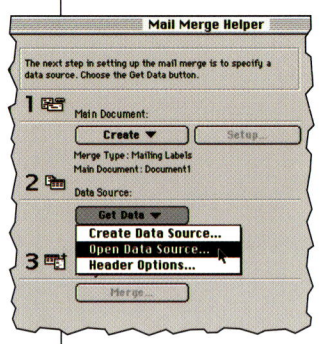

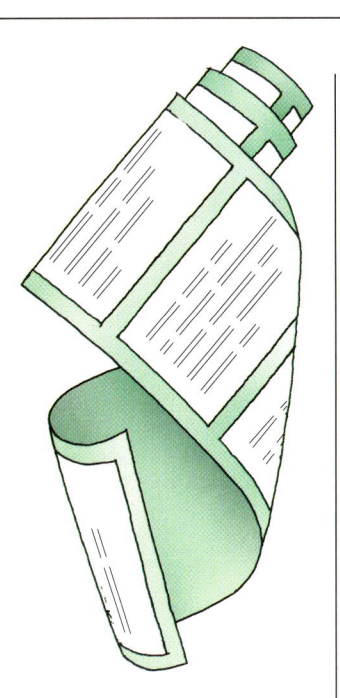

DESIGNER LABELS

Word now displays the *Create Labels* dialog box. In this dialog box, you insert the merge field names from your data source in a sample label. Word then automatically duplicates the set of merge field names from the sample label onto each label. Follow these steps to design your labels:

Creating Your Label Layout

1 In the *Create Labels* dialog box, the insertion point should be positioned inside the *Sample Label* box. Click on the *Insert Merge Field* button and choose *FirstName* from the pop-up list.

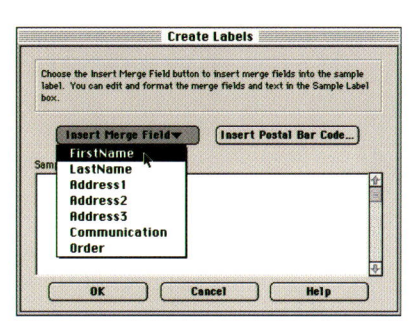

2 In the *Sample Label* box, you'll see the field you have just added. Press the Spacebar to insert a space after the first name and then choose *LastName* from the *Insert Merge Field* list to insert this merge field name into the *Sample Label* box.

3 To start a new line, press the Return key, and then add the three lines of the address in the same way. When you have inserted these merge fields, click on *OK* to close the *Create Labels* dialog box.

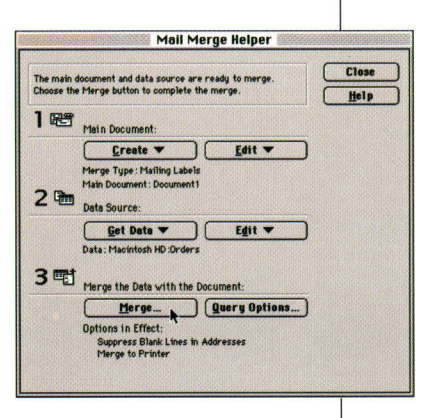

4 The *Mail Merge Helper* dialog box appears. Under *Merge the Data with the Document*, click on the *Merge* button.

5 The *Merge* dialog box appears. Click on the *Merge To* box and select *Printer*. Then click on the *Merge* button to merge the information from your data source and print the finished mailing labels. Click on *Print* in the dialog box that appears.

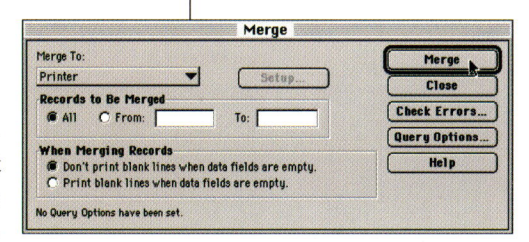

⚠ A Sticky Ending!
Your labels must be specifically designed for use with the printer you're using. If they are not, the labels may peel off the backing sheet and get stuck inside the printer, causing extensive internal damage. If you are using a laser printer, use label sheets specifically designed for a laser printer, as indicated by the manufacturer. If you have a dot-matrix printer, use continuous feed labels and set your printer to use a straight-through paper path, if it has one, to reduce the chance of labels getting stuck.

5

CHAPTER FIVE

Timesavers

With features such as templates, styles, AutoCorrect, AutoText, and macros, Word allows you to automate or speed up tasks that you perform frequently. Through just a little extra effort in understanding and setting up these features, you can save yourself a great deal of time in the long run. In this chapter, you'll see how to use these features to create your own Word tools designed to suit your specific needs. The chapter also introduces you to some Word Wizards that show you step by step how to create various types of documents.

TEMPLATES AND WIZARDS • STYLES
AUTOCORRECT AND AUTOTEXT • MACROS

Templates and Wizards *104*

Every document you create is based on a template. Find out all about templates — what they are, how to use them, and how to create your own custom templates. Then discover how using a Wizard is often the fastest way to create an agenda, letter, resume, or other common type of document — Word does most of the thinking for you!

Styles *108*

Learn to format with styles. Styles are easy to use, they save time, and they help ensure a consistent format within or between documents. Discover how to use them to format your documents quickly and efficiently.

AutoCorrect and AutoText *110*

With Word's AutoCorrect and AutoText features, you can store text, graphics, and other items that you use frequently and quickly insert them into documents whenever they are needed. Find out how to use these time-saving features.

Macros *112*

Macros are little programs you can create yourself for accomplishing everyday tasks in Word. Find out how easy it is to create a macro that will save you valuable time.

Templates and Wizards

A TEMPLATE PROVIDES A READY-MADE PATTERN FOR DOCUMENTS. A template can contain formatting, text, and graphics, and can provide styles (see page 108). It can also store AutoText entries and macros (see pages 110 and 112) that the documents based on that template will inherit. Using templates helps you avoid certain routine tasks that occur when you create documents from scratch. You can also use a Wizard to help you create a new document. Wizards take you step by step through the creation of certain common types of documents.

Document Blueprints

Every Word document is based on a template. A template not only helps you create a particular type of document, it also ensures an overall consistency among documents created from the same template. So far in this book, you have used only the Normal template to create your documents. But a number of other templates come with more specific features. Word offers templates for letters, invoices, and fax cover sheets, among others. You can use any template as it is or you can modify it to suit your individual needs.

THE NORMAL TEMPLATE
You select a template on which to base your document when you create a new document. Word opens a copy of the template as a new document — the new document contains all the information from that template.

Unless you select another template in the *New* dialog box, Word automatically bases any new document on the Normal template — a general-purpose template for any document. Documents you create by clicking on the New button on the Standard toolbar are also based on the Normal template. In addition, when you start Word and begin typing in the empty document window, Word bases the document on the Normal template. The Normal template provides more than just an empty document — it also stores the AutoText entries and macros and the toolbar, menu, and keyboard settings that you routinely use in Word. Items stored in the Normal template are global — which means they are available to all Word documents. If you were to delete the Normal template, you would lose all of these items. Items stored in any other template are available only to documents based on that template.

Choosing the Normal Template

> ⚠️ **Beware of Changes!**
> It is not advisable to modify the Normal template, because any changes to the Normal template affects all new documents that are based on the Normal template.

USING A TEMPLATE

If you want to create new documents such as memos, letters, and fax cover sheets, you can save time by basing the document on one of the templates that come with Word. To demonstrate how easy to use templates are, let's create a fax cover sheet. When you choose the template from the list, Word opens a document copy of the template on the screen. All you have to do is insert your own text. Choose *New* from the *File* menu, and then follow the steps below.

Wrong Type of File?
If you accidentally open and edit a template file instead of a document file, don't worry. You can still save it as a document and leave the template unchanged. Choose *Save As* from the *File* menu, and then save the template with a new name — doing this will preserve the original template with its original name.

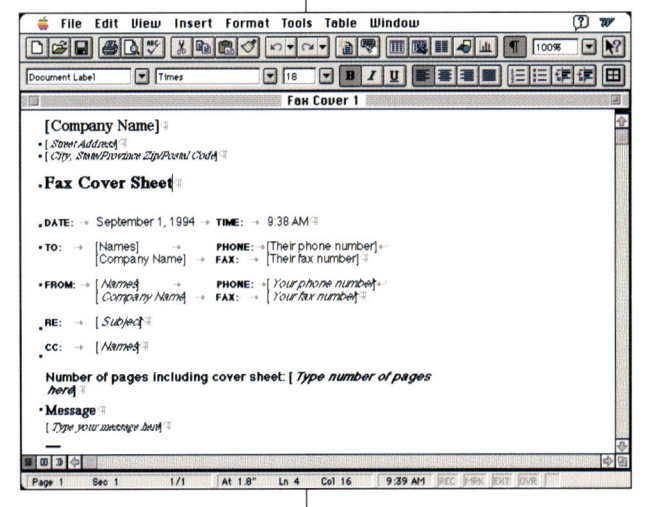

Creating a Fax Cover Sheet

1 In the *New* dialog box, make sure the *Document* option is selected under *New*, and then choose *Fax Cover 1* from the *Template* list. Note that a brief description of the template appears under *Description*. Click on *OK*.

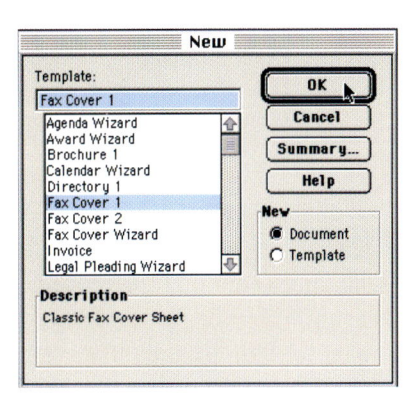

2 A document copy of the template appears on the screen as shown here. Highlight the sample text and replace it with your own text. Then save your fax cover sheet with a name before printing it.

Modifying and Creating Templates

You can produce professional-looking documents just by using the templates that Word provides. But if you prefer, you can modify a template to suit your needs. You modify a template just as you would a document — open the template, edit and format the text and graphics, and then save the changes you have made. You should bear in mind, however, that any changes you make will apply to any new documents based on that template. If you want to maintain the original features of the template, you should create a new template based on that template. On the following page, you'll learn how to create a new template. In the "Styles" section (see page 108), you'll practice modifying this template by adding new styles.

TEMPLATES AND WIZARDS

CREATING A NEW TEMPLATE

Word lets you create your own document templates. The easiest way to create a template is to open the Normal template, rename it, and then adapt it as you choose. The scope for customizing templates is limited only by your imagination! For now, let's adapt the Normal template to begin the process of creating a template for a bulletin board notice. You'll finish the template in the "Styles" section on page 108. Choose *New* from the *File* menu, and then follow these steps.

Creating a Bulletin Template

1 In the *New* dialog box, choose *Normal* from the *Template* list. Click on the *Template* option button under *New*, and then click on *OK*.

2 Word creates a template called *Template1*. Choose *Save As* from the *File* menu. In the dialog box that opens, *Template1* appears in the *Save Current Document as* box. Check that **Templates** is the folder in the pop-up list box above the file list. Then replace *Template1* by typing **Bulletin** in the *Save Current Document as* box, and click on *Save*.

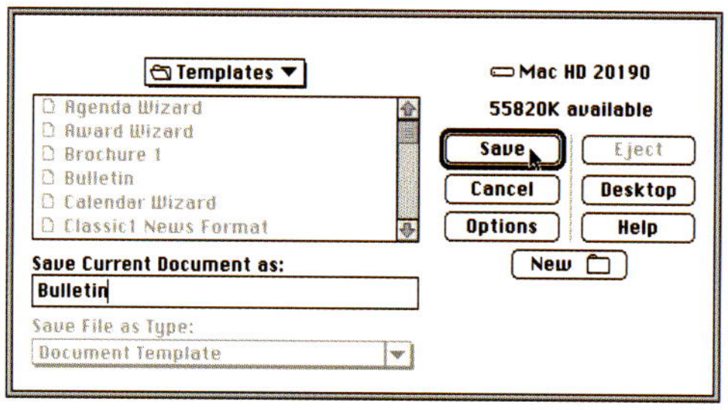

3 Choose *Document Layout* from the *File* menu. In the *Margins* flipcard of the *Document Layout* dialog box, change the margin settings as shown here and click on *OK*. Then save and close your **Bulletin** template.

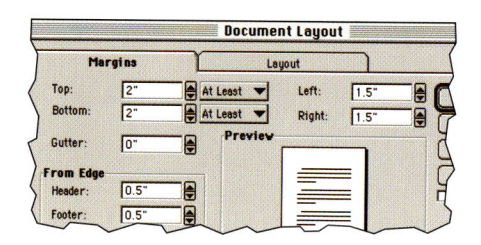

Wonderful Wizards

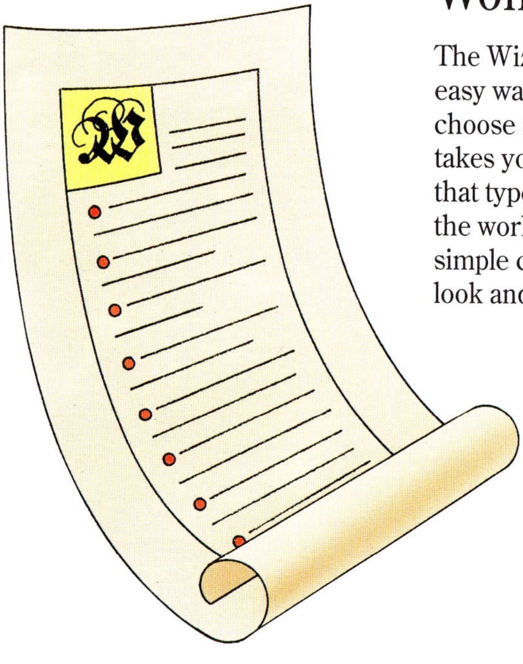

The Wizards supplied with Word provide a fast and easy way to create new documents. Each time you choose a specific Wizard to create a document, Word takes you step by step through the process of creating that type of document. In fact, the Wizard does most of the work for you — all you have to do is make a few simple choices about how you want the document to look and then type in your text.

STEP BY STEP

Word provides ten Wizards to help create the following commonly used documents: agenda, award, calendar, fax, legal plea, letter, memo, newsletter, resume, and table. Whichever Wizard you choose, the process is the same — you follow the on-screen instructions, selecting options along the way. To see how easy it is to use a Wizard, let's create an agenda. Choose *New* from the *File* menu, and then follow these steps:

Using the Agenda Wizard

1 In the *New* dialog box, choose *Agenda Wizard* from the *Template* list and click on *OK*. This begins the Agenda Wizard.

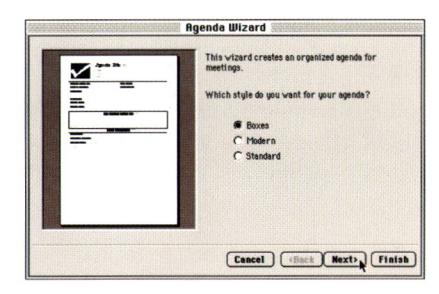

2 In the first box that appears, you choose a style for your agenda. Click on *Boxes*, and then click on *Next* to open the next box.

3 Enter a date and time for your meeting in the relevant text boxes, then click on *Next*. If you want to change the style you selected in step 2, click on *Back* to return to the last stage.

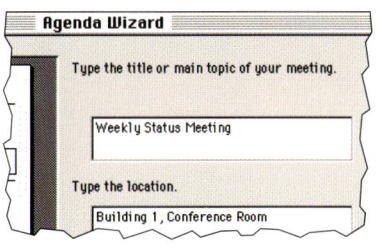

4 Type in a title and location for your meeting, and then click on *Next*.

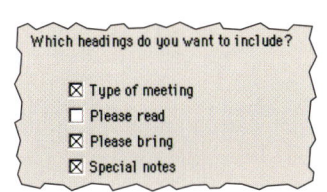

5 Word provides a number of headings that will be included in your agenda. Deselect the checked options you don't want, and then click on *Next*. In the next box, deselect any names you don't want. Then click on *Next*.

6 When the box at right appears, type the relevant information in the text boxes, and then click on *Next*. A new box appears, allowing you to reorder information. For now, click on *Next*.

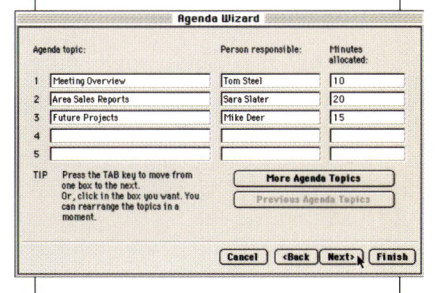

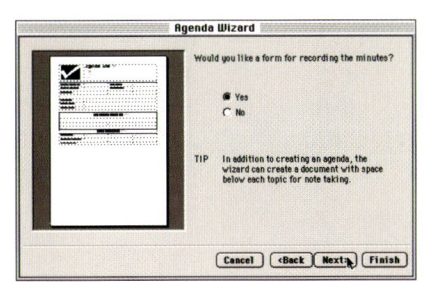

7 Choose whether or not you want any minutes recorded, and then click on *Next*.

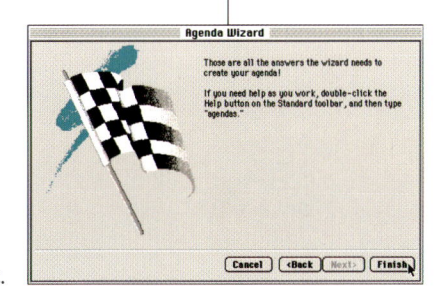

8 Word tells you that you have answered all the necessary questions. Choose whether you want to display Help, and then click on *Finish*. The Wizard will close and your agenda will appear on the screen. Now save your agenda with a name, print it, and finally close it.

Finished Business

Each time you use a Wizard, Word saves the settings you have selected. The next time you use the Wizard, you don't have to go through the whole process again if you want to use the options you previously set. Simply click on the *Finish* button in the first box that appears.

STYLES

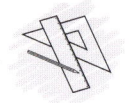

Styles

IN WORD, A STYLE IS A SPECIFIC SET OF CHARACTER and paragraph formats identified by a name. Word has several built-in styles designed for specific uses, such as a variety of headings styles and the Normal style, which is the standard style you'll probably use most often. You can also create your own styles to suit your particular formatting requirements.

Choosing a Style

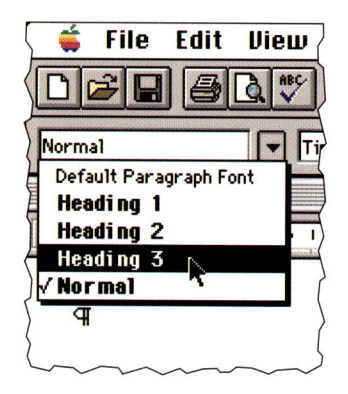

The Function of Styles

Styles help ensure a consistent format within a long document or among documents of a certain type. Styles also make global formatting changes simple because any changes to the style will automatically apply to all the paragraphs assigned to that style.

Styles are applied at paragraph level — to apply one of Word's built-in styles, for example, you select the paragraph(s) you want to style and choose a style from the Style pop-up list on the Formatting toolbar (see left). The selected text will be formatted accordingly.

Changed Your Mind?
It's easy to change the attributes of a style. Choose *Style* from the *Format* menu to open the *Style* dialog box. Under *Styles*, choose the style you want to change, click on *Modify*, and then make your changes by clicking on the *Format* button and choosing commands from the pop-up list. Once you have modified the style, click on *OK* in the *Modify Style* box, and then close the *Style* dialog box. Word automatically reformats any text assigned to this style.

HOW TO DEFINE A NEW STYLE

You can define styles for documents or templates. If you define a style for a document, the only way to make that style available in other documents is to add it to a document template (see step 7 on page 109). If you define a style for a template, however, it is automatically available in any new document based on that template. The easiest way to define a new style is to adapt an existing style. Let's create a new style for your **Bulletin** template. Choose *Open* from the *File* menu. In the dialog box that appears, choose *Microsoft Word* from the pop-up list box, and then double-click on *Templates* in the scrolling list box. Choose *Bulletin* in the list. Finally, click on *Open*.

1 Choose *Style* from the *Format* menu.

2 The *Style* dialog box opens, with *Normal* highlighted under *Styles*. To adapt the Normal style to create a new style, click on *New*.

3 The *New Style* dialog box appears, revealing more options. Under *Name,* choose a name for the new style you want to create; in this case type **Banner**. Click on the *Format* button to display a pop-up list, and then choose *Font*.

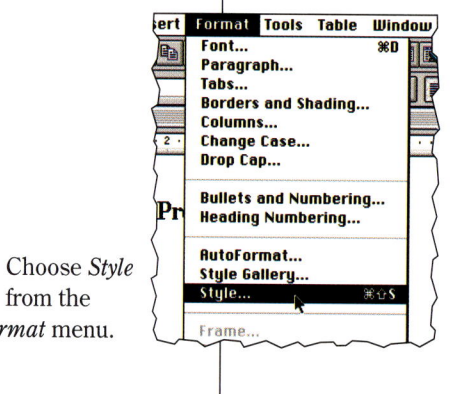

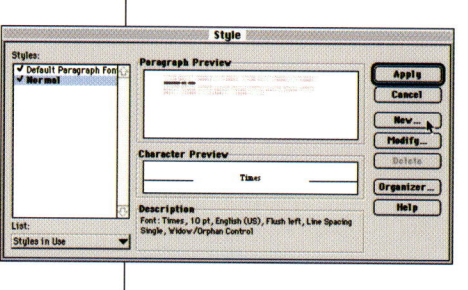

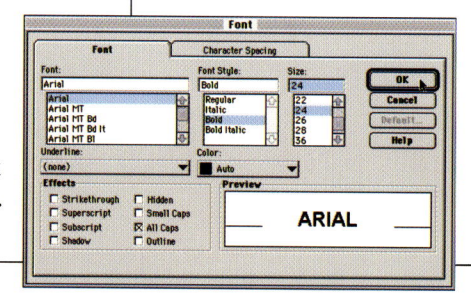

4 The *Font* dialog box appears. Choose *Arial* in the *Font* list box, click on *Bold* in the *Font Style* box, set the *Size* at *24* pt, and then check *All Caps* under *Effects*. Click on *OK* to return to the *New Style* dialog box.

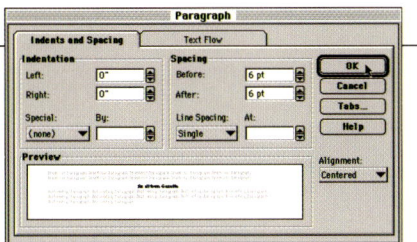

5 In the *New Style* dialog box, choose *Paragraph* from the *Format* pop-up list. In the *Paragraph* dialog box, choose *Centered* from the *Alignment* pop-up list. Under *Spacing,* set both *Before* and *After* to *6 pt*. Click on *OK* to return to the *New Style* dialog box.

6 In the *New Style* dialog box, choose *Border* from the *Format* pop-up list. In the *Paragraph Borders and Shading* dialog box, click on *Shadow* under *Presets*. Increase the value in the *From Text* box under *Border* to *4 pt*. Under *Line* choose the ¾ *pt* double-line border. Then click on *OK* to return to the *New Style* dialog box.

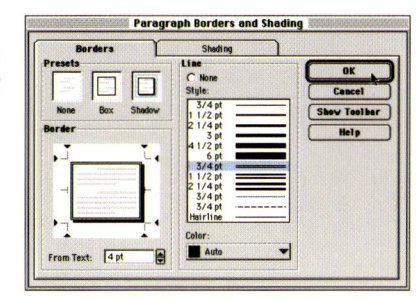

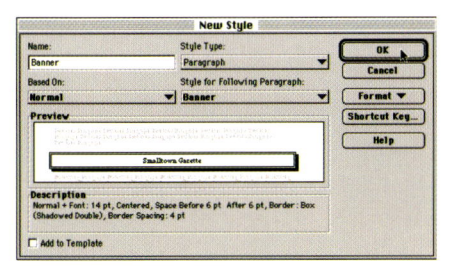

7 You've now defined your **Banner** style. Its details are listed in the *Description* box and a sample is shown in the *Preview* box. Click on *OK* to add the style to your template. If you had defined a style for a document, you could add it to the template on which the document was based by checking the *Add to Template* box. Click on *Close* in the *Style* dialog box.

In a Hurry?
After you've typed a document, you can save time by letting Word format the text for you. If you click on the AutoFormat button on the Standard toolbar, Word analyzes each paragraph and determines how it is used — for example, as a heading — and then applies an appropriate style to that paragraph. Word also makes small changes to improve the document's appearance, such as indenting paragraphs.

Selling Out

Now let's add another style to your template and then apply both of the new styles you've created to complete the template. Follow the procedure described in steps 1 and 2 on page 108. When the *New Style* dialog box opens, make sure that the *Based on* list box is set on *Normal,* call the new style **Contact**, and then do the following:

■ Access the *Font* dialog box via the *Format* pop-up list, and select *Bold* under *Font Style*. Click on *OK*.

■ Access the *Paragraph* dialog box, and choose *Centered* from the *Alignment* pop-up list. Click on *OK*.

You have now defined your **Contact** style. Click on *OK* in the *New Style* dialog box to add this style to your template and then close the *Style* dialog box to return to your **Bulletin** template. If you open the Style list on the Formatting toolbar, you'll see both of your new styles in the list. Now enter the text of your template:

■ Click at the top of the text area, type **For Sale**, and then press Return twice.

■ Choose *Date and Time* from the *Insert* menu and select an option. Then press Return two times.

■ Type **Main text here** and press Return three times.

■ Type **Contact:** and type your name and address.

Now apply the new styles you have created:

■ Select **For Sale** and choose *Banner* from the Style pop-up list on the Formatting toolbar.

■ Select the last part, from **Contact** through the end of your address, and choose *Contact* from the Style pop-up list. Finally, save and close **Bulletin**.

Now whenever you want to use the template, choose *New* from the *File* menu and then choose *Bulletin* in the *New* dialog box. This opens a new document with your "boilerplate" text in place. Then replace the line **Main text here** with your new text.

Your New Template
*When you have finished the **Bulletin** template, it should look like the example at right.*

AUTOCORRECT AND AUTOTEXT

AutoCorrect and AutoText

AUTOCORRECT AND AUTOTEXT ARE TWO of Word's most useful timesavers. Using AutoCorrect, you can quickly store and retrieve graphics and text that you use frequently in your documents. You store the item with a short code — then whenever you type this code, AutoCorrect automatically inserts the stored item in its place as you type. AutoText is a similar feature that inserts a stored item when you choose a specific command.

Speed Up Your Typing

AutoCorrect is especially useful for phrases that are repetitive or difficult to type. Let's suppose your company's name is All Nations Exports. Because you use this name regularly, you can save time by storing it as an AutoCorrect entry called **ANE** (a sort of codename). From now on, if you type **ANE** followed by a punctuation mark or space, AutoCorrect will automatically replace it, as you type, with **All Nations Exports**.

Let's create an AutoCorrect entry. First open a new document based on the Normal template and call it **Nature Letter**. Then follow these steps:

Creating an AutoCorrect Entry

1 Choose *AutoCorrect* from the *Tools* menu. The *AutoCorrect* dialog box appears, with a set of predefined AutoCorrect entries listed by default.

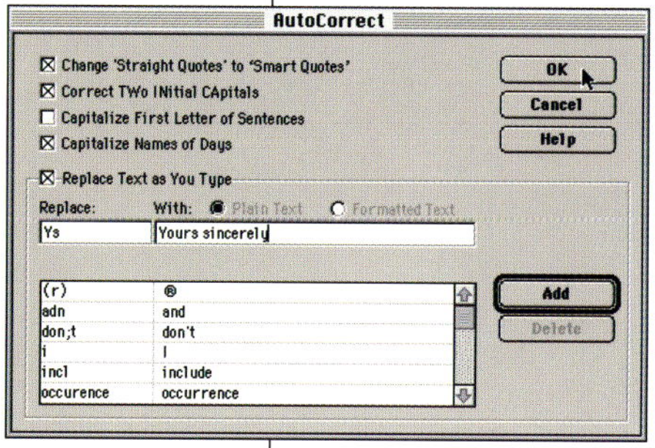

2 Type **Ys** in the *Replace* box. Then type **Yours sincerely** in the *With* box and click on *OK*. If you want to add more than one entry at a time, click on *Add* after each entry and then click on *OK* when you finish.

Now whenever you want to include the words **Yours sincerely** in a document, you simply type **Ys** followed by a space or punctuation mark.

STORING COMPLEX TEXT AND GRAPHICS

To store a graphic, a long piece of text, or formatted text, select the item before you open the *AutoCorrect* dialog box. The item appears in the *With* box. To save the entry with its original formatting, select the *Formatted Text* option. To save it as plain text, in which Word matches the formatting of the surrounding text, select the *Plain Text* option — but bear in mind that a plain text entry can only contain up to 255 characters. Then type a name for the entry in the *Replace* box.

⚠ Check That Name!
An AutoCorrect name can have up to 31 characters but it must not have any spaces. Don't give an AutoCorrect entry a name that is a real word because you might type the word as part of your text and have it inadvertently replaced! To cancel an AutoCorrect entry, click on the Undo button on the Standard toolbar.

❓ Habitual Misspeller?
You can set up AutoCorrect to correct any word that you habitually misspell. (Make sure the misspelling is not itself a proper word!) To do so, open the *AutoCorrect* dialog box, type the misspelling in the *Replace* box, and then type the correct spelling in the *With* box. Click on *OK*.

110

Controlled Entry

You can create AutoText entries for text and graphics that you don't want Word to insert automatically. Unlike AutoCorrect, AutoText allows you to insert a particular entry only by typing the name of the entry and pressing a combination of keys or by choosing *AutoText* from the *Edit* menu and then choosing the entry's name.

CREATING AN AUTOTEXT ENTRY

To practice creating an AutoText entry, let's use procedures you learned in Chapter Three to prepare a letterhead consisting of a graphic and some text. Open the file **Nature Letter** if it's not already open, and insert the graphic *Leaf.eps* from the **Clip Art\EPS Clip Art** folder (see page 77). Press Return twice and type the name and address for the Nature Society beneath the leaf graphic, as shown at right. Change the type size to 16 point and the type style to bold. You're now ready to store this letterhead as an AutoText entry:

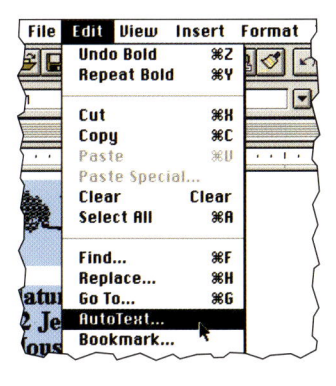

Example Letterhead

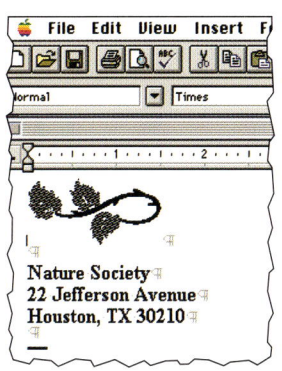

1. Select the graphic and text you've just entered, including the paragraph mark at the end of the text. This retains the paragraph formatting in the AutoText entry. Then choose *AutoText* from the *Edit* menu.

2. The *AutoText* dialog box appears with the letterhead displayed in the *Selection* box. Under *Name*, type **NS logo,** and then click on *Add*. (An AutoText name can have up to 32 characters, including spaces.) The letterhead is now stored as an AutoText entry.

Magic Touch
A quick way to insert an AutoText entry is to type the name of the entry into your document wherever you want the entry to appear, and then press Command-Option-V.

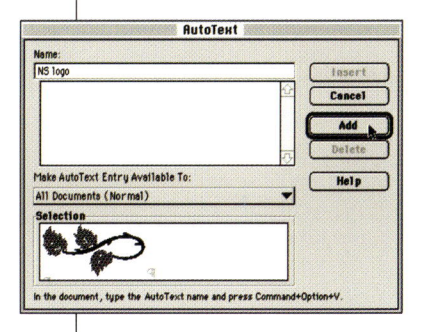

INSERTING AN AUTOTEXT ENTRY

Once you've saved an AutoText entry, adding it to a document is easy — you call up the entry and insert it wherever you want it to appear. Delete the graphic and name from your **Nature Letter** document and follow these steps:

1. Choose *AutoText* from the *Edit* menu. The *AutoText* dialog box appears.

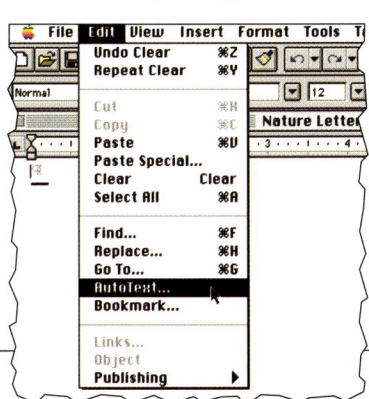

2. Choose **NS logo** from the *Name* list. Word displays the letterhead with its original formatting in the *Preview* window. You'll see the *Formatted Text* option selected under *Insert As*. Click on *Insert* to enter the logo into your document. Then save and close **Nature Letter**.

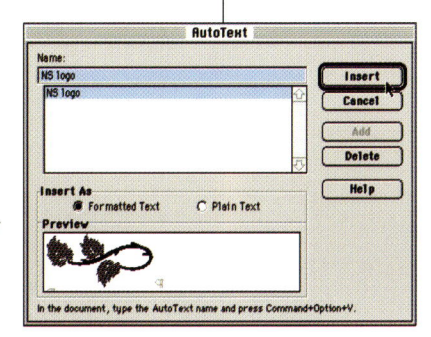

111

MACROS

Macros

A MACRO IS A SERIES OF COMMANDS that are grouped together in one single command, which is then assigned to a menu, toolbar button, or key combination. Macros provide shortcuts for accomplishing certain routine tasks. For example, you can create a macro that hides the Standard toolbar, Formatting toolbar, and Ruler all at once or one that opens a document with an address and the date already inserted. You can then assign this macro to a toolbar button and run the macro by clicking on that button.

Using Macros

To produce a macro, you must record the commands you want the macro to perform. Before you start recording, decide which commands you'll use and in which order. Let's create a macro that opens a new document with a company logo, an address, the date, and the opening greeting already inserted. The commands you'll need to record are shown in the box at right.

How to Record a Macro

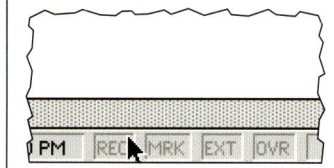

1 Double-click on *REC* on the status bar to open the *Record Macro* dialog box.

- Choose *New* from the *File* menu.
- Choose the *Normal* template in the *New* dialog box.
- Choose *AutoText* from the *Edit* menu.
- Choose a logo in the *AutoText* dialog box.
- Choose the *Date and Time* command from the *Insert* menu.
- Choose a Date format in the *Date and Time* dialog box.
- Type the opening to your letter.

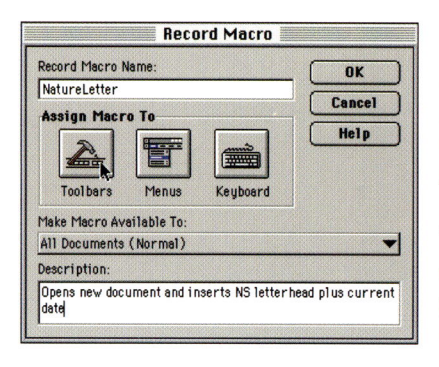

2 In the *Record Macro Name* text box, type the name **NatureLetter**. Make sure that the *Make Macro Available To* box is set on *All Documents (Normal)*. This makes your macro available in any document you are working on. Then in the *Description* text box type **Opens new document and inserts NS letterhead plus current date**. Now click on the *Toolbars* icon to assign the macro to a toolbar button.

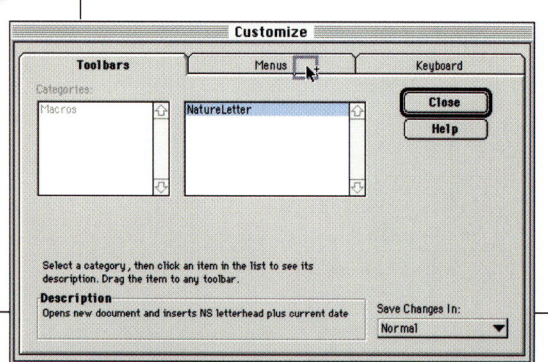

3 The *Customize* dialog box appears, with the *Toolbars* flipcard displayed. Select **NatureLetter** from the list of macros, and then drag it to a position on a toolbar — you'll see the outline of a square accompanied by a plus sign move on screen as you move the mouse. For now, position this square between the Underline button and the Left Align button on the Formatting toolbar.

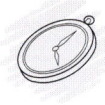

Cast a Macro Spell
To use a ready-made macro, choose *Open* from the *File* menu and double-click on the **Macros** folder within the **Microsoft Word** folder. Check that the *List Files of Type* box displays *Document Templates*, choose *Word 6.0 Macros* from the *File Name* list, and then click on *Open*. Choose *Macro* from the *Tools* menu, select a macro in the *Macro* dialog box, and click on *Run*.

112

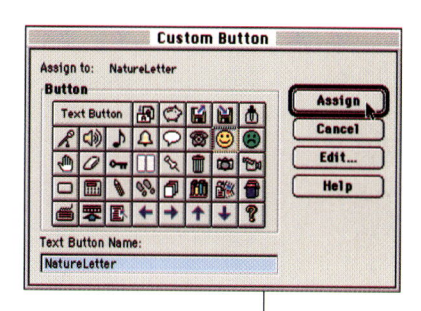

4 As soon as you release the mouse button, the *Custom Button* dialog box opens. Choose a symbol for your new toolbar button by clicking on the symbol, for example, the smiley, and then click on *Assign*. The smiley appears on the new button on the Formatting toolbar. Click on *Close* in the *Customize* dialog box.

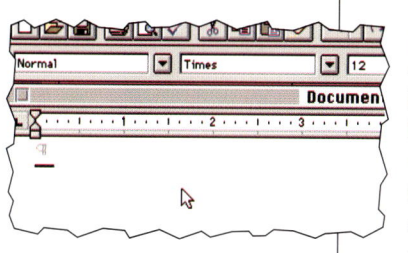

Macro Mistake?
If you make mistakes when you are recording a macro, you can cancel previously recorded actions by clicking on the arrow next to the Undo button and selecting the actions you want to undo. But remember that the actions can be undone in sequential order only.

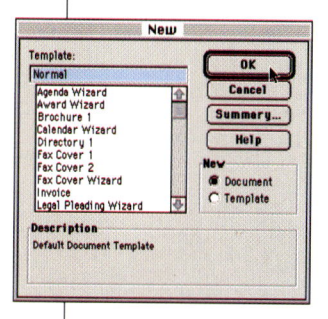

5 Any command you choose now will be recorded. To indicate this, the mouse pointer becomes a transparent arrow (see left). You'll also see two buttons appear on your screen — one to stop and one to pause the macro recording (see right).

Stop Button

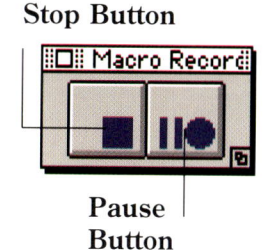

Pause Button

6 Start by choosing *New* from the *File* menu to access the *New* dialog box. In this box, click on *OK* to base your document on the Normal template.

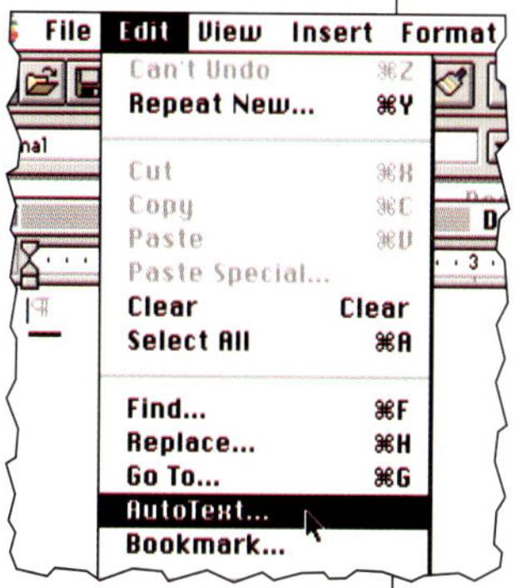

7 Now choose *AutoText* from the *Edit* menu.

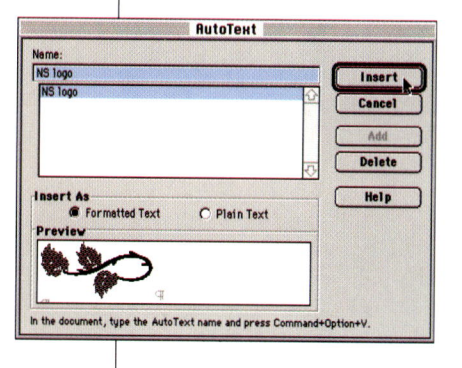

8 In the *AutoText* dialog box, choose *NS logo* from the *Name* list, and then click on *Insert*.

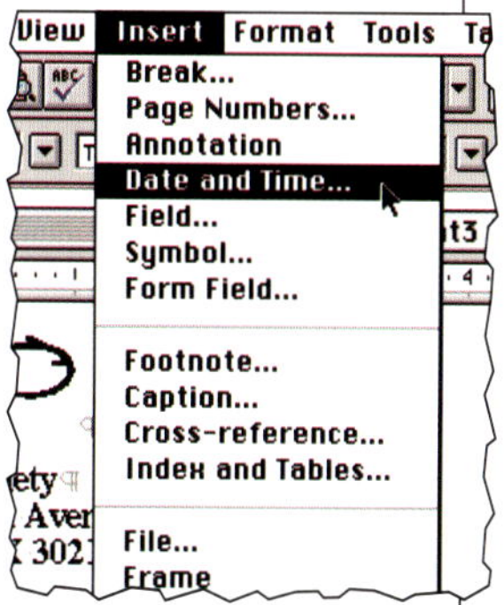

9 Press Return twice, and then choose *Date and Time* from the *Insert* menu. When the *Date and Time* dialog box appears, choose a date format, and then click on *OK*.

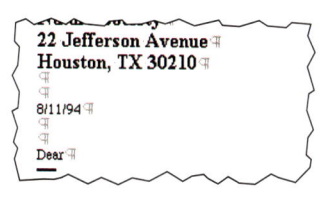

10 Press Return three times, and then type **Dear**.

The Finished Product
This is the letter heading that the macro you've created will produce each time you run the macro.

11 To stop recording your macro, click on the Stop Macro Recording button. Your macro has now been recorded.

113

MACROS

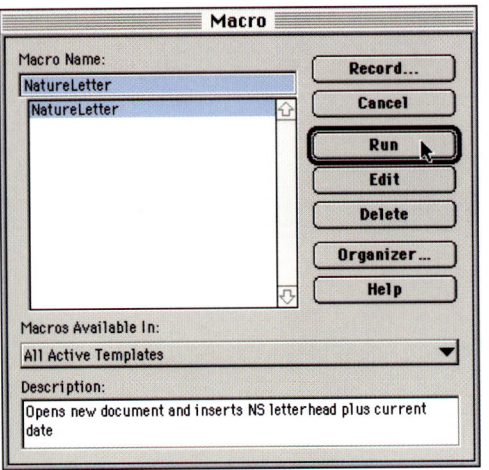

Macro **Dialog Box**

RUNNING A MACRO

When you run a macro, Word "plays back" all the actions you performed when you recorded that macro, but at a much higher speed. Because you have assigned your **NatureLetter** macro to a toolbar button, you only have to click on that button to begin running the macro. If you do not assign the macro to a toolbar button, a menu command, or a combination of keys when you record the macro, you have to access the *Macro* dialog box to run the macro. To do this, choose *Macro* from the *Tools* menu. When the *Macro* dialog box opens, choose the name of the macro and click on *Run* to use the macro.

Bear in mind that you can also use the *Macro* command when you want to record a macro. You choose *Macro* from the *Tools* menu, and then click on *Record* to access the *Record Macro* dialog box — but this method is not as quick and easy as double-clicking on *REC* on the status bar.

Give Me a Break!

When you're recording a macro, you may need to pause, for example, if there are actions you want to perform that you don't want recorded. To pause while recording a macro, click on the Pause Macro Recording button. When you're ready to resume, click again on the button.

Managing Macros

If you want to copy a macro to a different template, delete a macro, or rename a macro, you can do so in the *Organizer* dialog box. First choose *Macro* from the *Tools* menu to open the *Macro* dialog box, and then click on the *Organizer* button; the *Organizer* dialog box appears on the screen with the *Macros* flip-card displayed (see at right).

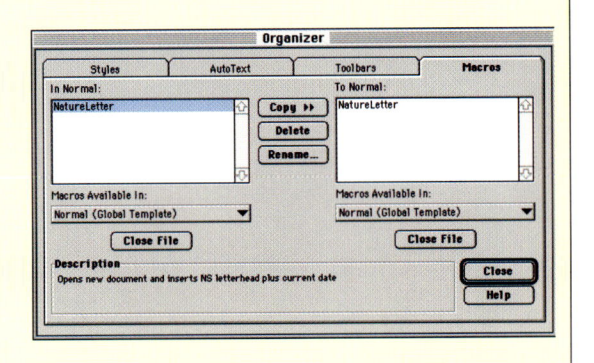

■ To copy a macro to another template: In the *Macros Available In* box on the left-hand side of the *Organizer* dialog box, choose the template in which the macro you want to copy is stored. Then select your destination template in the *Macros Available In* box on the right-hand side. Finally, click on the *Copy* button.

■ To delete a macro: Choose the relevant template from the *Macros Available In* box on the left side of the dialog box, select the macro you want to delete, and then click on *Delete*.

■ To rename a macro: Choose the relevant template from the *Macros Available In* box on the left side of the dialog box, select the name of the macro you want to rename, and then click on the *Rename* button. When the *Rename* box appears, simply type in the new name, and then click on *OK*. Don't use spaces, commas, or periods in your macro name.

Reference Section

The first few pages of this section list some useful keyboard and mouse shortcuts and also describe how to outline a document. The next two pages show you how you can install a printer and discuss the different types of fonts. You'll also find some additional help on managing your files, converting files, and linking files with those created in other applications. You'll then learn how to customize Word to suit your methods of working. Finally, you'll find an index to the whole volume.

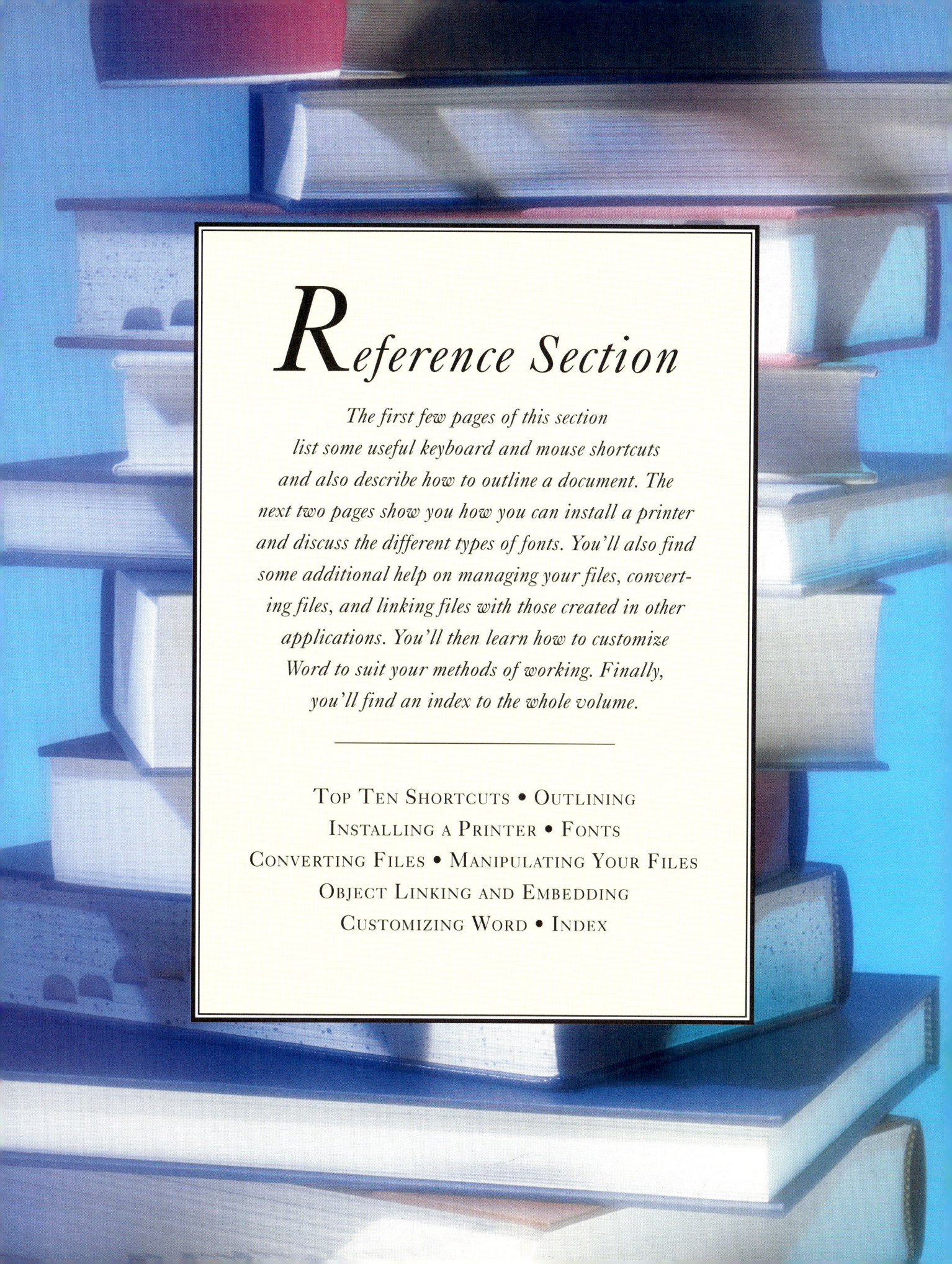

TOP TEN SHORTCUTS • OUTLINING
INSTALLING A PRINTER • FONTS
CONVERTING FILES • MANIPULATING YOUR FILES
OBJECT LINKING AND EMBEDDING
CUSTOMIZING WORD • INDEX

REFERENCE SECTION

Top Ten Shortcuts

IN THIS SECTION, we provide a list of "top ten" shortcuts, for both the keyboard and the mouse. As you become proficient in Word, you'll find you may prefer to carry out some commands with the keyboard and others with the mouse — and you'll gradually build up a repertoire of shortcuts. Below we've listed some of our own favorites.

Keyboard Shortcuts

Command	Keyboard Keys
Move to the beginning of a document.	Command and Home
Move to the end of a document.	Command and End
Obtain context-sensitive help.	Help (ins)
Save a document.	Command and S
Close the application window.	Command and W
Delete a single word (after the insertion point).	Command and Del
Repeat previous command.	Command and Y
Insert "soft" return (start a new line without creating a new paragraph).	Shift and Return
Restore a maximized document window to its previous size.	Command and F5
Capitalize initial letters of selected words.	Shift and F3

Mouse Shortcuts

Command	Mouse Action
Select an entire document.	Triple-click anywhere in the selection bar.
Select multiple paragraphs.	Double-click in the selection bar, then drag to select paragraphs
Make a toolbar "floating."	Double-click on an empty area on the toolbar.
Return a "floating" toolbar to its original position.	Double-click on an empty area on the toolbar.
Open *Go To* dialog box.	Double-click anywhere on the status bar.
Open *Margins* flip-card in *Document Layout* dialog box.	In Page Layout view, double-click on the corner of the page, outside the margins.
Maximize a document window.	Click on the zoom box.
Open *Layout* flip-card in *Document Layout* dialog box.	Double-click on any section break.
Open *Tabs* dialog box.	Double-click on any tab stop.
Resize a document window.	Drag on the size box.

116

Outlining

OUTLINING IS A USEFUL PROCESS for structuring a document and organizing your ideas in relation to each other. In an outline you view headings rather than text, making it easy to reorganize the document's structure, scroll through the document, and get a quick overview.

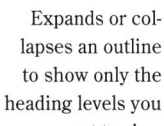

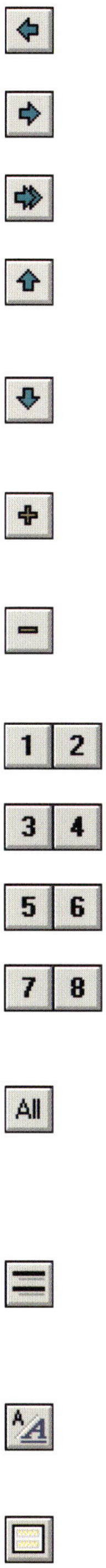

Promotes a selection up one level	⬅
Demotes a selection down one level	➡
Demotes a heading to body text	⇒
Moves a selection above the preceding heading	⬆
Moves a selection below the following heading	⬇
Displays the next level beneath a heading	+
Collapses the next level beneath a heading	−
Expands or collapses an outline to show only the heading levels you want to view	1 2 3 4 5 6 7 8
Expands the entire outline to display all heading levels and body text	All
Displays all body text or only the first line of body text	≡
Shows or hides all character formatting	A
Switches between Outline and Master Document view	

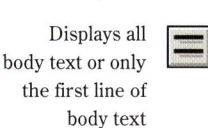

Using the Outline Toolbar

Whether you want to create a document from scratch using outlining, or apply outlining to an existing document, you must put the document into Outline view by clicking on the Outline button above the status bar, or choose *Outline* from the *View* menu.

In Outline view, a new toolbar — the Outline toolbar — appears. The Outline feature gives you eight heading levels (heading 1 for the top level, heading 8 for the lowest level). Each heading level comes with its own predefined style that you assign to your headings. If you assign a level to a heading but then change your mind about its significance within the document, you can easily "promote" the heading to a higher level or "demote" it to a lower level.

When outlining has been applied, you can collapse an outline so that only the main headings show while the supporting text gets hidden. You can then quickly scroll through the headings, and rearrange them by selecting a heading and clicking on the up- or down-arrow button. This moves the heading a paragraph up or down, taking any supporting text with it automatically.

Once you've finished rearranging your document, you can expand the outline again to work on the details. The buttons on the Outline toolbar and the actions they perform are explained at left.

CREATING AN OUTLINE

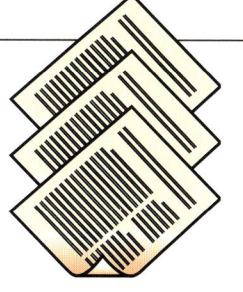

The steps below show you how to assign levels to headings and how to move them around. If you want to create an outline, make sure you are in Outline view first.

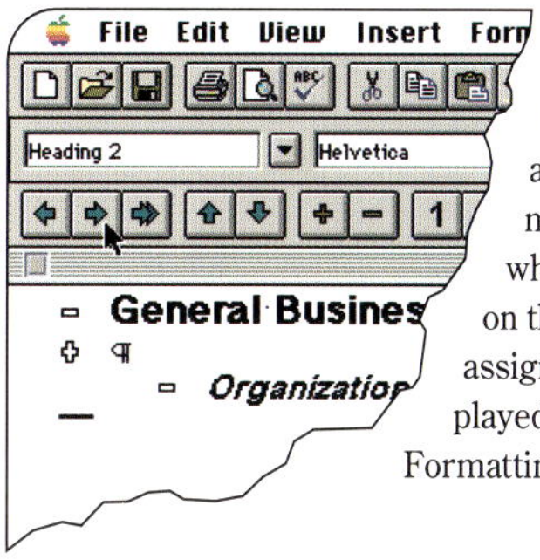

1 When you first start typing, Word automatically assigns heading 1 level to the text. To assign a lower level to a heading, move your insertion point anywhere within that heading and click on the Demote button. The level assigned to a selected heading is displayed in the Style box on the Formatting toolbar.

2 To turn a paragraph into body text, move the insertion point anywhere within that paragraph and click on the Demote to Body Text button. Outline view indents headings and body text to show how they relate to one another — in Normal view, however, they are not indented.

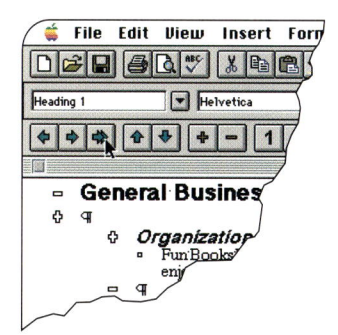

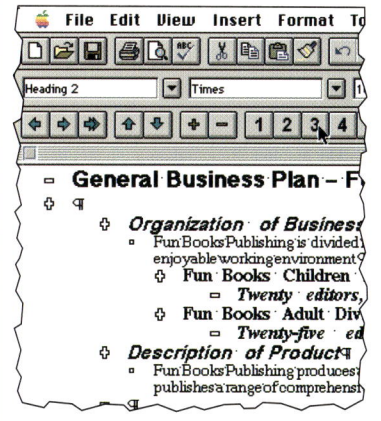

3 To collapse an outline, select the heading level that you want to display. In the example shown here, three heading levels were used to create the document. You would therefore click on the 3 button to collapse the outline so that the body text disappeared and only the headings were visible.

4 To move text to a new location further up in the document, select the heading you want to move and click on the Move Up button — any supporting text automatically moves with the heading. To view the "normal" appearance of the document, click on the Normal button above the status bar.

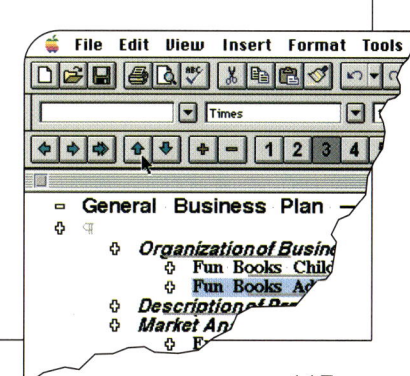

Installing a Printer

STRICTLY SPEAKING, INSTALLING A PRINTER isn't a feature of Word — it's something that is done within the Macintosh **System Folder**, which serves all Macintosh applications, including Word. As well as installing a printer, you'll also have to prepare the printer itself by plugging it in, adding paper and a ribbon or toner depending on the type of printer you have, and then connecting it to your computer before you can print any Word documents.

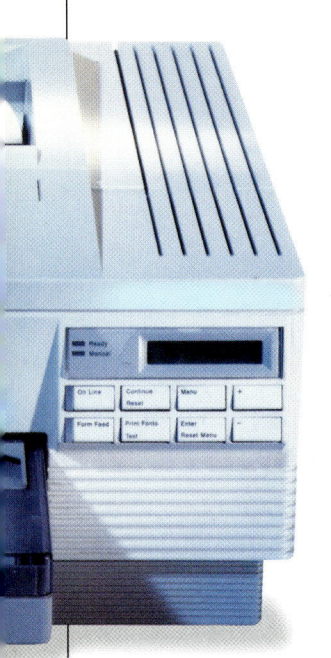

Printer-Driver Files

Every printer needs a printer-driver file to make it work. The printer-driver file processes data it receives from an application, such as Word, and then issues the commands to the printer.

It is possible to install more than one printer driver or different types of printer drivers to your Macintosh. For example, you may be connected to a network on which you have access to more than one printer. Macintosh System software is supplied with printer-driver files for the most commonly used printers. You need to know the name and model of your printer before you install a printer driver for it. If your printer is not supported by any of the printer-driver files that come with your Macintosh System software, you'll need to get a special printer driver. You should follow the instructions from the printer manufacturer.

To install a printer-driver file to your Macintosh, follow the steps below.

Installing a Printer-Driver File

1 Double-click on the folder or disk icon containing the printer driver you want to install to open it.

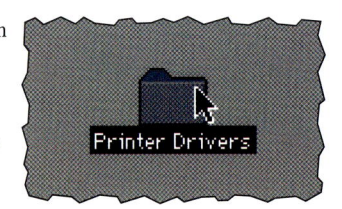

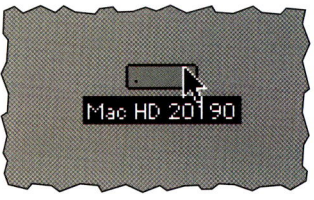

2 Double-click on the hard disk icon and locate your **System Folder**.

3 Now drag the printer-driver icon to the **System Folder**. The Macintosh will ask you to confirm that you want to place the new printer driver in the **Extensions** folder in the **System Folder**. Click on *OK* in the confirmation dialog box.

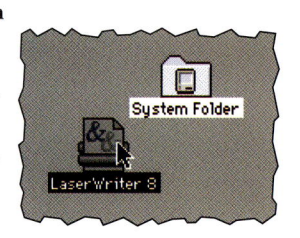

Choosing a Printer

If your Macintosh has more than one printer driver installed so that it can print to more than one printer, you may find that you sometimes want to change the printer you're using (for example, you may want to use the least busy printer or one that prints a larger page size). To do this, you need to specify the new printer that you want to use. (You only need to do this when changing printers; you don't need to do it every time you print.) To specify a printer, follow the steps below.

1 Choose *Chooser* from the Apple menu.

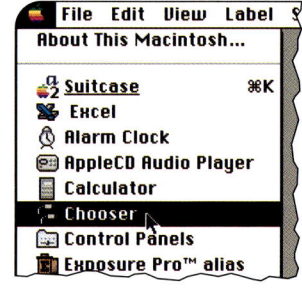

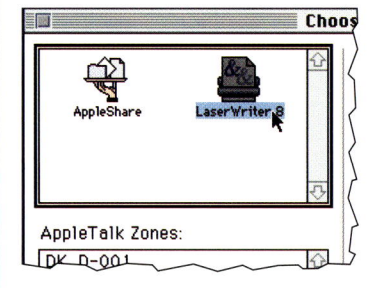

2 In the *Chooser* dialog box, click on the printer-driver icon for the printer you want to use.

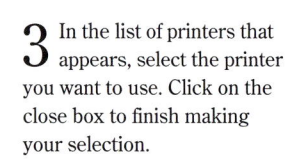

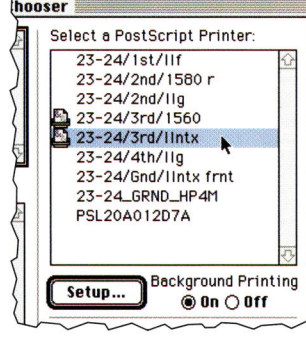

3 In the list of printers that appears, select the printer you want to use. Click on the close box to finish making your selection.

118

Fonts

A FONT IS ONE COMPLETE COLLECTION of letters, punctuation marks, numbers, and special characters that have a particular design. The fonts and font sizes you can use in your Word documents depend on the fonts you have available on your printer and the fonts installed on your Macintosh.

Types of Fonts

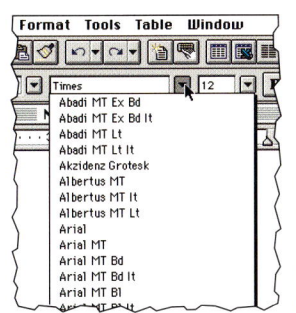

Font List

If you click on the down arrow next to the Font list box on the Formatting toolbar or if you open the *Font* dialog box by choosing *Font* from the *Format* menu, you'll see a list of the fonts available to you in Word.

All of the fonts that your Macintosh uses are stored in a particular location in the **System Folder** on your hard disk and are available to any application that is run on your Macintosh.

There are three types of fonts — TrueType fonts, PostScript fonts, and fixed-size fonts. TrueType fonts are scaleable to any point size and look exactly the same when printed as they do on screen. PostScript fonts are provided with your System software. These produce high-quality documents, but you need a PostScript printer, or emulation software, to print them. Fixed-size fonts are bitmapped (made up of a pattern of dots). For each font size you choose, your Macintosh must have a font of that size installed. If it doesn't, your Macintosh rescales the font from a size that is installed, with variable results.

If you use icon view to inspect the contents of the folder that holds your font files, you can identify TrueType fonts by their icons, which show the letter A in several different sizes.

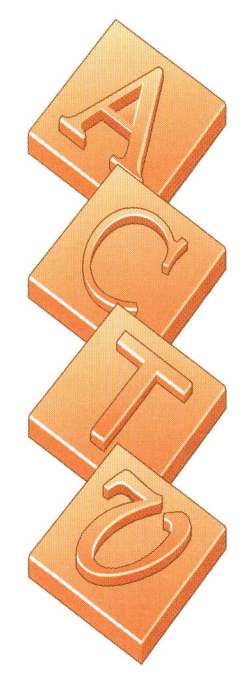

STICK TO TRUETYPE!
If you stick to TrueType fonts, you can be sure that your fonts look the same when printed as they do on screen. TrueType fonts also ensure that documents look the same when printed on different printers and when exchanged between the Macintosh and Windows.

Where Are My TrueType Fonts?

Word installs the TrueType fonts supplied with Word 6 only if you choose full installation. If you choose another installation option, Word stores the TrueType fonts in a **Fonts** subfolder in the **Microsoft Word** folder on your hard disk. You can install these at any time by closing any applications you have running and dragging the font icons to your **System Folder**.

Want More Fonts?

If you want to add more fonts for use in your Word documents, you must install them in the Macintosh's **System Folder**. To install extra fonts, follow the steps below:

1 Close all the applications you have running, making sure to save your work before you do so.

2 Double-click on the hard disk icon to open the hard disk window. The **System Folder** icon should be visible.

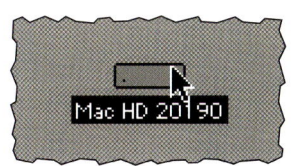

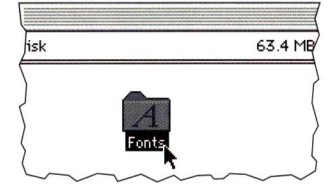

3 Locate the folder or disk icon that contains the fonts you want to install and double-click on it.

4 Hold down Shift and click on the font names to highlight them, then drag them to the **System Folder** icon in your hard disk window.

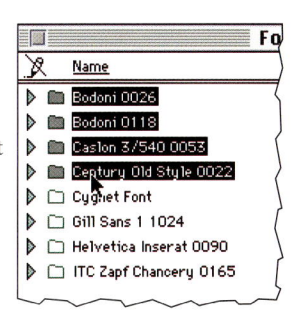

5 In the box that appears, click on *OK*.

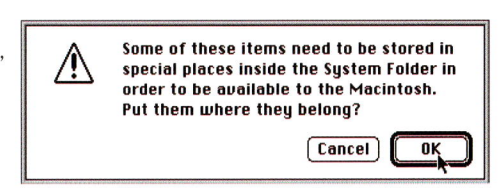

REFERENCE SECTION

Converting Files

WITH WORD, you can open and work with documents created in other applications, such as Word for Windows. Word recognizes the formats of many applications and can convert the documents to the Word for the Macintosh format when you open them. You can also save Word files in formats used by other applications.

Converters

To convert documents, you must have the appropriate converters. If there is no converter for the application you're using, you can still import the text, but you may lose some formatting elements.

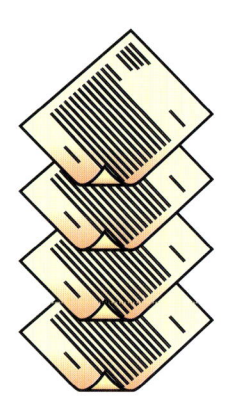

OPENING DOCUMENTS CREATED IN OTHER APPLICATIONS

To convert most types of documents created in other applications, you only have to open the document. Word performs the conversion automatically once you have confirmed the format that the file should be converted from. But bear in mind that if the document contains fonts that are not available on your Macintosh (see page 119), Word will use substitute fonts — you may need to alter the text to account for this.

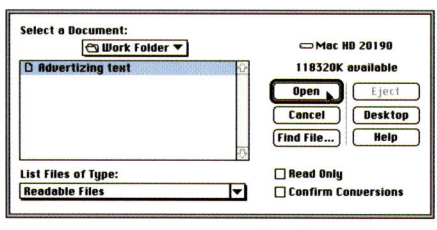

1 Choose *Open* from the *File* menu to access the dialog box shown at left. From the *List Files of Type* pop-up list, choose the type of file you want to open. If you're not sure of its format, choose *All Files*. Use the location and scrolling list boxes to locate the folder containing the file, and then choose the name of the file from the list displayed. Finally, click on *Open*.

2 If you attempt to open a file that is not in Word format, the *Convert File* dialog box appears. The current file format is highlighted. Click on *OK* to convert it and open it. (If you can't find the appropriate converter for a particular application, you may have to install it.)

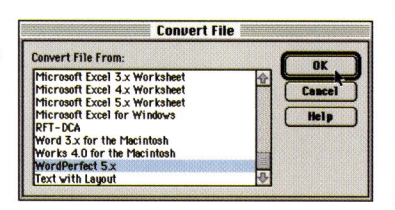

SAVING WORD FILES IN DIFFERENT FORMATS

You may need to save a Word document in another format — for example, if you want to share a file with someone who uses a different application. First choose *Save As* from the *File* menu. In the dialog box displayed, scroll through the *Save File as Type* pop-up list and choose the format in which you want to save the file. Specify a destination folder, and name the file in the *Save Current Document as* box. Then click on *Save* in order to store the file in the new format.

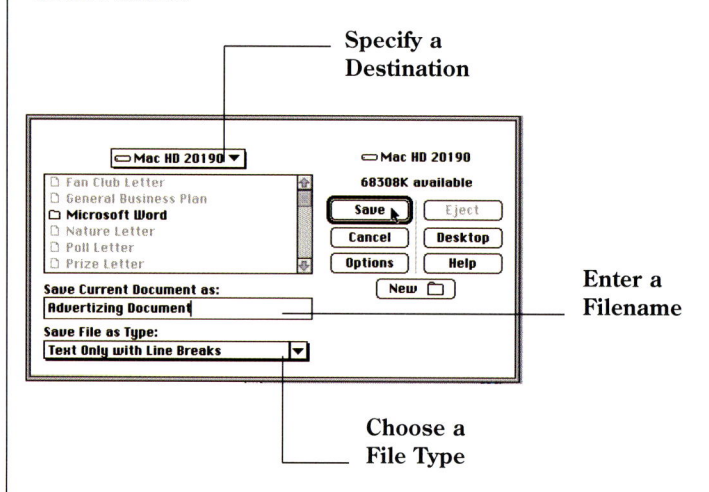

Specify a Destination

Enter a Filename

Choose a File Type

Importing Picture Files

You can also import and export pictures among different applications. To import and interpret a graphics file created in another application, Word uses a device called a graphics filter. Here are some popular graphics file formats that Word for the Macintosh allows you to import:

■ Paint program bitmap (PNTG)

■ Windows metafile (WMF)

■ Macintosh PICT (PICT and PICT2)

■ WordPerfect graphics (WPG)

■ Encapsulated PostScript (EPS)

■ Tagged image file format (TIFF)

For example, you can import an image created in the Paint program into a Word document. To do this, you create your image in Paint and save it to a specific folder as a PNTG file. You then open a Word document and choose *Picture* from the *Insert* menu. Locate your image file in the relevant folder, and finally click on *Insert* to import the image.

Manipulating Your Files

EARLIER IN THIS BOOK, you learned about the organization of the files and folders on your Macintosh's hard disk. Here we show you how to move and copy files from one folder to another, how to change the name of a file or folder, and how to delete files or folders that you no longer need.

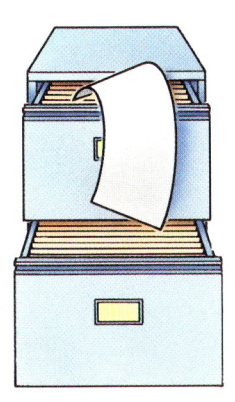

Making Changes

On the Macintosh, it's easy to move, copy, rename, or delete files or folders. Using the Finder if necessary (see page 49), first display the relevant files or folders on your Macintosh desktop. For example, if you want to move a file from the **Microsoft Word** folder to a **My Letters** folder that you have created on the desktop, display both the **Microsoft Word** folder and the **My Letters** icon.

Moving or Copying a File or Folder

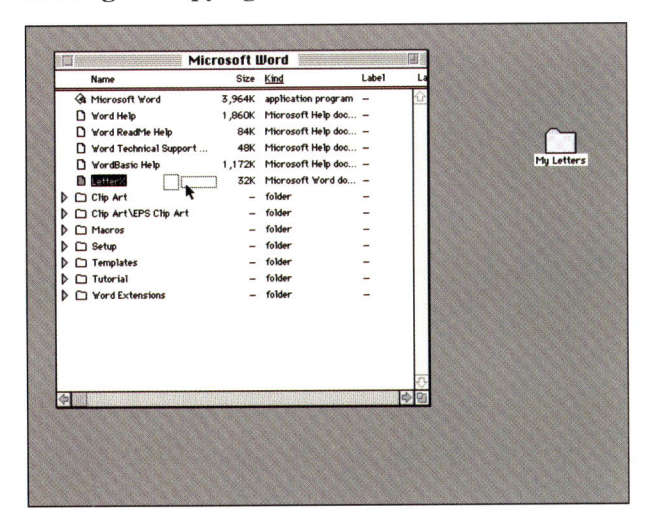

1 Place the mouse pointer over the file or folder you want to move. Then hold down the mouse button and drag the file or folder symbol toward the target folder. If you want to copy the file instead of moving it, hold down the Option key while you do this.

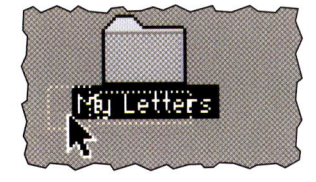

2 Position the file symbol over the target folder so that the icon's title box goes black as shown here, and then release the mouse button. The file has now been moved or copied to the target folder. If you want, double-click on the folder to check that the file is there.

Renaming a File or Folder

1 Click once on the name of the file or folder you want to rename. The text appears with its normal background highlight color.

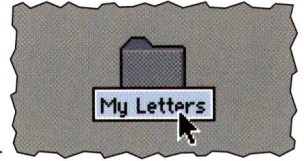

2 Type the new name in the box. If you only want to modify the existing filename, click again in the box. The insertion pointer appears and you can change the name as you wish.

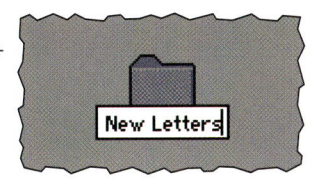

3 Click anywhere outside the filename box to finish renaming the file.

Deleting a File or Folder

1 Click on the file or folder you want to delete and drag it to the *Trash* icon. Release the mouse button, and the file or folder disappears. The *Trash* icon bulges (unless the folder it represents already contains some files).

2 Any items you want to delete remain in the trash until you choose *Empty Trash* from the *Special* menu. You can see the contents of the trash by double-clicking on the *Trash* icon.

Moving vs. Copying

When you drag files or folders to new locations on the same disk or volume, the Macintosh moves them and does not copy them unless you specifically tell it to do so (see "Moving or Copying a File or Folder" at left). When you drag files or folders to different disks or volumes, the Macintosh automatically copies them.

Multiple Actions

To move or copy several files at once, click on the first file you want to move or copy, hold down Shift, and then click on any other files you want to move or copy. All the files you select are highlighted. Then drag all the highlighted files at once to the new folder, making sure that the folder's name is highlighted before you release the mouse button.

To delete several files at once, you can use the same procedure. Select the files you want to delete, and then drag them to the *Trash* icon. All the files will be deleted when you next choose *Empty Trash* from the *Special* menu.

Object Linking and Embedding

THE OBJECT LINKING AND EMBEDDING features available in Word provide ways of exchanging information, or "objects," between documents or applications. The main difference between linking and embedding is where the linked or embedded data is stored. Linked objects remain in the original source file, whereas embedded objects become part of the Word document itself.

Linking

Creating a link is easy — you just copy information, called an object, from one document (the source) and paste it into another document (the destination) using the *Paste Special* command. If you then change the information in the source file, Word updates the destination document. You can create links between two Word documents, or between a Word document and a file in another application.

CREATING A LINK

A typical use of linkage might be a table in a Word document that is linked to a Microsoft Excel spreadsheet. Let's create a link between two documents in different applications. First open your Word document, then start Microsoft Excel. (If you don't have Microsoft Excel, open another Word document.) Next, open the source file containing the information you want to link and follow these steps:

From the Source...

1 In the source file, highlight the information you want to paste as a linked object into your Word document.

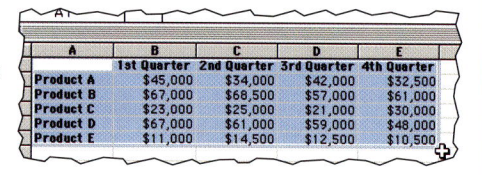

2 Choose *Copy* from the *Edit* menu of the source application.

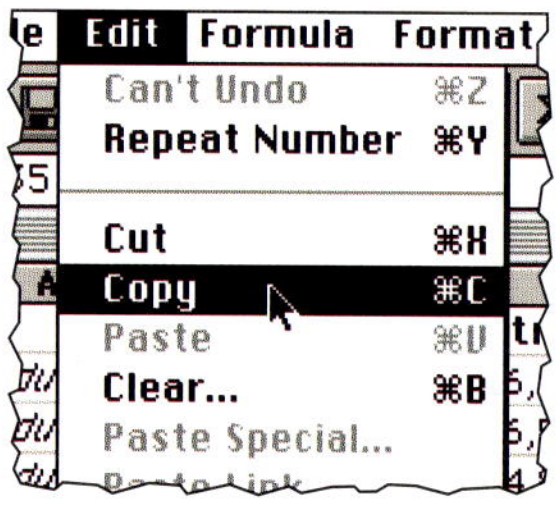

To the Destination

1 Switch to your Word document. Position the insertion point in the document where you want the linked information to appear. Then choose *Paste Special* from the *Edit* menu.

2 In the *Paste Special* dialog box, click on the *Paste Link* option, and then select the type of linked object in the *As* box, in this case *Excel Worksheet Object*. Finally, click on *OK* to insert the information into your Word document.

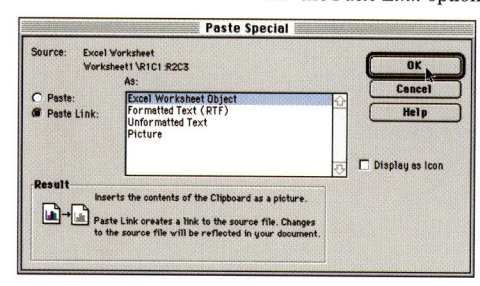

Updating or Breaking a Link

By default, Word automatically updates the information in a linked document whenever the original (source) document changes. But you can change a link to manual updating so that you can choose how frequently to update the information. To do this, select the linked information in your Word document, and then choose *Links* from the *Edit* menu. In the *Links* dialog box, click on the *Manual* option, and then click on *OK*. Now whenever you want to update your document, you select the linked information, open the *Links* dialog box, and click on *Update Now*. Alternatively, select the information to be updated and press F9.

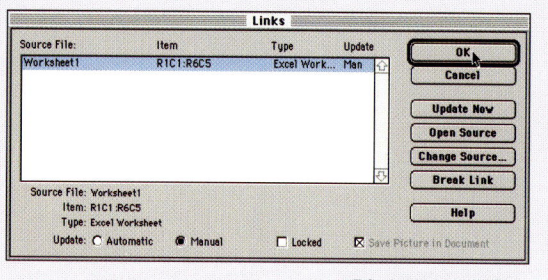

***Links* Dialog Box**

If you don't want further changes to occur in a linked document, you can cancel the link to prevent it from updating. To do this, select the linked information, open the *Links* dialog box, and then click on *Break Link*. Click on *Yes* in the box asking you to confirm the action. Once a link is broken, it can't be reconnected unless you set it up from scratch again.

Embedding

Embedding also means inserting information such as a chart, image, or equation from another application into a Word document. Once you have embedded the information, called an object, it becomes part of the Word document.

You can embed objects created using Microsoft WordArt, Microsoft Graph, and Equation Editor, all of which are supplied with Word. You can also embed objects from other applications installed on your Macintosh, and you can even embed one Word document in another.

EMBEDDING A NEW OBJECT IN A WORD DOCUMENT

You use embedding instead of linking when you don't need to share the information with other documents, but you want to be able to edit and format the information quickly and easily within Word. An object to be embedded can either be newly created or copied from an existing file. To see how easy it is to embed an object in a Word document, let's embed an equation created in Equation Editor — a companion application that provides you with a range of symbols for technical documents.

In Word

1 Position the insertion point in your Word document where you want to embed the equation, and then choose *Object* from the *Insert* menu.

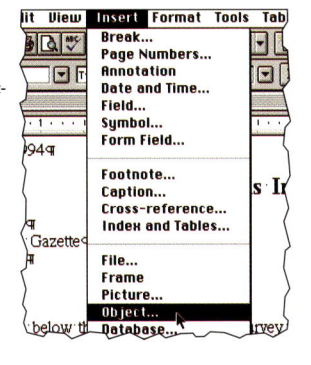

2 In the *Object* dialog box, under *Object Type,* you'll see a list of the types of objects you can create and embed. Choose *Microsoft Equation 2.0,* and then click on *OK*.

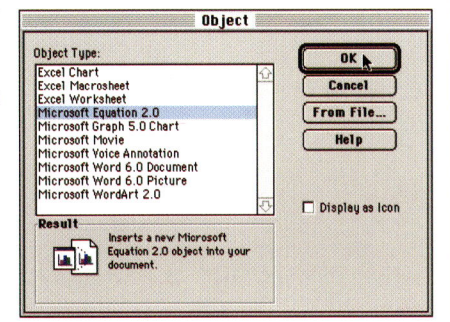

In Equation Editor

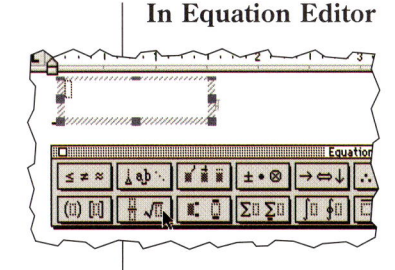

1 The Equation Editor toolbar and special menus appear in the document window. A rectangular box with a shaded gray border also appears; this is where you enter your equation. Create the equation, choosing the relevant symbols from the Equation Editor toolbar.

2 When you've finished creating the equation, click anywhere outside the gray-bordered rectangle. The equation is inserted into the document, and the regular Word menus and toolbars reappear.

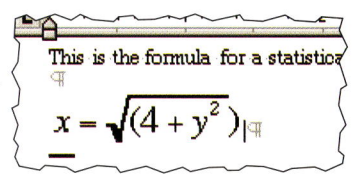

This is the formula for a statistic

$$x = \sqrt{(4 + y^2)}$$

You can use the same method to insert any other object, such as a WordArt image. To insert an object created in Microsoft Graph, choose *Exit and Return to ...* from the application's *File* menu and click on *Yes* when asked if you want to update the object in your document.

OBJECT ALREADY EXISTS?

To embed an existing file, click on the *From File* button in the *Object* dialog box. In the dialog box that appears, choose the location and name of your file, then click on *Insert*.

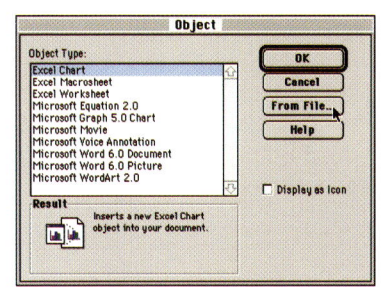

The *Object* Dialog Box

Making Changes

If you want to change an embedded object in any way, all you have to do is double-click on the object in your Word document. After a pause, the relevant toolbars and special menus appear or the application window in which the object was created opens, with the object displayed. You then make your changes and either click outside the object in your Word document or choose *Exit* from the application's *File* menu to return to your Word document and insert the updated object.

REFERENCE SECTION

Customizing Word

To suit your individual style of working, you can customize Word. You can, for example, change the appearance of your Word application window. You can change some of the default settings; you can alter the appearance of a toolbar; or you can assign a command or macro to a toolbar, menu, or shortcut key so that you don't have to wade through layers of menus to carry out a specific action or series of actions.

Modifying Screen Items

If you want, you can easily customize your Word application window. You may, for example, want to hide screen items, such as the scroll bars, the status bar, the Ruler, and so on, in order to see more of the document that you are working on. You can also customize your toolbars — changing the buttons that appear on a particular toolbar, for example.

How to Hide Screen Elements

1 Choose *Options* from the *Tools* menu. In the *Options* dialog box, you'll find twelve tabs. When you click on a particular tab, the dialog box changes to show you the settings assigned to that flipcard.

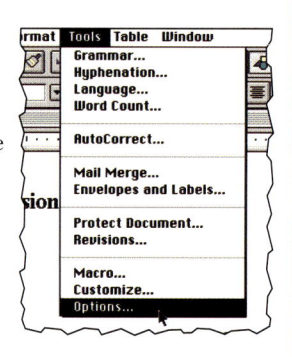

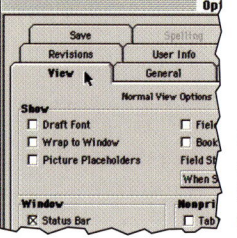

2 In the *Options* dialog box, click on the *View* tab (if it isn't already selected) to reveal the *View* flipcard.

3 Here, you can modify a number of screen items. For example, you can hide the scroll bars and status bar by clearing the relevant check boxes under *Window*; or you can choose which nonprinting characters are displayed by checking the relevant boxes under *Nonprinting Characters*. To make your changes apply, click on *OK*.

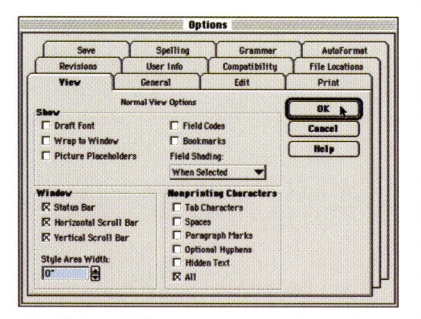

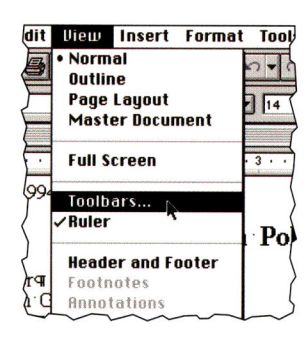

How to Change the Display of the Toolbars

1 Choose *Toolbars* from the *View* menu.

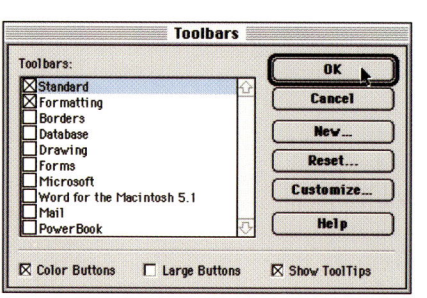

2 In the *Toolbars* dialog box, you can switch off the color of your toolbar buttons by clearing the *Color Buttons* check box; enlarge the toolbar buttons by clicking on the *Large Buttons* check box; or hide the brief descriptions of the toolbar buttons that appear when the mouse pointer pauses over a button by clearing the *Show ToolTips* box. Make your changes, and then click on *OK*.

Changing Your Display and Command Settings

You can also change a number of default settings that come with Word. Make yourself familiar with the various options by choosing *Options* again from the *Tools* menu to open the *Options* dialog box. You are already familiar with the options available under *View*; now explore the other flipcards and their settings. Clicking on the *Help* button gives you additional information about a particular setting.

YOUR GENERAL OPTIONS

In the *General* flipcard, you can decide whether or not a sound is made to indicate an error; whether links are updated automatically when opening files; how many files appear in the *File* menu as recently opened files; the units of measurement that appear on the rulers; and so on.

The Options Dialog Box

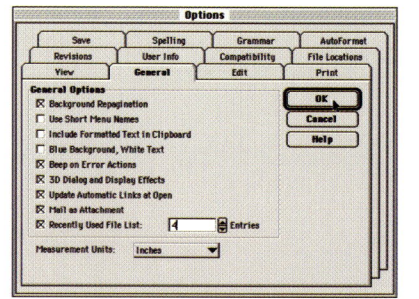

Customizing Toolbars, Menus, and Shortcut Keys

Word lets you customize your toolbars, menus, or shortcut keys to suit your personal needs. In Chapter Five, on page 112, you were shown how to assign a macro to a button on a toolbar. Using the same procedure you can also assign other items to a toolbar, such as a command, a style, a font, an AutoText entry, or a special character. You can further optimize your Word application by customizing your menus and shortcut keys in a similar fashion. Let's suppose you want to add a new command to your *File* menu that closes all the Word files that you currently have open on your screen.

How to Assign a Command to a Menu

1 Choose *Customize* from the *Tools* menu.

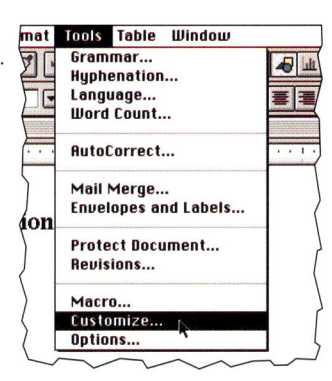

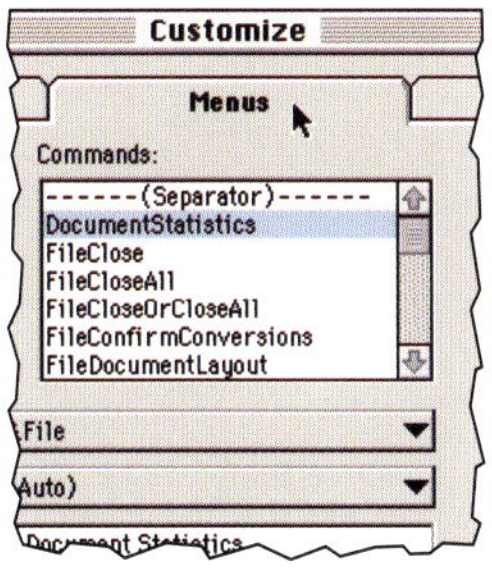

2 When the *Customize* dialog box appears, click on the *Menus* tab to display the *Menus* flipcard.

3 In the *Menus* flipcard, choose the options as shown in the illustration below. In the *Save Changes In* box, leave *Normal* highlighted so the new command is stored as part of the Normal template. When you're finished, click on *Add*, and then click on *Close*. You'll find the new *Close All* command on your *File* menu.

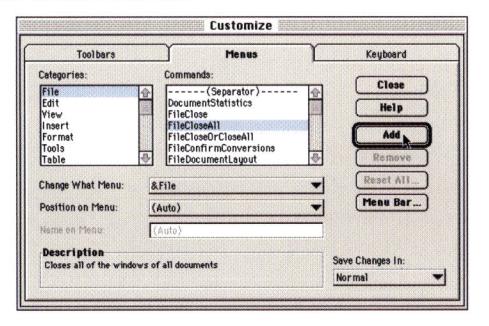

CUSTOMIZING SHORTCUT KEY ASSIGNMENTS

Let's assume that you use the copyright symbol regularly in your letters. Currently, you have to choose *Symbol* from the *Insert* menu, and then locate and click on the copyright symbol. You can make this routine task much simpler by assigning the copyright symbol to a key combination that is easy for you to remember and use. Follow the steps below to assign the copyright symbol to a key combination:

How to Assign a Keyboard Shortcut to a Common Symbol

1 Choose *Customize* from the *Tools* menu.

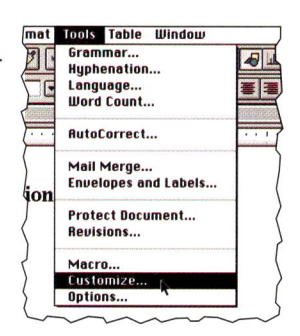

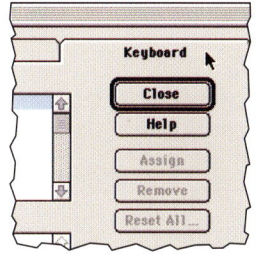

2 When the *Customize* dialog box appears, click on the *Keyboard* tab.

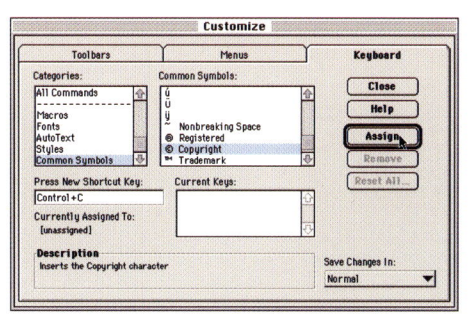

3 In the *Keyboard* flipcard, choose the options shown at left. The *Current Keys* box may show that a keyboard shortcut for © already exists. If so, highlight the shortcut in the *Current Keys* box and then click on *Remove*. Click in the *Press New Shortcut Key* box, and then press Control and C together to assign this combination to ©. The words *Currently Assigned To:* appear, followed by *[unassigned]*, indicating that this combination is unassigned. Check that the *Save Changes In* box is set to *Normal*. Click on *Assign*, and then on *Close*.

Now you press Control and C together whenever you want to insert the copyright symbol in a Word document.

INDEX

a
accented characters 28
active window 46
adding up numbers 81
Agenda Wizard 107
Align Drawing Objects toolbar button 73
aligning paragraphs 55, 59
Align Left and Right toolbar buttons 56
antonyms 42
Apple
    icon 12
    Macintosh 10, 48
    menu 12, 13, 94, 118
Application
    icon 13, 49, 50
    menu 13, 17, 49, 50
application window 12-13
    closing 116
Arc drawing tool 73, 74
Arrange All command 46
AutoCorrect 41
    command and dialog box 29, 110
AutoFormat 23, 109
    toolbar button 15, 23, 109
automatic saving 27
AutoText
    command and dialog box 111, 113
    toolbar button 15
Avery labels 100

b
Balloon help 13, 16
Bold toolbar button 23, 56, 57, 79
Bookmark command and dialog box 37
bookmarks 37
borders 68
Borders
    flipcard 68
    toolbar button 56, 68
Borders and Shading command 68, 70
Break command and dialog box 69
breaking pages and sections 69
Bring in Front of Text toolbar button 73
Bring to Front toolbar button 73
browsing files and folders 49
bullets 60
Bullets toolbar button 56, 60
Bullets and Numbering command and dialog box 60

c
calculations 81
callout 73
Callout drawing tool 73
capitalizing text 116
cells in tables 78, 80
Center toolbar button 22, 56, 59
centered tab 63
centering text 22, 59

character-level formatting 22-23, 54, 55, 56-58
characters
    definition of 56
    nonprinting 20
    special *see* special characters
Chart Type command 84
ChartWizard dialog boxes 82-83
charts 82-85
    choosing types of 84
    defining titles for 83
    inserting 83, 85
    moving 83, 85
    resizing 83, 85
check boxes 15
Check for Errors toolbar button 98
checking
    grammar 43
    spelling 40-41
Chooser dialog box 90, 94, 118
clicking 11
Clip Art images 77, 111
Clipboard 34, 35, 36
close box 12
Close command 17
closing
    documents 17
    split screen 44
    see also quitting Word
coloring objects and lines 76
column chart 84
    creating 82
columns 69
Columns toolbar button 15, 69
command buttons 15
commands 12, 14
    assigning to menus 125
    see also individual commands, e.g., Copy command
Command key 7, 14, 22, 29, 31, 32, 36, 57, 66, 111, 116
context-sensitive help 116
Control key 7, 30, 36, 58, 125
Control Panels command 13
Convert File dialog box 120
converting files 120
Copy
    command 36, 122
    toolbar button 15, 36
copying
    character formatting 58
    files and folders 121
    and pasting 36
    text 35-36
Create Data Source dialog box 97
Create Labels dialog box 101
Create Picture toolbar button 73
Custom Button dialog box 113
custom dictionary 41-42
    adding a word to 41
    creating an additional 42
Customize
    command 125
    dialog box 112, 125
customizing Word 124-125
Cut
    command 35
    toolbar button 15, 35
cutting and pasting 34-35

d
Data Form dialog box 97
Data menu (Microsoft Graph) 84
datasheet 82
data source 96-99
date, inserting current 28, 113
Date and Time command and dialog box 28, 113
Date toolbar button 67
Decrease Indent toolbar button 56
decimal tab 63
Del key 20, 32, 33
Delete Cells command and dialog box 80
Delete key 20, 32, 33
deleting
    cells in a table 80
    drawn objects 74
    files and folders 121
    selected text 33
    single characters 20
    single words 32, 116
Demote To Body Text toolbar button 117
Demote toolbar button 117
deselecting text 30
desktop 10, 48, 121
dialog box 15
    see also individual boxes, e.g., Options dialog box
direction keys 14, 18, 29
dividing numbers 81
document
    closing 17
    displaying in Print Preview 90-91
    examples of different types 86-87
    finding text in 38
    formatting 54-71
    layout 54
    moving around in 18, 29, 116
    naming 21
    opening existing 27
    opening new 26
    printing 23, 92-95
    saving 21, 50-51, 116
    scaling view of 45, 66
    steps to creating 18
Document Layout
    button 67
    command and dialog box 65, 67, 68, 85, 106, 116
document-level formatting 54, 64-65
document window
    fitting text to 45
    moving 47
    resizing 13, 45
    restoring 13, 45, 116
    zooming 13, 45
double-clicking 11, 116
dragging 11
dragging and dropping 34, 35
drawing objects 73-76
    coloring 76
    resizing 74

Drawing toolbar 73, 77
    button 15, 73
    example graphics created with 74-76, 86, 87
drop-down menu 14

e
Edit menu 35-39, 111, 113, 122
Ellipse drawing tool 73, 75
embedding objects 123
em dash 29
Empty Trash command 121
End key 29, 30, 116
entering text 19, 27
Envelopes flipcard 95
Envelopes and Labels command and dialog box 95
envelopes, printing 95
Equation editor 123
Exclude Row/Col command 84
exiting Word *see* quitting Word

f
F3 key 36, 116
F4 key 38
F5 key 32, 116
F7 key 41
Field command 81
File menu 14, 17, 21, 23, 26, 27, 46, 50, 51, 65, 85, 90, 92, 93, 105, 106, 112, 113, 120
files
    browsing 49, 51
    converting 120
    copying 121
    deleting 51, 121
    moving 121
    naming 21
    renaming 49, 121
    saving 21, 27, 50-51
    searching for 51
Fill Color toolbar button 73, 76
Find command and dialog box 38
Finder 13, 49, 50
    command 49
Find File command and dialog box 51
finding text and other items in document 38-39
Find Record toolbar button 98
first-line indent
    using dialog box to create 62
    using Ruler to create 61
    using Tab key to create 18, 19
first-line indent marker 61
First Record toolbar button 98
Flip Horizontal toolbar button 73
Flip Vertical toolbar button 73
floating toolbar 14, 116
folders 48, 51
    copying 121
    creating 50
    deleting 121
    displaying contents of 49
    moving 121
    naming 50
    renaming 49, 121
    saving files to 50-51

font 95, 119
    changing 22, 57
    choice of 55
    size 23, 57
    styles 57
Font
    command and dialog box 58, 93, 95, 108
    flipcard 108
    list box 22, 56, 57, 119
Fonts icon 119
Font Size list box 23, 56, 57
footers 67
Format Callout toolbar button 73
Format menu 58, 60, 61, 64, 68, 71, 108
Format Painter toolbar button 15, 58
formatting
    character-level 22-23, 54, 55, 56-58
    different levels of 54
    document-level 54, 64-65
    general principles of 54-55
    introduction to basic 22-23
    paragraph-level 54, 55, 59-64, 68
    section-level 54, 64, 67, 68-69
Formatting toolbar 12, 13, 56
Formula command and dialog box 81
frames 70-71
Frame
    command (Format menu) 71
    command (Insert menu) 70
    dialog box 71
Freeform drawing tool 73

g

General flipcard 124
Go To
    command 37
    dialog box 37, 116
Go to Record toolbar button 98
grammar checker 43
Grammar command and dialog box 43
graphics
    examples of different 86-87
    files, importing 120
    moving 34
    using Drawing toolbar to create 74-76
    using ready-made 77, 111
    using WordArt to create 72
graphs *see* charts
Gridlines command 78
Group toolbar button 73

h

hanging indent 62
hard disk icon and window 11, 49, 50
hardware requirements 10
headers 67
Header and Footer command and toolbar 67
help, obtaining 16, 116

Help
    Balloon 13, 16
    icon 13
    menu 13, 16
    pointer 16
    toolbar button 15, 16
hidden text 93
Hide Balloons command 16
Hide Microsoft Word command 17
highlight color 13
Home key 29, 30, 116
hyphenation 71
Hyphenation command and dialog box 71

i

I-beam pointer 11, 13, 18, 20, 30
Increase Indent toolbar button 56
indents
    using Paragraph dialog box to set 61-62
    using Ruler to set 61
    using Tab key to create first-line 18
Indents and Spacing flipcard 61, 62
Insert Cells dialog box 80
Insert Chart toolbar button 15, 82, 84
Insert Columns command 80
Insert Frame toolbar button 73
insertion point 18, 19, 20
Insert menu 28, 64, 69, 70, 72, 77, 81, 85, 113, 120, 123
Insert Merge Field toolbar button 98
Insert Microsoft Excel Worksheet toolbar button 15
Insert Table command and dialog box 78
Insert Word Field toolbar button 98
Italic toolbar button 23, 56

j-k

Justify toolbar button 56, 59
justifying text 59
Keyboard flipcard 125
keyboard shortcuts 116

l

Label Options dialog box 100
landscape orientation 93, 94
Last Record toolbar button 98
Layout flipcard 116
left-aligned
    tab 63
    text 59
left-indent marker 61
legend
    deleting from chart 85
    including in chart 83
Line Color toolbar button 73, 76
Line drawing tool 73, 75
line spacing 55, 62
Line Style toolbar button 73, 75
linking objects 122

Links command and dialog box 122
logo *see* graphics and WordArt objects

m

Macro command and dialog box 114
macros 112-114
Macros flipcard 114
magnifying text 45
mailing labels, printing 100-101
Mail Merge 96-99
    command 97
    toolbar 98
    toolbar button 98
Mail Merge Helper
    dialog box 97, 100, 101
    toolbar button 98, 99
manipulating windows 44-47
margins 55, 64-65
    creating different document 68
    using Document Layout dialog box to change 65, 85, 106
    using rulers in Print Preview to change 65, 90
Margins flipcard 65, 85, 106, 116
maximizing windows 13, 45, 116
measurement, changing units of 65
menu bar 12, 14
menu commands 12, 14
menus 12, 14
    customizing 125
    see also individual menus, e.g., File menu, Insert menu
Menus flipcard 125
Merge dialog box 101
merge field names 96
Merge to New Document toolbar button 98, 99
Merge to Printer toolbar button 98, 99
Microsoft Excel 122
    toolbar button 15
Microsoft Graph 82-85, 123
    toolbar button 15, 82, 84
    see also charts
Microsoft Word application window *see* application window
Microsoft WordArt *see* WordArt; WordArt objects
Microsoft Word folder 11, 48, 49
misspelled words *see* spelling check and AutoCorrect
Modify Bulleted list dialog box 60
mouse 11
    shortcuts 116
Move Up toolbar button 117
moving
    around in document 18, 29
    charts 83, 85
    files and folders 121
    graphics 34
    mouse 11
    text 34-35
    windows 47
multiple windows 46-47
    on one document 47
multiplying numbers 81

n

naming documents 21
New
    command and dialog box 26, 104, 105, 113
    document toolbar button 15, 26
New Folder command 50
New Style dialog box 108, 109
New Window command 47
Next Record toolbar button 98
nonprinting
    area 93
    characters 20
Normal template 104
    adapting 106
Normal view 12, 66
numbering lists 60
Numbering toolbar button 56, 60

o

Object command and dialog box 72, 123
OLE (object linking and embedding) 122-123
Online Help toolbar button 15, 16
Open
    command 27, 46, 120
    toolbar button 15, 27
opening
    existing document 27
    new document 26
    recently worked-on file 46
    several documents at once 46
    Word 11
option buttons 15
Option key 7, 30, 35, 66, 74, 111, 121
Options command and dialog box 27, 31, 42, 65, 93, 124
Organizer dialog box 114
Outline
    toolbar 117
    view 66, 117
outlining 117
overtyping text 33
OVR (status bar) 33

p-q

page breaks 69
Page Down key 18, 29, 90
Page Layout view 66, 67, 73
Page Number Format dialog box 64
page numbering 64
Page Numbers
    command and dialog box 64
    toolbar button 67
Page Setup command 93, 94
Page Up key 18, 29, 90
paper orientation 93, 94
paper size 94
paragraph
    alignment 55, 59
    definition of 59
    marks 20, 59
    spacing 62
    width 55

127

Paragraph Borders and Shading dialog box 68, 109
Paragraph command and dialog box 61, 62, 109
paragraph-level formatting 54, 55, 59-64, 68
Paste
   command 35, 36
   toolbar button 15, 35
   see also copying and pasting; cutting and pasting
Paste Special command and dialog box 122
Pause Macro Recording button 113, 114
Picture command 77
pictures see graphics
pie chart, creating 84
point size see font size
pop-up list boxes 15
portrait orientation 93, 94
PostScript fonts and printers 119
Previous Record toolbar button 98
Print
   command 14, 15, 92, 94
   flipcard 93
   toolbar button 15, 23, 92
printer 10
   changing settings of 94
   fonts 95
   installing and choosing 118
printer-driver files 118
printing
   documents 23, 92-94
   envelopes 95
   mailing labels 100-101
   options 92-94
   part of a document 92
Print Preview
   changing margins in 90
   command 90
   toolbar 91
   toolbar button 15, 90
Quit command 17
quitting Word 17
quotes, changing straight to smart 29

r

readability statistics 43
Record Macro dialog box 112
REC (status bar) 112
Rectangle drawing tool 73
redoing actions 33
Redo toolbar button 15, 33
renaming files and folders 121
repeating a command 116
Replace command and dialog box 39
replacing text and other items in document 39
Reshape toolbar button 73
resizing
   chart 83, 85
   drawing object 74
   frame 70
   windows 13, 45
   WordArt object 76
restoring document window 45, 116

Return key 19, 116
reverse print order 93
right-aligned
   tab 63
   text 59
right-indent marker 61
Rotate Right toolbar button 73
Ruler(s) 13, 61
   changing margins using 65, 90
   changing measurements on 65
   setting indents using 61, 62
   setting tab stops using 63

s

Save As command 51, 105, 120
Save
   command 21
   toolbar button 15, 21, 23, 98
saving 21, 50-51, 116
   automatically 27
screen
   modifying 124
   shots and fragments 7
   splitting 44
scroll
   arrow buttons 29, 90
   bars 13, 29, 90
   boxes 13, 29
Search dialog box 51
searching for files 51
section breaks 68-69
section-level formatting 54, 64, 67, 68-69
sections 54, 68
Select Column command 80
Select Drawing Objects toolbar button 73, 75
selecting text 30-31, 116
selection bar 12, 30
Send Behind Text toolbar button 73
Send to Back toolbar button 73, 76
Series in Columns command 84
Shift key 7, 30, 32, 38, 74, 75, 116, 119, 121
shortcut keys, customizing 125
shortcut menus 36, 58
shortcuts, keyboard and mouse 116
Show Balloons command 16
Show/Hide ¶ toolbar button 15, 20
shrinking document to fit 91
size box 13, 45
smart quotes 29
Snap to Grid toolbar button 73
soft return 116
Sort command and dialog box 81
sorting data in table 81
spacing
   between lines 55, 62
   between paragraphs 62
special characters
   finding and replacing 39
   inserting 28-29
Special Characters flipcard 29
spelling check 40
Spelling
   command and dialog box 40, 41
   toolbar button 15, 40

Spike feature 36
split box 44
splitting screen 44
Standard toolbar 12, 13, 14-15
status bar 12
Stop Macro Recording button 113
Style command and dialog box 108
Style list box (Formatting toolbar) 56, 109, 117
styles 108-109
subfolders 48, 49
subtracting numbers 81
summary info 93
Switch Between Header and Footer toolbar button 67
switching between windows 46
Symbol command and dialog box 28, 116
synonyms see thesaurus
System Folder 48, 118, 119
System 7 119

t

Tab key 14, 18, 19
Table
   menu 78, 80, 81
   toolbar button 15, 79, 80
tables 78-81
Tabs
   command 64
   dialog box 64, 116
tab stops 61, 63-64
   removing 63
   templates 26, 104-106
text
   area 13
   attributes 57
   boxes 15
   copying 35-36
   entering 19, 27
   moving 34-35
   selecting 30-31, 116
Text Box drawing tool 73
thesaurus 42
Thesaurus command and dialog box 42
timesavers 104-114
Time toolbar button 67
Tip of the Day 12
title bar 13
toolbar
   buttons 14, 124
   Drawing 73, 77
   Equation Editor 123
   floating 14, 116
   Formatting 12, 13, 56
   Header and Footer 67
   how to use 14
   Mail Merge 98
   modifying 124, 125
   Outline 117
   Print Preview 91
   Standard 12, 13, 14-15
   WordArt 72
Toolbars
   command and dialog box 13, 56, 124
   flipcard 112
Tools menu 40, 42, 43, 71, 93, 95, 97, 110, 114, 124, 125

Trash icon 121
TrueType fonts 95, 119
type size see font size
typing see entering text and overtyping text
typographical effects see font styles and WordArt objects

u-v

Underline toolbar button 56, 57
Undo toolbar button 15, 33
undoing actions 33
Ungroup toolbar button 73
View
   buttons 12, 66
   flipcard 124
   menu 13, 45, 49, 56, 66, 67, 117, 124
View Merged Data toolbar button 98, 99
views 66
   see also Normal view; Outline view; Page Layout view

w-z

Window menu 46, 47
windows
   manipulating 44-47
   maximizing 13, 45, 116
   moving 47
   multiple 46-47
   resizing 13, 45, 116
   switching between 46
Wizards 106-107
Word
   application window
      see application window
   customizing 124-125
   Help contents 16
   opening 11
   quitting 17
WordArt 2.0
   dialog box 72
   toolbar 72
WordArt objects
   embedding 123
   examples of different 87
   modifying 72
   resizing 76
wristwatch symbol 14
WYSIWYG (What You See Is What You Get) 6
zoom box 13, 45
Zoom command and dialog box 45
Zoom Control box and button 15, 45, 66, 91

Equipment suppliers:
The facsimile machine on page 105 was supplied by Panasonic, UK. The type blocks on pages 88-89 were loaned by James Robinson, Covent Garden, London, UK. The shoe photographed on page 67 was supplied by Hobbs, UK, and the boot on page 67 is courtesy of Shelleys Shoes, UK.

font 95, 119
    changing 22, 57
    choice of 55
    size 23, 57
    styles 57
Font
    command and dialog box 58, 93, 95, 108
    flipcard 108
    list box 22, 56, 57, 119
Fonts icon 119
Font Size list box 23, 56, 57
footers 67
Format Callout toolbar button 73
Format menu 58, 60, 61, 64, 68, 71, 108
Format Painter toolbar button 15, 58
formatting
    character-level 22-23, 54, 55, 56-58
    different levels of 54
    document-level 54, 64-65
    general principles of 54-55
    introduction to basic 22-23
    paragraph-level 54, 55, 59-64, 68
    section-level 54, 64, 67, 68-69
Formatting toolbar 12, 13, 56
Formula command and dialog box 81
frames 70-71
Frame
    command (Format menu) 71
    command (Insert menu) 70
    dialog box 71
Freeform drawing tool 73

g

General flipcard 124
Go To
    command 37
    dialog box 37, 116
Go to Record toolbar button 98
grammar checker 43
Grammar command and dialog box 43
graphics
    examples of different 86-87
    files, importing 120
    moving 34
    using Drawing toolbar to create 74-76
    using ready-made 77, 111
    using WordArt to create 72
graphs *see* charts
Gridlines command 78
Group toolbar button 73

h

hanging indent 62
hard disk icon and window 11, 49, 50
hardware requirements 10
headers 67
Header and Footer command and toolbar 67
help, obtaining 16, 116

Help
    Balloon 13, 16
    icon 13
    menu 13, 16
    pointer 16
    toolbar button 15, 16
hidden text 93
Hide Balloons command 16
Hide Microsoft Word command 17
highlight color 13
Home key 29, 30, 116
hyphenation 71
Hyphenation command and dialog box 71

i

I-beam pointer 11, 13, 18, 20, 30
Increase Indent toolbar button 56
indents
    using Paragraph dialog box to set 61-62
    using Ruler to set 61
    using Tab key to create first-line 18
Indents and Spacing flipcard 61, 62
Insert Cells dialog box 80
Insert Chart toolbar button 15, 82, 84
Insert Columns command 80
Insert Frame toolbar button 73
insertion point 18, 19, 20
Insert menu 28, 64, 69, 70, 72, 77, 81, 85, 113, 120, 123
Insert Merge Field toolbar button 98
Insert Microsoft Excel Worksheet toolbar button 15
Insert Table command and dialog box 78
Insert Word Field toolbar button 98
Italic toolbar button 23, 56

j-k

Justify toolbar button 56, 59
justifying text 59
Keyboard flipcard 125
keyboard shortcuts 116

l

Label Options dialog box 100
landscape orientation 93, 94
Last Record toolbar button 98
Layout flipcard 116
left-aligned
    tab 63
    text 59
left-indent marker 61
legend
    deleting from chart 85
    including in chart 83
Line Color toolbar button 73, 76
Line drawing tool 73, 75
line spacing 55, 62
Line Style toolbar button 73, 75
linking objects 122

Links command and dialog box 122
logo *see* graphics and WordArt objects

m

Macro command and dialog box 114
macros 112-114
Macros flipcard 114
magnifying text 45
mailing labels, printing 100-101
Mail Merge 96-99
    command 97
    toolbar 98
    toolbar button 98
Mail Merge Helper
    dialog box 97, 100, 101
    toolbar button 98, 99
manipulating windows 44-47
margins 55, 64-65
    creating different document 68
    using Document Layout dialog box to change 65, 85, 106
    using rulers in Print Preview to change 65, 90
Margins flipcard 65, 85, 106, 116
maximizing windows 13, 45, 116
measurement, changing units of 65
menu bar 12, 14
menu commands 12, 14
menus 12, 14
    customizing 125
    see also individual menus, e.g., File menu, Insert menu
Menus flipcard 125
Merge dialog box 101
merge field names 96
Merge to New Document toolbar button 98, 99
Merge to Printer toolbar button 98, 99
Microsoft Excel 122
    toolbar button 15
Microsoft Graph 82-85, 123
    toolbar button 15, 82, 84
    see also charts
Microsoft Word application window *see* application window
Microsoft WordArt *see* WordArt; WordArt objects
Microsoft Word folder 11, 48, 49
misspelled words *see* spelling check and AutoCorrect
Modify Bulleted list dialog box 60
mouse 11
    shortcuts 116
Move Up toolbar button 117
moving
    around in document 18, 29
    charts 83, 85
    files and folders 121
    graphics 34
    mouse 11
    text 34-35
    windows 47
multiple windows 46-47
    on one document 47
multiplying numbers 81

n

naming documents 21
New
    command and dialog box 26, 104, 105, 113
    document toolbar button 15, 26
New Folder command 50
New Style dialog box 108, 109
New Window command 47
Next Record toolbar button 98
nonprinting
    area 93
    characters 20
Normal template 104
    adapting 106
Normal view 12, 66
numbering lists 60
Numbering toolbar button 56, 60

o

Object command and dialog box 72, 123
OLE (object linking and embedding) 122-123
Online Help toolbar button 15, 16
Open
    command 27, 46, 120
    toolbar button 15, 27
opening
    existing document 27
    new document 26
    recently worked-on file 46
    several documents at once 46
    Word 11
option buttons 15
Option key 7, 30, 35, 66, 74, 111, 121
Options command and dialog box 27, 31, 42, 65, 93, 124
Organizer dialog box 114
Outline
    toolbar 117
    view 66, 117
outlining 117
overtyping text 33
OVR (status bar) 33

p-q

page breaks 69
Page Down key 18, 29, 90
Page Layout view 66, 67, 73
Page Number Format dialog box 64
page numbering 64
Page Numbers
    command and dialog box 64
    toolbar button 67
Page Setup command 93, 94
Page Up key 18, 29, 90
paper orientation 93, 94
paper size 94
paragraph
    alignment 55, 59
    definition of 59
    marks 20, 59
    spacing 62
    width 55

Paragraph Borders and Shading
  dialog box 68, 109
Paragraph command and dialog
  box 61, 62, 109
paragraph-level formatting 54, 55,
  59-64, 68
Paste
  command 35, 36
  toolbar button 15, 35
  see also copying and pasting;
    cutting and pasting
Paste Special command and dialog
  box 122
Pause Macro Recording button
  113, 114
Picture command 77
pictures *see* graphics
pie chart, creating 84
point size *see* font size
pop-up list boxes 15
portrait orientation 93, 94
PostScript fonts and printers 119
Previous Record toolbar button 98
Print
  command 14, 15, 92, 94
  flipcard 93
  toolbar button 15, 23, 92
printer 10
  changing settings of 94
  fonts 95
  installing and choosing 118
printer-driver files 118
printing
  documents 23, 92-94
  envelopes 95
  mailing labels 100-101
  options 92-94
  part of a document 92
Print Preview
  changing margins in 90
  command 90
  toolbar 91
  toolbar button 15, 90
Quit command 17
quitting Word 17
quotes, changing straight to smart
  29

r

readability statistics 43
Record Macro dialog box 112
REC (status bar) 112
Rectangle drawing tool 73
redoing actions 33
Redo toolbar button 15, 33
renaming files and folders 121
repeating a command 116
Replace command and dialog box
  39
replacing text and other items in
  document 39
Reshape toolbar button 73
resizing
  chart 83, 85
  drawing object 74
  frame 70
  windows 13, 45
  WordArt object 76
restoring document window 45,
  116

Return key 19, 116
reverse print order 93
right-aligned
  tab 63
  text 59
right-indent marker 61
Rotate Right toolbar button 73
Ruler(s) 13, 61
  changing margins using 65, 90
  changing measurements on 65
  setting indents using 61, 62
  setting tab stops using 63

s

Save As command 51, 105, 120
Save
  command 21
  toolbar button 15, 21, 23, 98
saving 21, 50-51, 116
  automatically 27
screen
  modifying 124
  shots and fragments 7
  splitting 44
scroll
  arrow buttons 29, 90
  bars 13, 29, 90
  boxes 13, 29
Search dialog box 51
searching for files 51
section breaks 68-69
section-level formatting 54, 64, 67,
  68-69
sections 54, 68
Select Column command 80
Select Drawing Objects toolbar
  button 73, 75
selecting text 30-31, 116
selection bar 12, 30
Send Behind Text toolbar button
  73
Send to Back toolbar button 73, 76
Series in Columns command 84
Shift key 7, 30, 32, 38, 74, 75, 116,
  119, 121
shortcut keys, customizing 125
shortcut menus 36, 58
shortcuts, keyboard and mouse
  116
Show Balloons command 16
Show/Hide ¶ toolbar button 15, 20
shrinking document to fit 91
size box 13, 45
smart quotes 29
Snap to Grid toolbar button 73
soft return 116
Sort command and dialog box 81
sorting data in table 81
spacing
  between lines 55, 62
  between paragraphs 62
special characters
  finding and replacing 39
  inserting 28-29
Special Characters flipcard 29
spelling check 40
Spelling
  command and dialog box
    40, 41
  toolbar button 15, 40

Spike feature 36
split box 44
splitting screen 44
Standard toolbar 12, 13, 14-15
status bar 12
Stop Macro Recording button 113
Style command and dialog box 108
Style list box (Formatting toolbar)
  56, 109, 117
styles 108-109
subfolders 48, 49
subtracting numbers 81
summary info 93
Switch Between Header and
  Footer toolbar button 67
switching between windows 46
Symbol command and dialog box
  28, 116
synonyms *see* thesaurus
System Folder 48, 118, 119
System 7 119

t

Tab key 14, 18, 19
Table
  menu 78, 80, 81
  toolbar button 15, 79, 80
tables 78-81
Tabs
  command 64
  dialog box 64, 116
tab stops 61, 63-64
  removing 63
templates 26, 104-106
text
  area 13
  attributes 57
  boxes 15
  copying 35-36
  entering 19, 27
  moving 34-35
  selecting 30-31, 116
Text Box drawing tool 73
thesaurus 42
Thesaurus command and dialog
  box 42
timesavers 104-114
Time toolbar button 67
Tip of the Day 12
title bar 13
toolbar
  buttons 14, 124
  Drawing 73, 77
  floating 14, 116
  Equation Editor 123
  Formatting 12, 13, 56
  Header and Footer 67
  how to use 14
  Mail Merge 98
  modifying 124, 125
  Outline 117
  Print Preview 91
  Standard 12, 13, 14-15
  WordArt 72
Toolbars
  command and dialog box 13,
    56, 124
  flipcard 112
Tools menu 40, 42, 43, 71, 93, 95,
  97, 110, 114, 124, 125

Trash icon 121
TrueType fonts 95, 119
type size *see* font size
typing *see* entering text and
  overtyping text
typographical effects *see* font
  styles and WordArt objects

u-v

Underline toolbar button 56, 57
Undo toolbar button 15, 33
undoing actions 33
Ungroup toolbar button 73
View
  buttons 12, 66
  flipcard 124
  menu 13, 45, 49, 56, 66, 67, 117,
    124
View Merged Data toolbar button
  98, 99
views 66
  see also Normal view; Outline
    view; Page Layout view

w-z

Window menu 46, 47
windows
  manipulating 44-47
  maximizing 13, 45, 116
  moving 47
  multiple 46-47
  resizing 13, 45, 116
  switching between 46
Wizards 106-107
Word
  application window
    see application window
  customizing 124-125
  Help contents 16
  opening 11
  quitting 17
WordArt 2.0
  dialog box 72
  toolbar 72
WordArt objects
  embedding 123
  examples of different 87
  modifying 72
  resizing 76
wristwatch symbol 14
WYSIWYG (What You See Is What
  You Get) 6
zoom box 13, 45
Zoom command and dialog box 45
Zoom Control box and button 15,
  45, 66, 91

Equipment suppliers:
The facsimile machine on page 105
was supplied by Panasonic, UK.
The type blocks on pages 88-89
were loaned by James Robinson,
Covent Garden, London, UK. The
shoe photographed on page 67 was
supplied by Hobbs, UK, and the
boot on page 67 is courtesy of
Shelleys Shoes, UK.

Register Today!

Return this
The Way Word for the Macintosh® Works
registration card for:

✔ a Microsoft Press catalog

✔ exclusive offers on specially priced books

Fill in information below and mail postage free.

1-55615-672-3A   The Way Word for the Macintosh Works

_____
NAME

_____
COMPANY

_____
ADDRESS

_____

_____
CITY   STATE   ZIP

Your feedback is important to us.

To help us make future editions even more useful, include your daytime telephone number and we might call to find out how you use *The Way Word for the Macintosh Works*. If we call you, we'll send you a **FREE GIFT** for your time!

(   ) _____
DAYTIME TELEPHONE NUMBER

More from the WYSIWYG Series
Microsoft Press and Dorling Kindersley

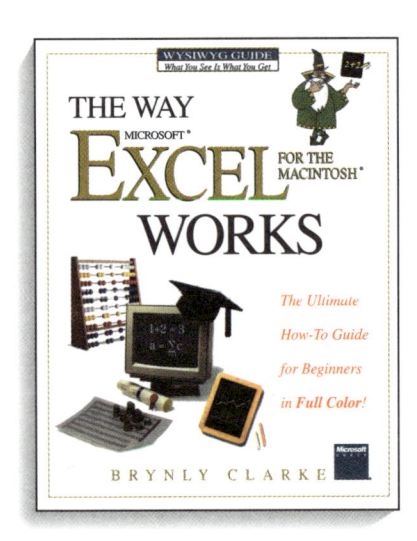

The Way Microsoft® Excel for the Macintosh® Works
Version 5
Brynly Clarke
$19.95 ($24.95 Canada)   ISBN 1-55615-671-5

Microsoft Press®

Microsoft Press® books are available wherever quality books are sold and through CompuServe's Electronic Mall—GO MSP. Call 1-800-MSPRESS for direct ordering information or for placing credit card orders.*

Please refer to BBK when placing your order. Prices subject to change.

*In Canada, contact Macmillan Canada, Attn: Microsoft Press Dept., 164 Commander Blvd., Agincourt, Ontario, Canada M1S 3C7, or call 1-800-667-1115. Outside the U.S. and Canada, write to International Coordinator, Microsoft Press, One Microsoft Way, Redmond, WA 98052-6399 or fax +(206) 936-7329.

NO POSTAGE
NECESSARY
IF MAILED
IN THE
UNITED STATES

BUSINESS REPLY MAIL
FIRST-CLASS MAIL   PERMIT NO. 53   BOTHELL, WA

POSTAGE WILL BE PAID BY ADDRESSEE

MICROSOFT PRESS REGISTRATION
THE WAY WORD FOR THE
   MACINTOSH WORKS
PO BOX 3019
BOTHELL WA   98041-9946